Financial Aggregation and Index Number Theory

Surveys on Theories in Economics and Business Administration

ISSN: 2010-1724

Published

Vol. 1 A Survey of Dynamic Games in Economics
by Van Long Ngo

Vol. 2 Financial Aggregation and Index Number Theory
by William A. Barnett & Marcelle Chauvet

Financial Aggregation and Index Number Theory

William A Barnett
University of Kansas, USA

Marcelle Chauvet
University of California at Riverside, USA

NEW JERSEY • LONDON • SINGAPORE • BEIJING • SHANGHAI • HONG KONG • TAIPEI • CHENNAI

Published by

World Scientific Publishing Co. Pte. Ltd.

5 Toh Tuck Link, Singapore 596224

USA office: 27 Warren Street, Suite 401-402, Hackensack, NJ 07601

UK office: 57 Shelton Street, Covent Garden, London WC2H 9HE

Library of Congress Cataloging-in-Publication Data

Financial aggregation and index number theory / by William A Barnett & Marcelle Chauvet.
p. cm. -- (Surveys on theories in economics and business administration ; vol. 2)
ISBN-13: 978-9814293099
ISBN-10: 9814293091
1. Index numbers (Economics) 2. Finance--Mathematical models.
3. Monetary policy--Mathematical models. I. Barnett, William A. II. Chauvet, Marcelle.
HB225.F46 2010
332.01'5195--dc22

2010020448

British Library Cataloguing-in-Publication Data

A catalogue record for this book is available from the British Library.

Typeset by Stallion Press
Email: enquiries@stallionpress.com

Printed in Singapore.

Contents

Introduction xi

1. International Financial Aggregation and Index Number Theory: A Chronological Half-Century Empirical Overview 1

William A. Barnett and Marcelle Chauvet

1.1 Introduction 2
1.2 Monetary Aggregation Theory 8
1.2.1 Monetary Aggregation 8
1.2.2 Aggregation Theory versus Index Number Theory 9
1.2.3 The Economic Decision 10
1.2.4 The Divisia Index 12
1.2.5 Risk Adjustment 13
1.2.6 Dual Space 14
1.2.7 Aggregation Error and Policy Slackness . 14
1.3 The History of Thought on Monetary Aggregation 16
1.4 The 1960s and 1970s 19
1.5 The Monetarist Experiment: November 1979–November 1982 26
1.6 End of the Monetarist Experiment: 1983–1984 . 29
1.7 The Rise of Risk Adjustment Concerns: 1984–1993 31
1.8 The Y2K Computer Bug: 1999–2000 37

1.9 The Supply Side 39
1.10 European ECB Data 44
1.11 The Most Recent Data: Would You Believe This? 44
1.12 Conclusion 49

2. The Exact Theoretical Rational Expectations Monetary Aggregate 53

William A. Barnett, Melvin J. Hinich and Piyu Yue

2.1 Introduction 53
2.2 Consumer Demand for Monetary Assets 56
2.3 Existence of a Monetary Aggregate for the Consumer 59
2.4 The Solution Procedure 62
2.5 Monetary Policy 64
2.6 The Risk Neutral Case 66
2.7 A Generalization 66
2.8 Data and Specification 69
2.9 Estimation 73
2.10 Frequency Domain Tests 76
2.11 Frequency Domain Results 80
2.12 Conclusions 84

3. On User Costs of Risky Monetary Assets 85

William A. Barnett and Shu Wu

3.1 Introduction 85
3.2 Consumer's Optimization Problem 88
3.3 Risk-adjusted User Cost of Monetary Assets . . 91
3.3.1 The Theory 91
3.3.2 Approximation to the Theory 98
3.4 Concluding Remarks 104

4. The Discounted Economic Stock of Money with VAR Forecasting . . . 107

William A. Barnett, Unja Chae and John W. Keating

4.1 Introduction . . . 107
4.2 Microfoundations of Consumer Demand for Money . . . 109
4.2.1 Overview . . . 109
4.2.2 User Cost of Money . . . 111
4.3 Economic Aggregation and Index Number Theory . . . 112
4.3.1 Definition of the Economic Stock of Money under Perfect Foresight . . . 113
4.3.2 Extension to Risk . . . 114
4.3.3 CE and Simple Sum Indexes as Special Cases of the ESM . . . 116
4.3.3.1 The CE Index . . . 116
4.3.3.2 The SSI Index . . . 117
4.4 Measurement of the Economic Stock of Money . . . 118
4.4.1 Method 1: Linearizing Around Current Values . . . 119
4.4.2 Method 2: Martingale Expectations for Only the Benchmark Rate . . . 121
4.4.3 Method 3: Setting Covariances to Zero . . . 121
4.5 Forecasting Models . . . 123
4.5.1 Unrestricted VARs . . . 123
4.5.2 Asymmetric VARs . . . 124
4.5.3 Bayesian VARs . . . 124
4.6 Model Specification . . . 125
4.6.1 Data Description . . . 125
4.6.2 Nonstationarity and Data Transformation . . . 126
4.6.3 Selection of Lag Length . . . 127

4.6.4 Criterion for Evaluation of Forecasting Performance 128
4.6.5 Specification of Priors 129
4.7 Empirical Results: Forecasting Performance and Evaluation 132
4.8 Empirical Results: Estimation of Money Stock . 136
4.8.1 Economic Stock of Money Computed using Actual Data 136
4.8.2 Economic Stock of Money Based on BVAR Forecasts 140
4.8.2.1 ESM Computed Using Forecasts from BVAR 141
4.8.2.2 Comparison across Computing Methods 146
4.9 Discussion and Conclusion 147

5. Exchange Rate Determination from Monetary Fundamentals: An Aggregation Theoretic Approach 151

William A. Barnett and Chang Ho Kwag

5.1 Introduction 151
5.2 The Role of Money Supply and Demand in Exchange Rate Models 153
5.3 Aggregation and Index Number Theory 156
5.4 Exchange Rate Forecasting with Divisia Money and User Cost Prices 158
5.4.1 Model Specification 158
5.4.2 Data Specification and Transformation . 159
5.4.3 Estimation and Forecasting 160
5.4.4 Forecast Comparisons 161
5.5 The Empirical Results 162
5.5.1 The MSE and DM Comparisons 162
5.5.2 The DOC Results 164
5.6 Conclusion 165

6. Multilateral Aggregation-Theoretic Monetary Aggregation over Heterogeneous Countries 167

William A. Barnett

6.1 Introduction 167
6.2 Definition of Variables 170
6.3 Aggregation within Countries 173
6.4 Aggregation Over Countries 175
6.5 Special Cases 184
6.5.1 Purchasing Power Parity 184
6.5.2 Multilateral Representative Agent over the Economic Union 185
6.5.2.1 Multilateral Representative Agent with Heterogeneous Tastes . . . 186
6.5.2.2 Multilateral Representative Agent with Homogeneous Tastes . . . 196
6.5.3 Existence of a Unilateral Representative Agent over the Economic Union 199
6.6 Interest Rate Aggregation 202
6.7 Divisia Second Moments 203
6.8 Conclusions 205

7. Measurement Error in Monetary Aggregates: A Markov Switching Factor Approach 207

William A. Barnett, Marcelle Chauvet and Heather L. R. Tierney

7.1 Introduction 208
7.2 Monetary Aggregation Theory 213
7.2.1 Monetary Aggregation 213
7.2.2 Aggregation Theory versus Index Number Theory 214
7.2.3 The Economic Decision 215
7.2.4 The Divisia Index 217

7.2.5 Risk Adjustment 218
7.2.6 Dual Space 219
7.3 The State Space Model 219
7.4 Empirical Results 225
7.4.1 Data 225
7.4.2 Specification Tests 226
7.4.3 High and Low Inflation and Interest Rate Phases 227
7.4.4 Estimates 229
7.4.5 Simple M1 Aggregate and Divisia M1 . . 232
7.4.6 Simple M2 Aggregate and Divisia M2 . . 237
7.4.7 Simple M3 Aggregate and Divisia M3 . . 241
7.5 Summary of Findings 245
7.6 Conclusions 247

References 251

Author Index 261

Introduction

William A. Barnett and Marcelle Chauvet

The modern formal theory of monetary and financial aggregation began with the seminal paper of Barnett (1980) for consumer demand, and extended to firm demand and financial intermediary supply by Barnett (1987). The result has been a large and growing theoretical and empirical literature, now drawing increasingly broad-based attention as a result of the current financial crisis and its origins in misperceived systemic risk. Since most of that literature is highly technical and has been spread over many analytically sophisticated journals, Barnett and Serletis (2000) collected together reprints of the most important published articles available at that time, to make that literature more easily and widely available. But the literature has grown dramatically since the publication of that book, especially in the areas of adjustment for risk and multilateral aggregation over multiple countries. The current book brings together the most important papers that have appeared since then.

Kar-yiu Wong, President of the Asia-Pacific Economic Association, runs an annual Advanced Training Program for Asian scholars at the University of Washington in Seattle. He invited William Barnett to write and present a survey paper on his research in monetary and financial aggregation as a keynote lecture at the 2008 Advanced Training Program, held August 11–29, 2008 in Seattle. That lecture surveys the entire literature up to that date, and produced the article reprinted in this book as chapter 1. Professor Wong also invited William Barnett to publish that survey, along with the relevant articles not previously reprinted, in a book to be published by World Scientific. This is the resulting book.

The invited survey, appearing as chapter 1, was first submitted to and published by a journal. The reason was to assure peer review and accuracy. Chapter 1 is reprinted from the resulting published journal article. As requested by Professor Wong, that paper surveys the entire literature from its origins in 1980. In the other chapters of this book, only the papers published subsequent to the Barnett and Serletis (2000) collection have been reprinted and are organized into the chronological order of the dates of their publication. As a result this book and Barnett and Serletis (2000) can be viewed as companion volumes, with chapter 1 of this book unifying the two collections.

Chapters 2 and 3 extend the theory to the case of risk, with chapter 2 producing the relevant microeconomic theory and chapter 3 deriving the index number theory consistent with the microeconomic theory. In addition, chapter 3 extends to the case of intertemporal nonseparability to avoid the equity premium puzzle problems associated with the conventional consumption capital asset pricing model (CCAPM) special case.

Chapter 4 derives the economic capital stock of money produced from discounting the expected service flow to present value with vector autoregressive (VAR) process forecasting of expectations. While service flows produced in accordance with chapters 2 and 3 are relevant to the demand and supply of money and market equilibrium, the capital stock is relevant to wealth effects of policy.

Chapter 5 investigates the implications of monetary aggregation theory for the theory of exchange rate determination. While simple sum monetary aggregation is well known to produce results inconsistent with rational exchange-rate theory, this chapter finds no conflicts with trade theory, when the monetary aggregates are produced from aggregation theory.

Chapter 6 extends to multilateral aggregation with emphasis on joint aggregation over, as well as within, countries. This research was motivated by problems of aggregation within the European Monetary Union, but is relevant to aggregation within any optimal currency area or potential candidate for an optimal currency area as well as aggregation over local regions of countries.

Chapter 7 explores the relationship between monetary aggregation theory and state-space time-series approaches to evaluation of measurement accuracy. By separating common factors, captured both by simple-sum monetary aggregates and aggregation-theoretic monetary aggregates, from idiosyncratic factors specific to each, this paper extracts the information-gain available only from the aggregation-theoretic monetary aggregates.

1

International Financial Aggregation and Index Number Theory: A Chronological Half-Century Empirical Overview[1]

William A. Barnett and Marcelle Chauvet

This paper comprises a survey of a half century of research on international monetary aggregate data. We argue that since monetary assets began yielding interest, the simple sum monetary aggregates have had no foundations in economic theory and have sequentially produced one source of misunderstanding after another. The bad data produced by simple sum aggregation have contaminated research in monetary economics, have resulted in needless "paradoxes," and have produced decades of misunderstandings in international monetary economics research and policy. While better data, based correctly on index number theory and aggregation theory, now exist, the official central bank data most commonly used have not improved in most parts of the world. While aggregation theoretic monetary aggregates exist for internal use at the European Central Bank, the Bank of Japan, and many other central banks throughout the world, the only central banks that currently make aggregation theoretic monetary aggregates available to the public are the Bank of England and the St. Louis Federal Reserve Bank. No other area of economics has been so seriously damaged by data unrelated to valid index number and aggregation theory. In this paper we chronologically review the

[1]Reprinted from *Open Economies Review* (2009), "International Financial Aggregation and Index Number Theory: A Chronological Half-Century Empirical Overview" by William A. Barnett and Marcelle Chauvet, vol. 20, no. 1, February, pp. 1–37; with kind permission of Springer Science+Business Media.

past research in this area and connect the data errors with the resulting policy and inference errors. Future research on monetary aggregation and policy can most advantageously focus on extensions to exchange rate risk and its implications for multilateral aggregation over monetary asset portfolios containing assets denominated in more than one currency. The relevant theory for multilateral aggregation with exchange rate risk has been derived by Barnett (2007) and Barnett and Wu (2005).

1.1. Introduction

Since Barnett (1980) derived the aggregation theoretic approach to monetary aggregation and advocated the use of the Divisia or Fisher Ideal index with user cost prices in aggregating over monetary services, Divisia monetary aggregates have been produced for many countries. For example, Divisia monetary aggregates have been produced for Britain (Batchelor (1989), Drake (1992), and Belongia and Chrystal (1991)), Japan (Ishida (1984)), the Netherlands (Fase (1985)), Canada (Cockerline and Murray (1981)), Australia (Hoa (1985)), and Switzerland (Yue and Fluri (1991)), among many others. More recently, Barnett (2007) has extended the theory to multilateral aggregation over different countries with potentially different currencies, and Barnett and Shu (2005) have extended to the case of risky contemporaneous interest rates, as is particularly relevant when exchange rate risk is involved. That research was particularly focused on the needs of the European Central Bank. But despite this vast amount of research, most central banks continue to supply the disreputable simple sum monetary aggregates having no connection with aggregation and index number theory, when different monetary asset components have different interest rate yields. The simple sum monetary aggregates have produced repeated inference errors, policy errors, and needless paradoxes. In this paper, we bring together the history of the problems produced by the use of simple sum monetary aggregates and demonstrate that these problems disappear, when Divisia monetary aggregates are used.

In this paper we survey the relevant theory and the most dramatic of the empirical evidence. We present the evidence in chronological order. The concerns, puzzles, and paradoxes in the literature have changed over time, in accordance with the evolving policy concerns. The first dramatic puzzle appeared in 1974, when it was purported that there had been a mysterious shift in both the demand and supply for money functions. We provide an overview of the issues and empirical evidence with emphasis on graphical displays. What has been happening in this literature and in policy is most clearly displayed graphically. We cite the original publications for those readers interested in the formal econometrics used in resolving the paradoxes.

We conclude with a discussion of the most recent research in this area, which introduces state space factor modeling into this literature. We also display the most recent puzzle regarding Federal Reserve data on nonborrowed reserves and show that the recent behavior of that data contradicts the definition of nonborrowed reserves: in short, is an oxymoron. Far from resolving the earlier data problems, the Federal Reserve's most recent data may be the most puzzling that the Federal Reserve has ever published.

There is a vast literature on the appropriateness of aggregating over monetary asset components using simple summation. Linear aggregation can be based on Hicksian aggregation (Hicks 1946), but that theory only holds under the unreasonable assumption that the user-cost prices of the services of individual money assets not change over time. This condition implies that each asset is a perfect substitute for the others within the set of components. Simple sum aggregation is an even more severe special case of that highly restrictive, linear aggregation, since simple summation requires that the coefficients of the linear aggregator function all be the same. This, in turn, implies that the constant user-cost prices among monetary assets be exactly equal to each other. Not only must the assets be perfect substitutes, but must be perfect one-for-one substitutes — i.e., must be indistinguishable assets, with one unit of each asset being a perfect substitute for exactly one unit of each of the other assets.

In reality, financial assets provide different services, and each such asset yields its own particular rate of return. As a result, the user costs, which measure foregone interest and thereby opportunity cost, are not constant and are not equal across financial assets. The relative prices of U.S. monetary assets fluctuate considerably, and the interest rates paid on many monetary assets are not equal to the zero interest rate paid on currency. These observations have motivated serious concerns about the reliability of the simple sum aggregation method, which has been disreputable in the literature on index number theory and aggregation theory for over a century. In addition, an increasing number of imperfect substitute short-term financial assets have emerged in recent decades. Since monetary aggregates produced from simple summation do not accurately measure the quantities of monetary services chosen by optimizing agents, shifts in the series can be spurious, as those shifts do not necessarily reflect a change in the utility derived from money holdings.

Microeconomic aggregation theory offers an appealing alternative approach to the definition of money, compared to the atheoretical simple-sum method. The quantity index under the aggregation theoretic approach extracts and measures the income effects of changes in relative prices and is invariant to substitution effects, which do not alter utility and thereby do not alter perceived services received. The simple sum index, on the other hand, does not distinguish between income and substitution effects, if the aggregate's components are not perfect substitutes in identical ratios, and thereby the simple sum index confounds together substitution effects with actual services received. The aggregation-theoretic monetary aggregator function, which correctly internalizes substitution effects, can be tracked accurately by the Divisia quantity index, constructed by using expenditure shares as the component growth-rate weights. Barnett (1978,1980) derived the formula for the theoretical user-cost price of a monetary asset, needed in computation of the Divisia index's share weights, and thereby originated the Divisia monetary aggregates. The growth rate weights resulting from this approach are different across assets, depending on all of the quantities and interest rates in each share, and those weights can be time-varying at each point in time. For a detailed description of the theory underlying this construction, see Barnett (1982, 1987).

It is important to understand that the direction in which an asset's growth-rate weight will change with an interest rate change is not predictable in advance. Consider Cobb-Douglas utility. Its shares are independent of relative prices, and hence of the interest rates within the component user cost prices. For other utility functions, the direction of the change in shares with a price change, or equivalently with an interest rate change, depends upon whether the own price elasticity of demand exceeds or is less than -1. In elementary microeconomic theory, this often overlooked phenomenon produces the famous "diamonds versus water paradox" and is the source of most of the misunderstandings of the Divisia monetary aggregates' weighting, as explained by Barnett (1983).

Several authors have studied the empirical properties of the Divisia index compared with the simple sum index. The earliest comparisons are in Barnett (1982) and Barnett, Offenbacher, and Spindt (1984). More recent examples include Belongia (1996), Belongia and Ireland (2006), and Schunk (2001), and the comprehensive survey found in Barnett and Serletis (2000). In particular, Belongia (1996) replicates some studies on the impact of money on economic activity and compares results acquired using a Divisia index instead of the originally used simple sum index, Schunk (2001) investigates the forecasting performance of the Divisia index compared with the simple sum aggregates, and Belongia and Ireland (2006) explore the policy implications in the dual space of aggregated user costs and interest rates. Barnett and Serletis (2000) collect together and reprint seminal journal articles from this literature.[2]

[2]Other overviews of published theoretical and empirical results in this literature are available in Barnett, Fisher, and Serletis (1992) and Serletis (2006).

The most recent research in this area is Barnett, Chauvet, and Tierney (2009), who compare the different dynamics of simple sum monetary aggregates and the Divisia indexes, not only over time, but also over the business cycle and across high and low inflation and interest rate phases. The potential differences between the series can be economically very important. If one of the indexes corresponds to a better measure of money, its dynamical differences from the official simple sum aggregates increase the already considerable uncertainty regarding the effectiveness and appropriateness of current monetary policy. Barnett, Chauvet, and Tierney aim to find the nature of the differences and whether they occur during particular periods. Information about the state of monetary growth becomes particularly relevant for policymakers, when inflation enters a high growth phase or the economy begins to weaken. In fact Barnett (1997) has argued and documented the connection between the decline in the policy credibility of monetary aggregates and defects that are peculiar to simple sum aggregation.

Although traditional comparisons of the monetary aggregates series sometimes suggest that the series share similar long run dynamics, there are differences during certain important periods, such as around turning points. These differences cannot be evaluated by long run average behavior. The Barnett, Chauvet, and Tierney (2009) proposed approach offers several ways in which these differences can be analyzed. The approach separates out the common movements underlying the monetary aggregate indexes, summarized in the dynamic factor, from individual variations specific to each of the indexes, captured by the idiosyncratic terms. The idiosyncratic terms and the measurement errors reveal where the monetary indexes differ.[3] The idiosyncratic terms show the movements that are peculiar

[3]In aggregation theory measurement error refers to the tracking error in a nonparametric index number's approximation to the aggregator function of microeconomic theory, where the aggregator function is the subutility or subproduction function that is weakly separable within tastes or technology of an economic agent's

to each series, whereas the measurement error captures the remaining noise inherent in the data. That is, the dynamic factor represents simultaneous downturn and upturn movements in money growth rate indexes. If only one of the indexes declines, this would be captured by its idiosyncratic term.

Barnett, Chauvet, and Tierney (2009) model both the common factor as well as the idiosyncratic terms for each index as following different Markov processes. Given that the idiosyncratic movements are peculiar to each index, the idiosyncratic terms' Markov processes are assumed to be independent of each other. In addition, Barnett, Chauvet, and Tierney allow the idiosyncratic terms to follow autoregressive processes. These assumptions entail a very flexible framework that can capture the dynamics of the differences across the indexes without imposing dependence between them.

Factor models with regime switching have been widely used to represent business cycles (see e.g., Chauvet (1998, 2001), Kim and Nelson (1998), among several others), but without relationship to aggregation theory. Barnett, Chauvet, and Tierney's proposed model differs from the literature in its complexity, as it includes estimation of the parameters of three independent Markov processes. In addition, the focus is not only on the estimated common factor, but on the idiosyncratic terms that reflect the divergences between the simple sum and Divisia monetary aggregate indexes in a manner relevant to aggregation theory.

---

complete utility or production function. Consequently, aggregator functions are increasing and concave and need to be estimated econometrically. On the other hand, state space models use the term measurement error to mean un-modeled noise, which is not captured by the state variable or idiosyncratic terms. In this paper, measurement error refers to this latter definition, which can be expected to be correlated with the former, when the behavior of the data process is consistent with microeconomic theory. But it should be acknowledged that neither concept of measurement error can be directly derived from the other. In fact the state space model concept of measurement error is more directly connected with the statistical ("atomistic") approach to index number theory than to the more recent "economic approach," which is at its best when data is not aggregated over economic agents.

To our knowledge, there is no parallel work in the literature that formally compares simple sum aggregate with the Divisia index directly, using a multivariate time-series framework to *estimate* the dynamical differences between these series in a manner extracting the idiosyncratic terms specific to each aggregate. Barnett, Chauvet, and Tierney's (2009) contribution goes beyond the simple comparison over time, as they also focus on major measurement errors that might have occurred during some periods, such as around the beginnings or ends of recessions or in transition times, as from low (high) to high (low) inflation or interest rate phases.

1.2. Monetary Aggregation Theory

1.2.1. *Monetary Aggregation*

Aggregation theory and index-number theory have been used to generate official governmental data since the 1920s. One exception still exists. The monetary quantity aggregates and interest rate aggregates supplied by many central banks are not based on index-number or aggregation theory, but rather are the simple unweighted sums of the component quantities and the quantity-weighted or arithmetic averages of interest rates. The predictable consequence has been induced instability of money demand and supply functions, and a series of 'puzzles' in the resulting applied literature. In contrast, the Divisia monetary aggregates, originated by Barnett (1980), are derived directly from economic index-number theory. Financial aggregation and index number theory was first rigorously connected with the literature on microeconomic aggregation and index number theory by Barnett (1980; 1987).

Data construction and measurement procedures imply the theory that can rationalize the aggregation procedure. The assumptions implicit in the data construction procedures must be consistent with the assumptions made in producing the models within which the data are to be used. Unless the theory is internally consistent, the data and its applications are incoherent. Without that coherence between aggregator function structure and the econometric models within which the aggregates are embedded, stable structure can appear to be unstable. This phenomenon has been called the 'Barnett critique' by Chrystal and MacDonald (1994).

1.2.2. *Aggregation Theory versus Index Number Theory*

The exact aggregates of microeconomic aggregation theory depend on unknown aggregator functions, which typically are utility, production, cost, or distance functions. Such functions must first be econometrically estimated. Hence the resulting exact quantity and price indexes become estimator- and specification-dependent. This dependency is troublesome to governmental agencies, which therefore view aggregation theory as a research tool rather than a data construction procedure.

Statistical index-number theory, on the other hand, provides indexes which are computable directly from quantity and price data, without estimation of unknown parameters. Within the literature on aggregation theory, such index numbers depend jointly on prices and quantities, but not on unknown parameters. In a sense, index number theory trades joint dependency on prices and quantities for dependence on unknown parameters. Examples of such statistical index numbers are the Laspeyres, Paasche, Divisia, Fisher ideal, and Törnqvist indexes.

The loose link between index number theory and aggregation theory was tightened, when Diewert (1976) defined the class of second-order 'superlative' index numbers, which track any unknown aggregator function up to the second order. Statistical index number theory became part of microeconomic theory, as economic aggregation theory had been for decades, with statistical index numbers judged by their non-parametric tracking ability to the aggregator functions of aggregation theory.

For decades, the link between statistical index number theory and microeconomic aggregation theory was weaker for aggregating over monetary quantities than for aggregating over other goods and asset quantities. Once monetary assets began yielding interest long ago, monetary assets became imperfect substitutes for each other, and the 'price' of monetary-asset services was no longer clearly defined. That problem was solved by Barnett (1978; 1980), who derived the formula for the user cost of demanded monetary services.[4]

Barnett's results on the user cost of the services of monetary assets set the stage for introducing index number theory into monetary economics.

1.2.3. *The Economic Decision*

Consider a decision problem over monetary assets. The decision problem will be defined in the simplest manner that renders the relevant literature on economic aggregation over goods immediately applicable.[5] Initially we shall assume perfect certainty.

Let $\mathbf{m}_t' = (m_{1t}, m_{2t}, \ldots, m_{nt})$ be the vector of real balances of monetary assets during period t, let $\mathbf{r}_t$ be the vector of nominal holding-period yields for monetary assets during period t, and let R_t be the one period holding yield on the benchmark asset during period t. The benchmark asset is defined to be a pure investment that

[4]Subsequently Barnett (1987) derived the formula for the user cost of supplied monetary services. A regulatory wedge can exist between the demand and supply-side user costs, if non-payment of interest on required reserves imposes an implicit tax on banks.

[5]Our research in this paper is not dependent upon this simple decision problem, as shown by Barnett (1987), who proved that the same aggregator function and index number theory applies, regardless of whether the initial model has money in the utility function, or money in a production function, or neither, so long as there is intertemporal separability of structure and certain assumptions are satisfied for aggregation over economic agents. The aggregator function is the derived function that has been shown in general equilibrium always to exist, if money has positive value in equilibrium, regardless of the motive for holding money.

provides no services other than its yield, R_t, so that the asset is held solely to accumulate wealth. Thus, R_t is the maximum holding period yield in the economy in period t.

Let y_t be the real value of total budgeted expenditure on monetary services during period t. Under simplifying assumptions for data within one country, the conversion between nominal and real expenditure on the monetary services of one or more assets is accomplished using the true cost of living index, $p_t^* = p_t^*(\mathbf{p}_t)$, on consumer goods, where the vector of consumer goods prices is $\mathbf{p}_t$.[6] The optimal portfolio allocation decision is:

$$\begin{gathered} \text{maximize } u(\mathbf{m}_t) \\ \text{subject to } \boldsymbol{\pi}_t'\mathbf{m}_t = y_t, \end{gathered} \tag{1.1}$$

where $\boldsymbol{\pi}_t' = (\pi_{1t}, \ldots, \pi_{nt})$ is the vector of monetary-asset real user costs, with

$$\pi_{it} = \frac{R_t - r_{it}}{1 + R_t}. \tag{1.2}$$

The function u is the decision maker's utility function, assumed to be monotonically increasing and strictly concave.[7] The user cost formula (1.2), derived by Barnett (1978; 1980), measures the forgone interest or opportunity cost of holding monetary asset i, when the higher yielding benchmark asset could have been held.

Let $\mathbf{m}_t^*$ be derived by solving decision (1.1). Under the assumption of linearly homogeneous utility, the exact monetary aggregate of economic theory is the utility level associated with holding the portfolio, and hence is the optimized value of the decision's objective

[6]The multilateral open economy extension is available in Barnett (2007).

[7]To be an admissible quantity aggregator function, the function u must be weakly separable within the consumer's complete utility function over all goods and services. Producing a reliable test for weak separability is the subject of much intensive research, most recently by Barnett and Peretti (2009).

function:

$$M_t = u(\mathbf{m}_t^*). \tag{1.3}$$

1.2.4. *The Divisia Index*

Although equation (1.3) is exactly correct, it depends upon the unknown function, u. Nevertheless, statistical index-number theory enables us to track M_t exactly without estimating the unknown function, u. In continuous time, the monetary aggregate, $M_t = u(\mathbf{m}_t^*)$, can be tracked exactly by the Divisia index, which solves the differential equation

$$\frac{d \log M_t}{dt} = \sum_i s_{it} \frac{d \log m_{it}^*}{dt} \tag{1.4}$$

for M_t, where

$$s_{it} = \frac{\pi_{it} m_{it}^*}{y_t}$$

is the i'th asset's share in expenditure on the total portfolio's service flow.[8] The dual user cost price aggregate $\Pi_t = \Pi(\boldsymbol{\pi}_t)$, can be tracked exactly by the Divisia price index, which solves the differential equation

$$\frac{d \log \Pi_t}{dt} = \sum_i s_{it} \frac{d \log \pi_{it}}{dt}. \tag{1.5}$$

The user cost dual satisfies Fisher's factor reversal in continuous time:

$$\Pi_t M_t = \boldsymbol{\pi}_t' \mathbf{m}_t. \tag{1.6}$$

As a formula for aggregating over quantities of perishable consumer goods, that index was first proposed by François Divisia (1925), with market prices of those goods inserted in place of the user costs in equation (1.4). In continuous time, the Divisia index, under

[8]In equation (1.4), it is understood that the result is in continuous time, so the time subscripts are a short hand for functions of time. We use t to be the time period in discrete time, but the instant of time in continuous time.

conventional neoclassical assumptions, is exact. In discrete time, the Törnqvist approximation is:

$$\log M_t - \log M_{t-1} = \sum_i \bar{s}_{it}(\log m_{it}^* - \log m_{i,t-1}^*), \quad (1.7)$$

where

$$\bar{s}_{it} = \frac{1}{2}(s_{it} + s_{i,t-1}).$$

In discrete time, we often call equation (1.7) simply the Divisia quantity index.[9] After the quantity index is computed from (1.7), the user cost aggregate most commonly is computed directly from equation (1.6).

1.2.5. *Risk Adjustment*

Extension of index number theory to the case of risk was introduced by Barnett, Liu and Jensen (2000), who derived the extended theory from Euler equations rather than from the perfect-certainty first-order conditions used in the earlier index number-theory literature. Since that extension is based upon the consumption capital-asset-pricing model (CCAPM), the extension is subject to the 'equity premium puzzle' of smaller-than-necessary adjustment for risk. We believe that the under-correction produced by CCAPM results from its assumption of intertemporal blockwise strong separability of goods and services within preferences. Barnett and Wu (2005) have extended Barnett, Liu, and Jensen's result to the case of risk aversion with intertemporally non-separable tastes.[10]

---

[9] Diewert (1976) defines a 'superlative index number' to be one that is exactly correct for a quadratic approximation to the aggregator function. The discretization (1.7) to the Divisia index is in the superlative class, since it is exact for the quadratic translog specification to an aggregator function.

[10] The Federal Reserve Bank of St. Louis Divisia database, which we use in this paper, is not risk corrected. In addition, it is not adjusted for differences in marginal taxation rates on different asset returns or for sweeps, and its clustering of components into groups was not based upon tests of weak separability, but rather on the Federal Reserve's official clustering. The St. Louis Federal Reserve

1.2.6. *Dual Space*

User cost aggregates are duals to monetary quantity aggregates. Either implies the other uniquely. In addition, user-cost aggregates imply the corresponding interest-rate aggregates uniquely. The interest-rate aggregate r_t implied by the user-cost aggregate Π_t is the solution for r_t to the equation:

$$\frac{R_t - r_t}{1 + R_t} = \Pi_t.$$

Accordingly, any monetary policy that operates through the opportunity cost of money (that is, interest rates) has a dual policy operating through the monetary quantity aggregate, and vice versa. Aggregation theory implies no preference for either of the two dual policy procedures or for any other approach to policy, so long as the policy does not violate principles of aggregation theory. In their current state-space comparisons, Barnett, Chauvet, and Tierney model in quantity space rather than the user-cost-price or interest-rate dual spaces. Regarding policy in the dual space, see Barnett (1987) and Belongia and Ireland (2006).

1.2.7. *Aggregation Error and Policy Slackness*

Figure 1 displays the magnitude of the aggregation error and policy slackness produced by the use of the simple sum monetary aggregates. Suppose there are two monetary assets over which the central bank aggregates. The quantity of each of the two component assets is y_1 and y_2. Suppose that the central bank reports, as data,

---

Bank is in the process of revising its MSI database, perhaps to incorporate some of those adjustments. Regarding sweep adjustment, see Jones, Dutkowsky, and Elger (2005). At the present stage of this research, we felt it was best to use data available from the Federal Reserve for purposes of replicability and comparability with the official simple sum data. As a result, we did not modify the St. Louis Federal Reserve's MSI database or the Federal Reserve Board's simple sum data in any ways. This decision should not be interpreted to imply advocacy by us of the official choices.

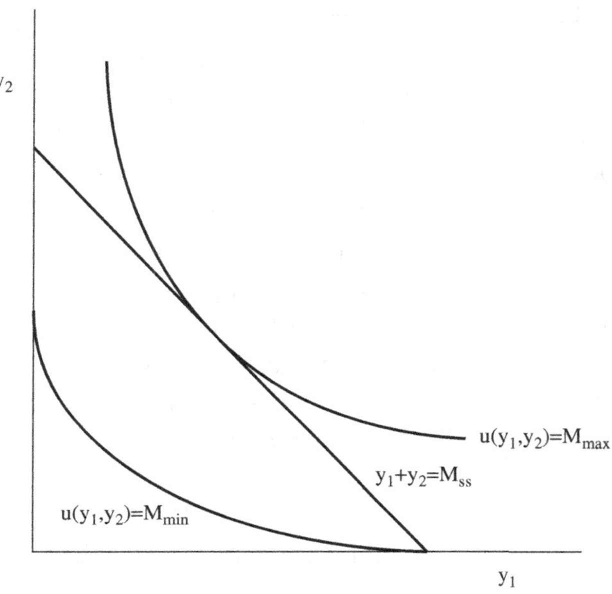

Fig. 1. Demand side aggregation error range.

that the value of the simple sum monetary aggregates is M_{ss}. The information content of that reported variable level is contained in the fact that the two components must be somewhere along the Figure 1 hyperplane, $y_1 + y_2 = M_{ss}$, or more formally that the components are in the set A:

$$A = \{(y_1, y_2) : \ y_1 + y_2 = M_{ss}\}.$$

But according to equation (1.3), the actual value of the service flow from those asset holdings is $u(y_1, y_2)$. Consequently the information content of the information set A regarding the monetary service flow is that the flow is in the set E:

$$E = \{u(y_1, y_2) : \ (y_1, y_2) \in A\}.$$

Note that E is not a singleton. To see the magnitude of the slackness in that information, observe from Figure 1 that if the utility level (service flow) is $M_{\min}$, then the indifference curve does touch the hyperplane, A, at its lower right corner. Hence that indifference curve cannot rule out the M_{ss} reported value of the simple sum monetary aggregate, although a lower level of utility is ruled out, since indifference curves at lower utility levels cannot touch the hyperplane, A.

Now consider the higher utility level of $M_{\max}$ and its associated indifference curve in Figure 1. Observe that indifference curve also does have a point in common with the hyperplane, A, at the tangency. But higher levels of utility are ruled out, since their indifference curves cannot touch the hyperplane, A. Hence the information about the monetary service flow, provided by the reported value of the simple sum aggregate, M_{ss}, is the interval

$$E = [M_{\min}, M_{\max}].$$

The supply side aggregation is analogous, but the lines of constant supplied service flow for financial firms are production possibility curves, not indifference curves, as shown by Barnett (1987). The resulting display of the information content of the simple sum aggregate is in Figure 2, with the analogous conclusions. To make the figure easy to understand, the same symbols are used as in Figure 1, with the exception of the replacement of the utility aggregator function, u, with production aggregator function, y_0.

1.3. The History of Thought on Monetary Aggregation

The field of aggregation and index number theory has a long history, going back for about a century. The first book to put together the properties of all of the available index numbers in a systematic manner was the famous book by Irving Fisher (1922). He made it clear in that book that the simple sum and arithmetic average indexes are the worst known indexes. On p. 29 of that book he wrote:

> "The simple arithmetic average is put first merely because it naturally comes first to the reader's mind, being the most common

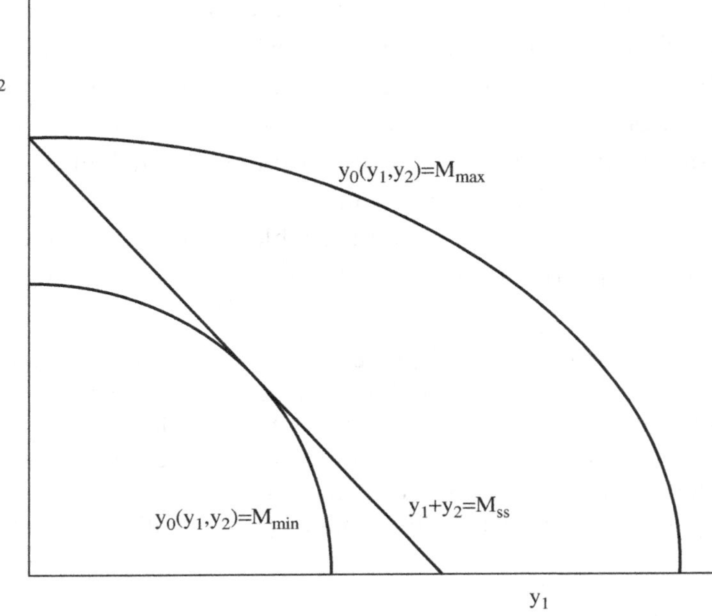

Fig. 2. Supply side aggregation error range.

form of average. In fields other than index numbers it is often the best form of average to use. But we shall see that the simple arithmetic average produces one of the very worst of index numbers, and if this book has no other effect than to lead to the total abandonment of the simple arithmetic type if index number, it will have served a useful purpose."

On p. 361 Fisher wrote:

"The simple arithmetic should not be used under any circumstances, being always biased and usually freakish as well. Nor should the simple aggregative ever be used; in fact this is even less reliable."

Indeed data producing agencies and data producing newspapers switched to reputable index numbers, following the appearance of Fisher's book. But there was one exception: the world's central banks, which produced their monetary aggregates as simple sums. While the implicit assumption of perfect substitutability in identical ratios might have made sense during the first half of the 20th century, that assumption has made unreasonable since then, as interest bearing substitutes for currency became available from banks, including interest bearing checking accounts.

Nevertheless, the nature of the problem was understood by Friedman and Schwartz (1970, pp. 151–152), who wrote the following:

> "The [simple summation] procedure is a very special case of the more general approach. In brief, the general approach consists of regarding each asset as a joint product having different degrees of 'moneyness,' and defining the quantity of money as the weighted sum of the aggregated value of all assets.... We conjecture that this approach deserves and will get much more attention than it has so far received."

More recently, subsequent to the work of Diewert on superlative index number theory and Barnett's derivation of the user cost of monetary assets and the Divisia monetary aggregates, Lucas (2000, p. 270) wrote:

> "I share the widely held opinion that M1 is too narrow an aggregate for this period [the 1990s], and I think that the Divisia approach offers much the best prospects for resolving this difficulty."

In a related vein, Lucas (1999) stated in a published interview:

> "I am happy about the successes of general equilibrium theory in macro and sad about the de-emphasis on money that those successes have brought about."

In light of recent events, the following statement appeared in *The Economist* magazine, June 9–15, 2007, p. 88.

> "Has the pendulum swung too far from monetarist overkill to monetary neglect? In a recent lecture, Mervyn King, the governor of Britain's inflation-targeting central bank, seemed to think so.... Money, if not monetarism, is making a comeback in the way central bankers think about and carry out policy....Money still matters — as it always has done."

Even more recently, the following statement appeared in the *Wall Street Journal*, April 9, 2008. The title of the article was "Volcker's Demarche":

> "You don't have to predict it. We're in it." Thus did Paul Volcker respond to a question Tuesday about whether he still predicts a "dollar crisis" in the coming years .... The world has been staging a run on the greenback .... The present climate, Mr. Volcker told his audience, reminded him of nothing so much as the early 1970s."

1.4. The 1960s and 1970s

Having surveyed the theory and some of the relevant historical background, we now survey some key results. We organize them chronologically, to make the evolution of views clear. The source of the results in this section, along with further details, can be found in Barnett, Offenbacher, and Spindt (1984) and Barnett (1982).

Demand and supply of money functions were fundamental to macroeconomics and to central bank policy until the 1970s, when questions began to arise about the stability of those functions. It was common for general equilibrium models to determine real values and relative prices, and for the demand and supply for money to determine the price level and thereby nominal values. But it was believed that something went wrong in the 1970s. In Figure 3, observe the behavior of the velocity of M3 and M3+ (later called *L*), which were the two broad aggregates often emphasized in that literature. For the demand for money function to have the correct sign for its interest elasticity (better modeled as user-cost price elasticity), velocity must increase

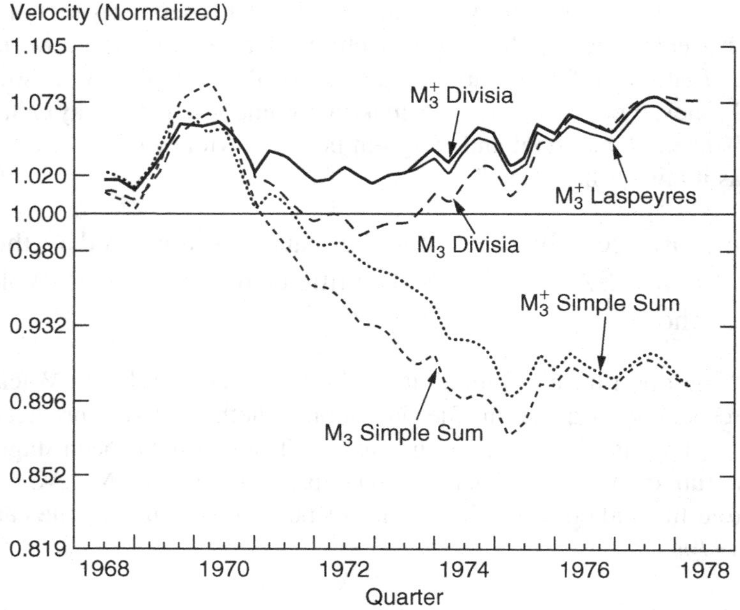

Fig. 3. Seasonally adjusted normalized velocity during the 1970s.

when nominal interest rates increase. In fact velocity should move in the same direction as nominal interest rates.

Figure 4 provides an interest rate during the same time period. Note that while nominal interest rates were increasing during the increasing inflation of that decade, the velocity of the simple sum monetary aggregates in Figure 3 were decreasing. While the source of concern is evident, note that the problem did not exist, when the data was produced from index number theory. The interest elasticity of velocity was positive for all three plots produced from index number theory.

Most of the concern in the 1970s was focused on 1974, when it was believed that there was a sharp structural shift in money markets. Figure 5 displays a source of that concern. In Figure 5, we have plotted velocity against a bond rate, rather than against time, as in Figure 3. As is evident from Figure 5, there appears to be a dramatic shift

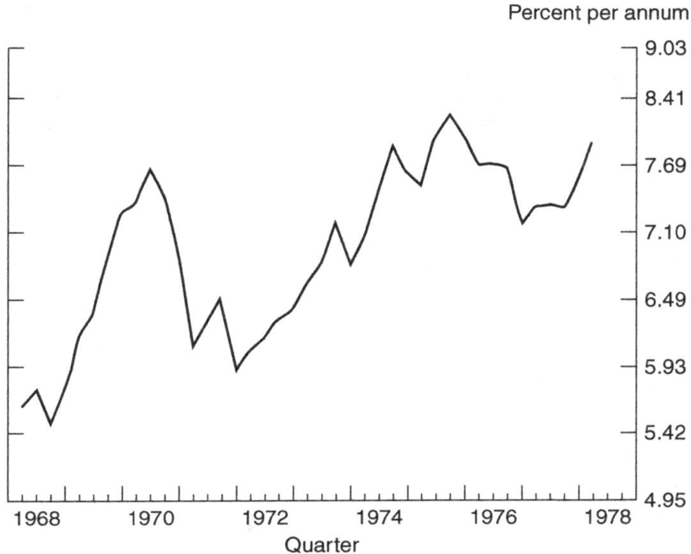

Fig. 4. Interest Rates during the 1970s: 10 year government bond rate.

downwards in that velocity function in 1974. But observe that this result was acquired using simple sum M3. Figure 6 displays the same cross plot of velocity against an interest rate, but with M3 computed as its Divisia index. Observe that velocity no longer is constant, either before or after 1974. But there is no structural shift.

There were analogous concerns about the supply side of money markets. The reason is evident from Figure 7, which plots the base multiplier against a bond rate's deviation from trend. The base multiplier is the ratio of a monetary aggregate to the monetary base. In this case, the monetary aggregate is again simple sum M3. Observe the dramatic structural shift. Prior to 1974, the function was a parabola. After 1974 the function is an intersecting straight line. But again this puzzle was produced by the simple sum monetary aggregate. In Figure 8, the same plot is provided, but with the monetary aggregate changed to Divisia M2. The structural shift is gone.

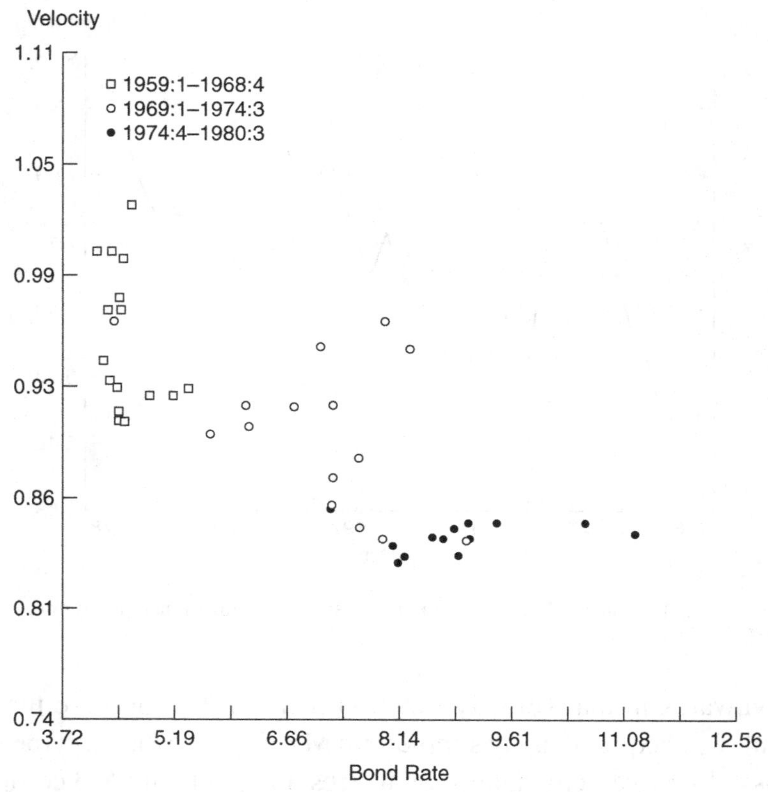

Fig. 5. Simple Sum M3 Velocity versus Interest Rate: Moody's AAA corporate bond rate, quarterly, 1959.1–1980.3.

The most formal methods of investigating these concerns at the time were based on the use of the Goldfeld demand for money function, which was the standard specification used by the Federal Reserve System. The equation was originated by Stephen Goldfeld (1973) at Princeton University. The equation was a linear function of a monetary aggregate on national income, a regulated interest rate, and an unregulated interest rate. It was widely believed that the function had become unstable in the 1970s. P. A. V. B. Swamy and Peter Tinsley (1980), at the Federal Reserve Board in Washington, DC, had produced a stochastic coefficients approach to estimating a

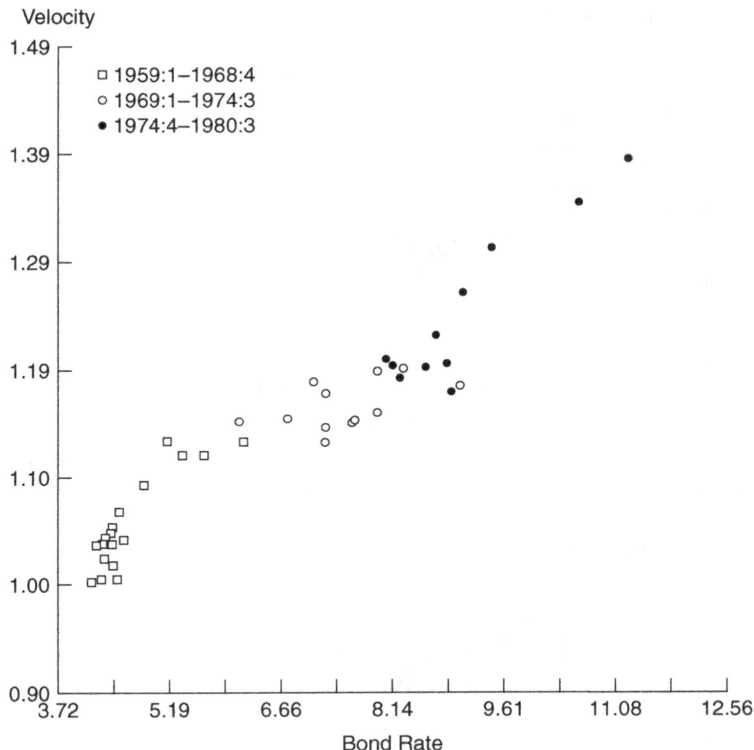

Fig. 6. Divisia M3 Velocity versus Interest Rate: Moody's AAA corporate bond rate, quarterly, 1959.1–1980.3.

linear equation. The result was an estimated stochastic process for each coefficient. The approach permitted testing the null hypothesis that all of the stochastic processes are constant.

Swamy estimated the processes for the model's three coefficients at the Federal Reserve Board with quarterly data from 1959:2–1980:4, and the results were published by Barnett, Offenbacher, and Spindt. The realizations of the three coefficient processes are displayed in Figures 9, 10, and 11. The solid line is the process's realization, when money is measured by simple sum M2. The dotted line is the realization, when the monetary aggregate is measured by the Divisia index. The instability of the coefficient is very clear, when

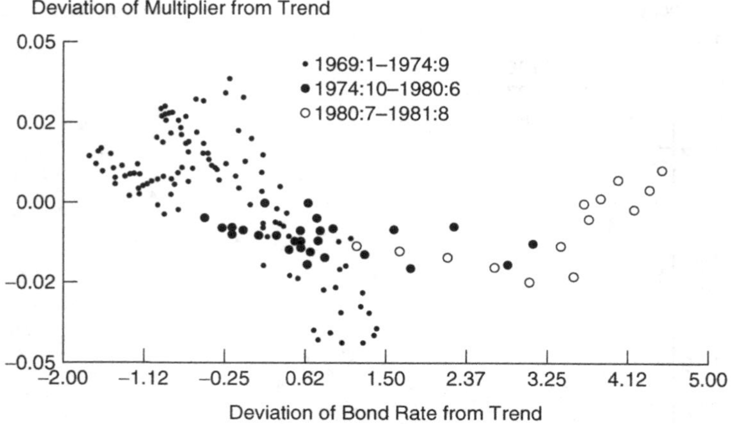

Fig. 7. Simple Sum M3 Base Multiplier versus Interest Rate: deviation from time trend of Moody's Baa corporate bond rate, monthly 1969.1–1981.8.

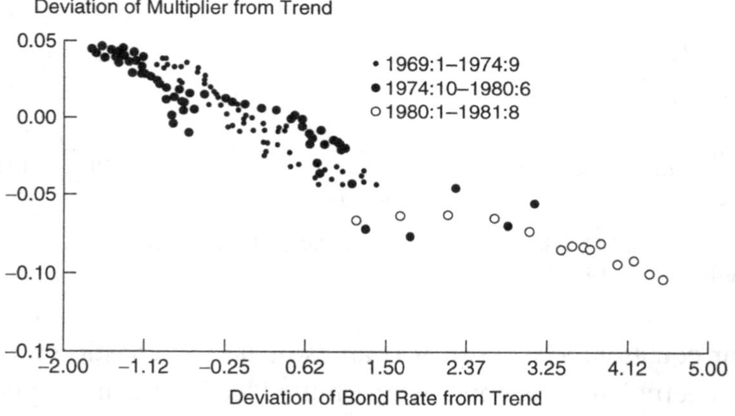

Fig. 8. Divisia M3 Monetary Aggregate Base Multiplier versus Deviation from time trend of Moody's Baa corporate bond Interest Rate, monthly 1969.1–1981.8.

the monetary aggregate is simple sum, but the processes look like noise around a constant, when the monetary aggregate is Divisia. The statistical test could not reject constancy (i.e., stability of the demand for money function), when Divisia was used. But stability was rejected, when the monetary aggregate was simple sum.

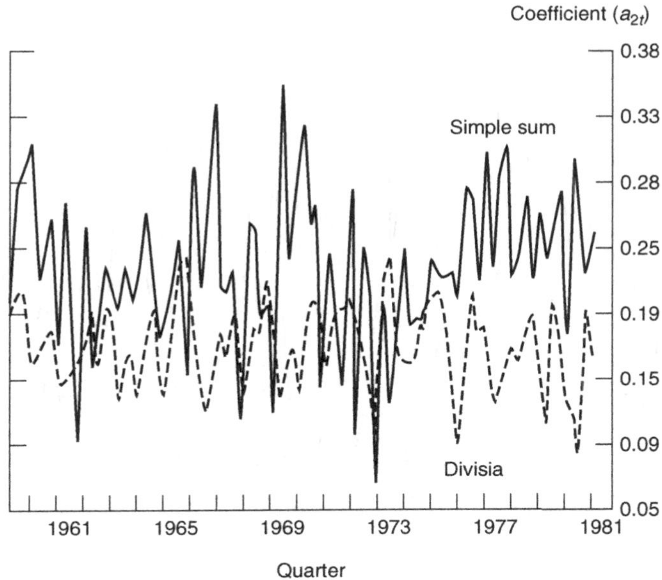

Fig. 9. Income coefficient time path.

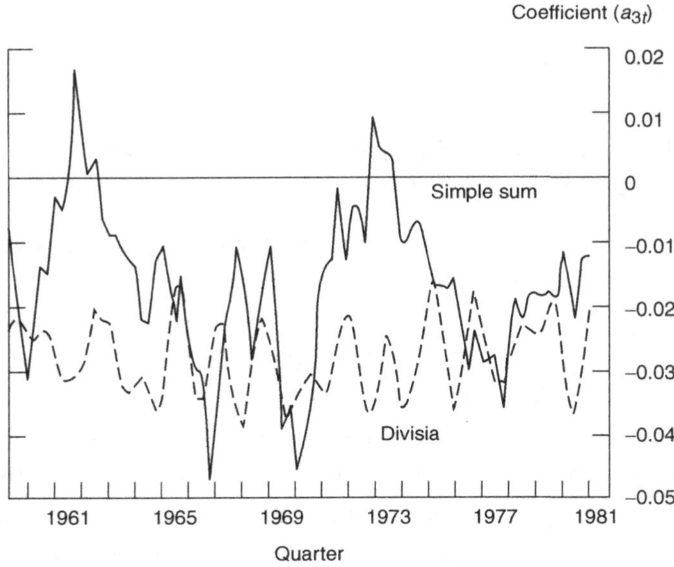

Fig. 10. Market interest rate (commercial paper rate) coefficient time path.

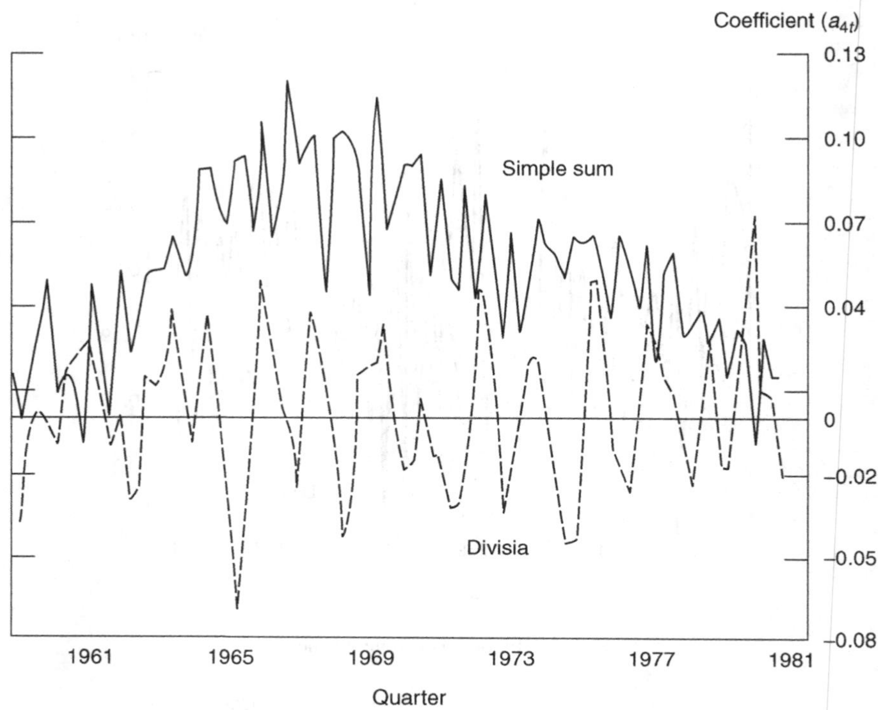

Fig. 11. Regulated interest rate (passbook rate) coefficient time path.

1.5. The Monetarist Experiment: November 1979–November 1982

Following the inflationary 1970s, Paul Volcker, as Chairman of the Federal Reserve Board, decided to bring inflation under control by decreasing the rate of growth of the money supply, with the instrument of policy being changed from the federal funds rate to nonborrowed reserves. The period, November 1979–November 1982, during which that policy was applied was called the "Monetarist Experiment." The policy succeeded in ending the escalating inflation of the 1970s, but was followed by a recession. That recession was not intended. The Federal Reserve decided that the existence of widespread 3-year negotiated wage contracts precluded a sudden decrease in the money supply growth rate to the intended long run growth rate. The decision was to decrease from the high double-digit growth rates to about 10% per year and then gradually decrease towards the intended long run growth rate.

It was believed that a sudden drop to the intended long run growth rate would produce a recession. Figures 12 and 13 and Table 1 reveal the cause of the unintended recession. As is displayed in Figures 12 and 13, for the M2 and M3 levels of aggregation, the rate of growth of the Divisia monetary aggregates was less than the rate of growth of the official simple sum aggregate intermediate targets.

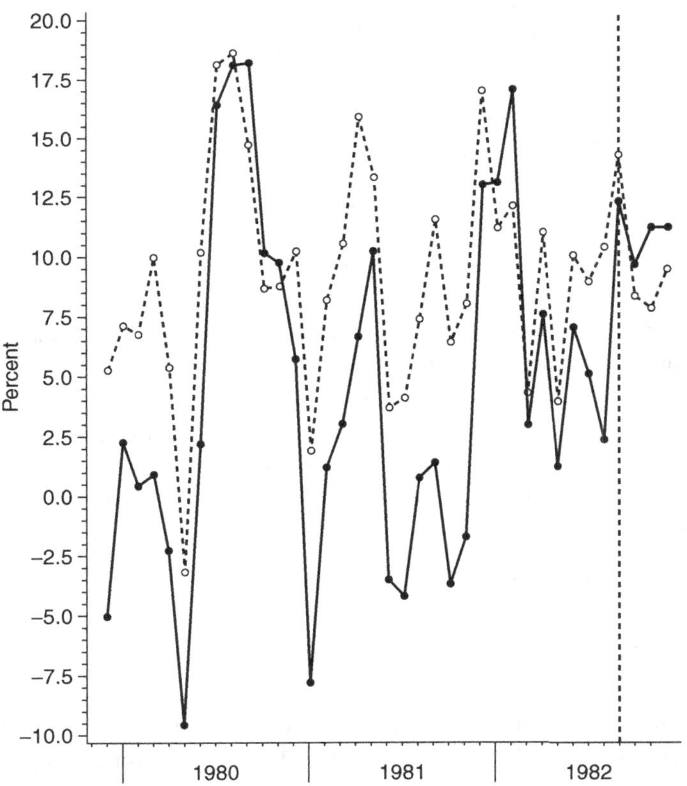

Fig. 12. Seasonally adjusted annual M2 Growth Rates. Solid line = Divisia, dashed line = simple sum. The last three observations to the right of the vertical line are post sample period.

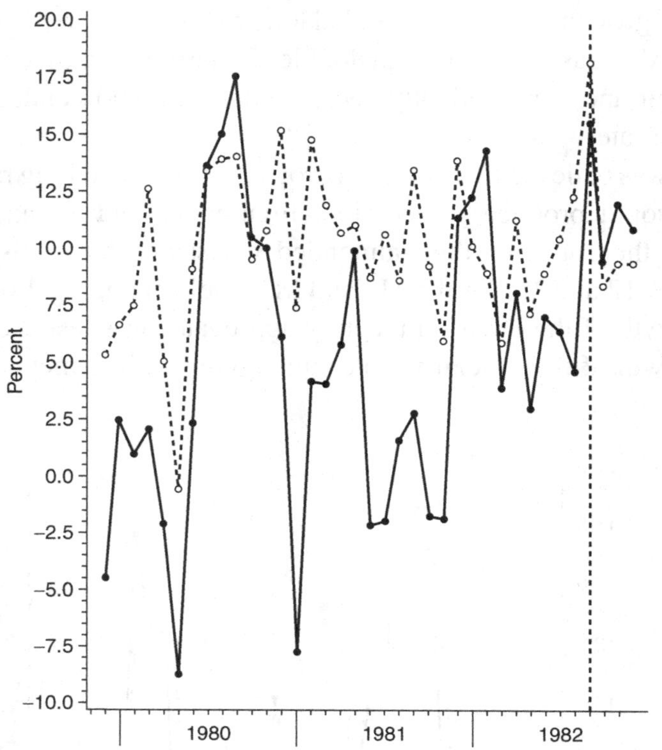

Fig. 13. Seasonally adjusted annual M3 Growth Rates. Solid line = Divisia, dashed line = simple sum. The last three observations to the right of the vertical line are post sample period.

Table 1. Mean Growth Rates During the Period.

Monetary Aggregate	Mean Growth Rate during Period
Divisia M2	4.5
Simple Sum M2	9.3
Divisia M3	4.8
Simple Sum M3	10.0

As Table 1 summarizes, the simple sum aggregate growth rates were at the intended levels, but the Divisia growth rates were half as large, producing an unintended negative shock of substantially greater magnitude than intended. When a recession occurred, that unintended consequence was an embarrassment to monetarists, who subsequently denied that a monetarist policy actually had been in effect. But it is well known to those who were on the staff of the Federal Reserve Board at the time that the Federal Reserve was doing what it said it was doing.

1.6. End of the Monetarist Experiment: 1983–1984

Following the end of the Monetarist Experiment and the unintended recession that followed, Milton Friedman became very vocal with his prediction that there had just been a huge surge in the growth rate of the money supply, and that surge would surely work its way through the economy and produce a new inflation. He further predicted that there would be an overreaction by the Federal Reserve, plunging the economy back down into a recession. He published this view repeatedly in the media in various magazines and newspapers, with the most visible being his *Newsweek* article that appeared on September 26, 1983. That article is provided in the Appendix in Figure A1.

We have excerpted some of the sentences from that *Newsweek* article below:

> "The monetary explosion from July 1982 to July 1983 leaves no satisfactory way out of our present situation. The Fed's stepping on the brakes will appear to have no immediate effect. Rapid recovery will continue under the impetus of earlier monetary growth. With its historical shortsightedness, the Fed will be tempted to step still harder on the brake — just as the failure of rapid monetary growth in late 1982 to generate immediate recovery led it to keep its collective foot on the accelerator much too long. The result is bound to be renewed stagflation — recession accompanied by rising inflation and high interest rates...The only real uncertainty is when the recession will begin."

But on exactly the same day, September 26, 1983, William Barnett published a very different view in *Forbes* magazine. That article is reprinted in the Appendix as Figure A2. The following is an excerpt of some of the sentences from that article:

> "people have been panicking unnecessarily about money supply growth this year. The new bank money funds and the super NOW accounts have been sucking in money that was formerly held in other forms, and other types of asset shuffling also have occurred. But the Divisia aggregates are rising at a rate not much different from last year's...the 'apparent explosion' can be viewed as a statistical blip."

Of course, Milton Friedman would not have taken such a strong position without reason. You can see the reason from Figure 14. The percentage growth rates in that figure are divided by 10, so should be multiplied by 10 to acquire the actual growth rates. Notice the large spike in growth rate, rising to near 30% per year. But that solid line is produced from simple sum M2, which was greatly overweighting the recent new availability of super NOW accounts

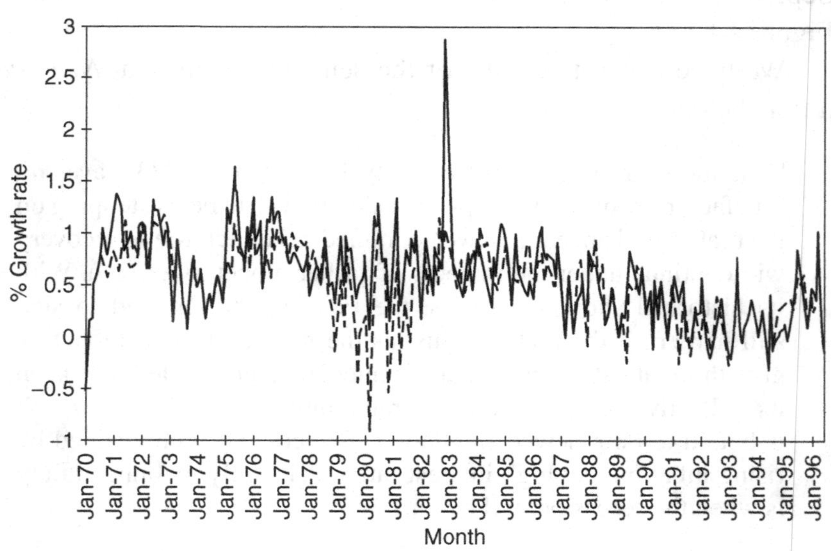

Fig. 14. Monetary growth rates, dashed line = Divisia, solid line = simple sum, 1970–1996, from St. Louis Federal Reserve's Database.

and money market deposit accounts. There was no spike in the Divisia monetary aggregate, represented by the dashed line.

If indeed the huge surge in the money supply had happened, then inflation would surely have followed, unless money is extremely non-neutral, a view held by very few economists. But there was no inflationary surge and no subsequent recession.

1.7. The Rise of Risk Adjustment Concerns: 1984–1993

The exact monetary quantity aggregator function $m_t = u(\mathbf{m}_t)$ can be tracked very accurately by the Divisia monetary aggregate, m_t^d, since that tracking ability is known under perfect certainty. However, when nominal interest rates are uncertain, the Divisia monetary aggregate's tracking ability is somewhat compromised. That compromise is eliminated by using the extended Divisia monetary aggregate derived by Barnett, Liu, and Jensen (1997) under risk. Let m_t^G denote the extended "generalized" Divisia monetary aggregate over the monetary assets. The only difference between m_t^G and m_t^d is the user cost formula used to compute the prices in the Divisia index formula.

Let π_{it}^G denote the generalized user cost of monetary asset i. Barnett, Liu, and Jensen (1997) prove that

$$\pi_{it}^G = \pi_{it}^e + \varphi_{it}$$

where

$$\pi_{it}^e = \frac{E_t(R_t - R_{it})}{E_t(1 + R_t)}$$

and

$$\varphi_{it} = \frac{E_t(1 + R_{it})}{E_t(1 + R_t)} \frac{Cov\left(R_t, \frac{\partial T}{\partial C_{t+1}}\right)}{\frac{\partial T}{\partial C_T}} - \frac{Cov\left(R_{it}, \frac{\partial T}{\partial C_{t+1}}\right)}{\frac{\partial T}{\partial C_t}},$$

where

$$T = E_t \sum_{t=0}^{\infty} \beta^t F(c_t, m_t^G).$$

Barnett, Liu, and Jensen (1997) show that the values of π_{it} determine the risk premia in interest rates. Note that π_{it}^G reduces to equation (1.2) under perfect certainty.

Using that extension, Barnett and Xu (1998) demonstrated that velocity will change, if the variance of an interest rate stochastic process changes. Hence the variation in the variance of an interest rate ARCH or GARCH stochastic process cannot be ignored in modelling monetary velocity. By calibrating a stochastic dynamic general equilibrium model, Barnett and Xu (1998) showed that the usual computation of velocity will appear to produce instability, when interest rates exhibit stochastic volatility. But when the CCAPM adjusted variables above are used, so that the variation in variance is not ignored, velocity is stabilized.

Figure 15 displays their simulated slope coefficient for the velocity function, treated as a function of the exact interest rate aggregate, but without risk adjustment. All functions in the model are stable, by construction. Series 1 was produced with the least stochastic volatility in the interest rate stochastic process, series 2 with greater variation in variance, and series 3 with even more stochastic volatility. Note that the velocity function slope appears to be increasingly unstable, as stochastic volatility increases. By the model's construction, the slope of the velocity function is constant, if the CCAPM risk adjustment is used. In addition, with real economic data, Barnett and Xu (1998) showed that the evidence of velocity instability is partially explained by overlooking the variation in the variance of interest rates over time.

Subsequently Barnett and Wu (2005) found that the explanatory power of the risk adjustment increases, if the assumption of intertemporal separability of the intertemporal utility function, T, is

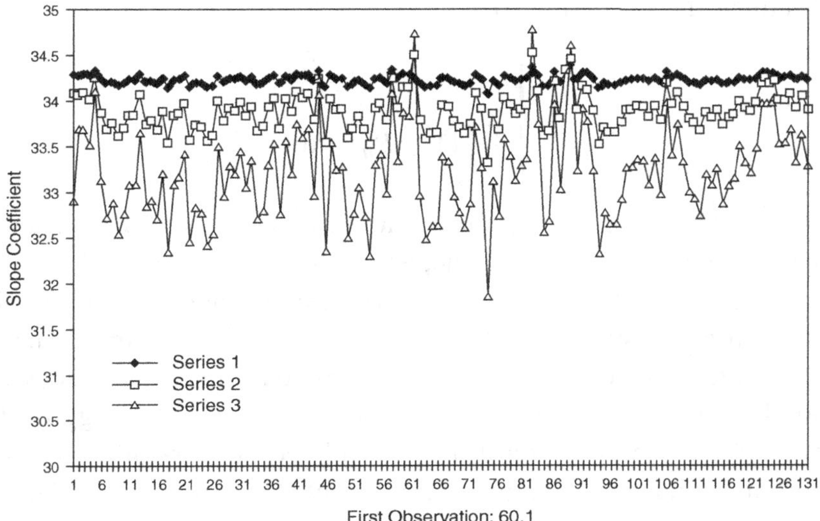

Fig. 15. Simulated velocity slope coefficient with stochastic volatility of interest rates.

weakened. The reason is the same as a source of the well known equity premium puzzle, by which CCAPM under intertemporal separability under-corrects for risk.

The Divisia index tracks the aggregator function measuring service flow. But for some purposes, the economic capital stock, computed from the discounted expected future service flow, is relevant, especially when investigating wealth effects of policy. The economic stock of money (ESM), as defined by Barnett (2000) under perfect foresight, follows immediately from the manner in which monetary assets are found to enter the derived wealth constraint, (2.3). As a result, the formula for the economic stock of money under perfect foresight is

$$V_t = \sum_{s=t}^{\infty} \sum_{i=1}^{n} \left[\frac{p_s^*}{\rho_s} - \frac{p_s^*(1 + r_{is})}{\rho_{s+1}} \right] m_{is}.$$

Where the true cost of living index on consumer goods is $p_s^* = p_s^*(\mathbf{p}_s)$, with the vector of consumer goods prices being $\mathbf{p}_s$, and where the discount rate for period s is

$$\rho_s = \begin{cases} 1 & \text{for } s = t \\ \prod_{u=t}^{s-1} (1 + R_u) & \text{for } s > t \end{cases}.$$

The CCAPM extension of the economic capital stock formula to risk is available from Barnett, Chae, and Keating (2006).

During the late 1980s and early 1990s, there was increasing concern about substitution of monetary assets within the monetary aggregates (especially money market mutual funds) with stock and bond mutual funds, which are not within the monetary aggregates. The Federal Reserve Board staff considered the possibility of incorporating stock and bond mutual funds into the monetary aggregates. Barnett and Zhou (1994a) used the formulas above to investigate the problem. They produced the figures that we reproduce below as Figures 16–19. The dotted line is the simple sum monetary aggregate, which Barnett (2000) proved is equal to the sum of economic capital stock of money, V_t, and the discounted expected investment return from the components.

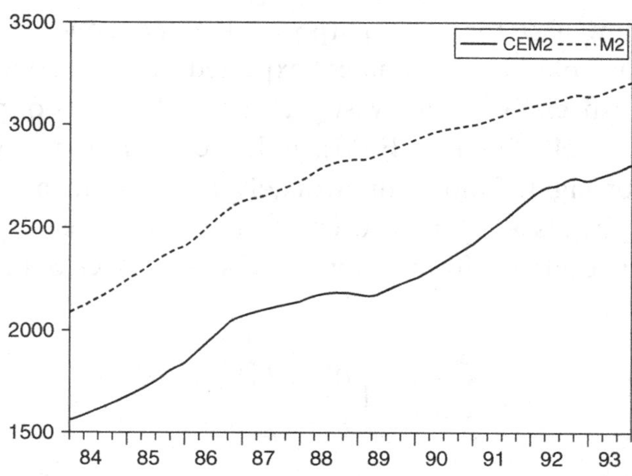

Fig. 16. M2 Joint Product and Economic Capital Stock of Money. M2 = simple sum joint product; CEM2 = economic capital stock part of the joint product.

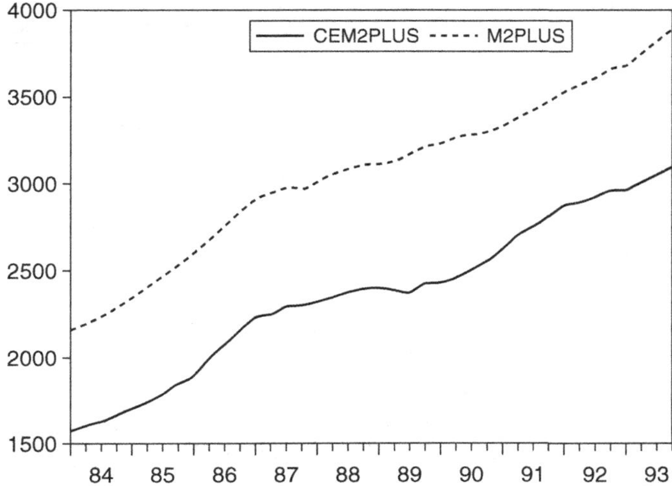

Fig. 17. M2+ Joint Product and Economic Capital Stock of Money. M2+ = simple sum joint product; CEM2+ = economic capital stock part of the joint product.

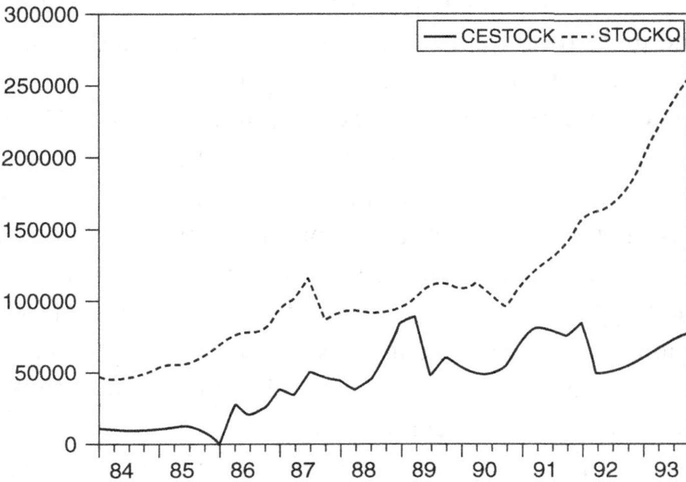

Fig. 18. Common stock mutual funds joint product and their economic capital stock. StockQ = simple sum joint product; CEstock = economic capital stock part of the joint product.

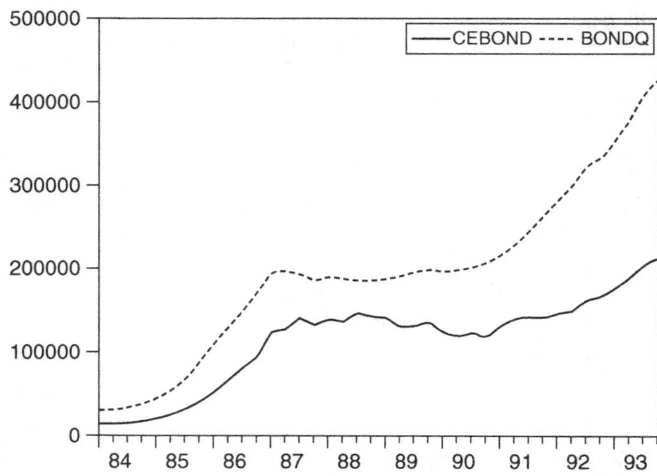

Fig. 19. Bond mutual funds joint product and their economic capital stock. BondQ = simple sum joint product; CEbond = economic capital stock part of the joint product.

Computation of V_t requires modeling expectations. In that early paper, Barnett and Zhou (1994a) used martingale expectations rather than the more recent approach of Barnett, Chae, and Keating, using VAR forecasting. When martingale expectations are used, the index is called CE. Since the economic capital stock of money, V_t, is what is relevant to macroeconomic theory, we should concentrate on the solid lines in those figures. Note that Figure 17 displays nearly parallel time paths, so that the growth rate is about the same in either. That figure is for M2+, which was the Federal Reserve Board staff's proposed extended aggregate, adding stock and bond mutual funds to M2. But note that in Figure 16, the gap between the two graphs is decreasing, producing a slower rate of growth for the simple sum aggregate than for the economic stock of money.

The reason can be found in Figures 18 and 19, which use a solid line to display the monetary (i.e., liquidity) services from stock and bond mutual funds and a dotted line for simple sum measure of those funds, where again the simple sum measures a joint product: the discounted investment yield plus the discounted service flow. Hence the gap between the two lines is the amount motivated by investment yield. Clearly those gaps have been growing. But it is precisely that gap which does *not* measure monetary services. By adding the value of stock and bond mutual funds into Figure 16 to get Figure 17, the growth rate error of the simple sum aggregate is offset by adding in an increased amount of assets providing nonmonetary services. Rather than trying to stabilize the error gap by adding in more and more nonmonetary services, the correct solution would be to remove the entire error gap by using the solid line in Figure 16 (or Figure 17), which measures the actual capital stock of money.

1.8. The Y2K Computer Bug: 1999–2000

Following the problems of risk that increased in importance in the 1990s with the increasing substitution of monetary assets into stock and bond mutual funds, the next major concern about monetary aggregates and monetary policy was at the end of 1999. In particular, the financial press became highly critical of the Federal Reserve for what was perceived by those commentators to be a large, inflationary surge in the monetary base. The reason is clear from Figure 20. But in fact there was no valid reason for concern, since the cause was again a problem with the data.

The monetary base is the sum of currency plus bank reserves. Currency is dollar for dollar pure money, while reserves back deposits in an amount that is a multiple of the reserves. Hence as a measure of monetary services, the monetary base is severely defective, even though it is a correct measure of "outside money." At the end of 1999, there was the so-called Y2K computer bug, which was expected to cause temporary problems with computers throughout the world, including at banks. Consequently many depositors withdrew funds from their checking accounts and moved them into cash. While the decrease in deposits thereby produced an equal increase in currency demand, the decrease in deposits produced a smaller decline in reserves, because of the multiplier from reserves to deposits. The

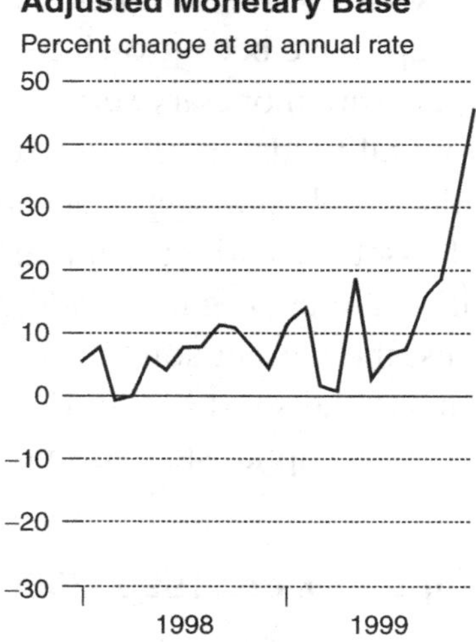

Fig. 20. Monetary base surge.

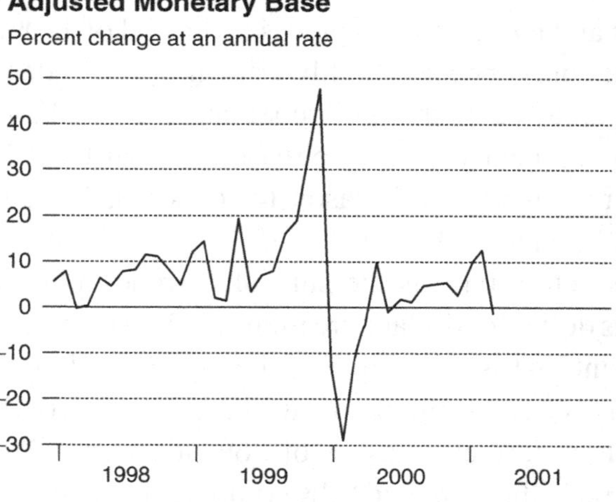

Fig. 21. Y2K computer bug.

result was a surge in the monetary base, even though the cause was a temporary dollar-for-dollar transfer of funds from demand deposits to cash, having little effect on economic liquidity. Once the computer bug was resolved, people put the withdrawn cash back into deposits, as is seen from Figure 21.

1.9. The Supply Side

While much of the concern in this literature has been about the demand for money, there is a parallel literature about the supply of money by financial intermediaries. Regarding the aggregation theoretic approach, see Barnett and Hahm (1994) and Barnett and Zhou (1994a). It should be observed that the demand-side Divisia monetary aggregate, measuring perceived service flows received by financial asset holders, can be slightly different from the supply side Divisia monetary aggregate, measuring service flows produced by financial intermediaries. The reason is the regulatory wedge resulting from non-interest-bearing required reserves. That wedge produces a difference between demand side and supply side user cost prices and thereby can produce a small difference between the demand side and supply side Divisia aggregates.

When there are no required reserves and hence no regulatory wedge, the general equilibrium looks like Figure 22, with the usual separating hyperplane determining the user cost prices, which are the same on both sides of the market. The production possibility surface

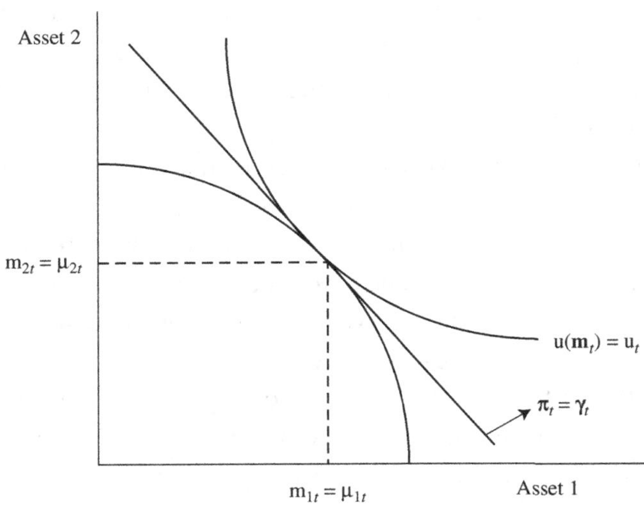

Fig. 22. Financial general equilibrium without required reserves.

between deposit types 1 and 2 is for a financial intermediary, as in Figure 2, while the indifference curve is for a depositor allocating funds over the two asset types, as in Figure 1. But now the separating hyperplane can have any slope and is not the same as the simple sum hyperplane displayed in Figures 1 and 2.

While this separating-hyperplane general-equilibrium diagram is elementary, it assumes that the same prices and user costs are seen on both sides of the market. But when noninterest-bearing required reserves exist, the foregone investment return to banks is an implicit tax on banks and produces a regulatory wedge between the demand and supply side. It was shown by Barnett (1987) that under those circumstances, the user cost of supplied financial services by banks is not equal to the demand price, (1.2), but rather is

$$\gamma_{it} = \frac{(1 - k_{it})R_t - r_{it}}{1 + R_t},$$

where k_{it} is the required reserve ratio for account type i. Note that this supply-side user cost is equal to the demand-side formula, (1.2), when $k_{it} = 0$.

The resulting general equilibrium diagram, with the regulatory wedge, is displayed in Figure 23. Notice that one tangency determines the supply-side prices, while the other tangency produces the demand-side prices, with the angle between the two straight lines being the "regulatory wedge." Observe that the demand equals the supply for each of the component assets, 1 and 2.

Although the component demands and supplies are equal to each other, the failure of tangency between the production possibility curve and the indifference curve at the equilibrium results in a wedge between the growth rates of aggregate demand and supply services, as reflected in the fact that the user cost prices in the Divisia index are not the same in the demand and the supply side aggregates. To determine whether this wedge might provide a reason to compute and track the Divisia monetary supply aggregate as well as the more common demand-side Divisia monetary aggregate, Barnett,

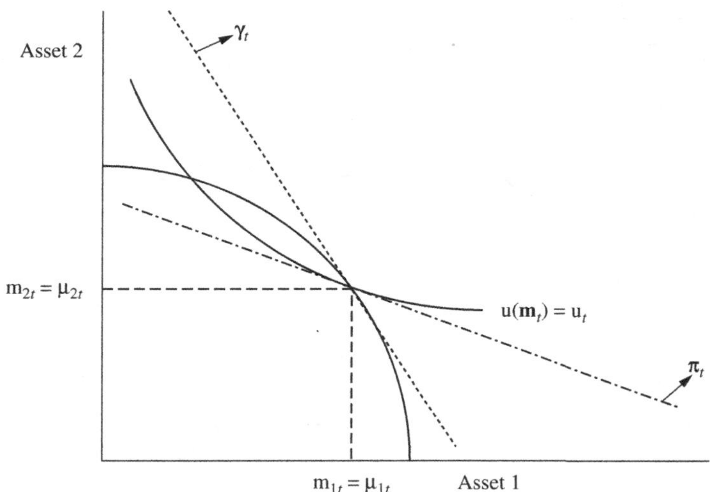

Fig. 23. Financial equilibrium with positive required reserves.

Hinich, and Weber (1986) conducted a detailed spectral analysis in the frequency domain. Some of the results are reprinted in Figures 24–26.

Figure 24 displays the supply and demand side Divisia M2 power spectrum. The demand side spectrum is displayed only at its estimated value, while the supply side spectrum is displayed as its confidence region. Notice that the supply side confidence region contains the demand side at all frequency. Hence the null hypothesis that the supply and demand side aggregates are the same cannot be rejected at any frequency, even though the computed aggregates are not exactly the same on the demand and supply sides. Figure 25 displays the squared coherence between the demand and supply side Divisia monetary aggregates, where coherence measures correlation as a function of frequency. The figure provides those plots at three levels of aggregation. Note that the correlation usually exceeds 95% for all three levels of aggregation at all frequencies, but the coherence begins to decline at very high frequencies (i.e., very short cycle periods in months). Hence the difference between the demand and supply side monetary aggregates is relevant only in modelling very short run phenomena.

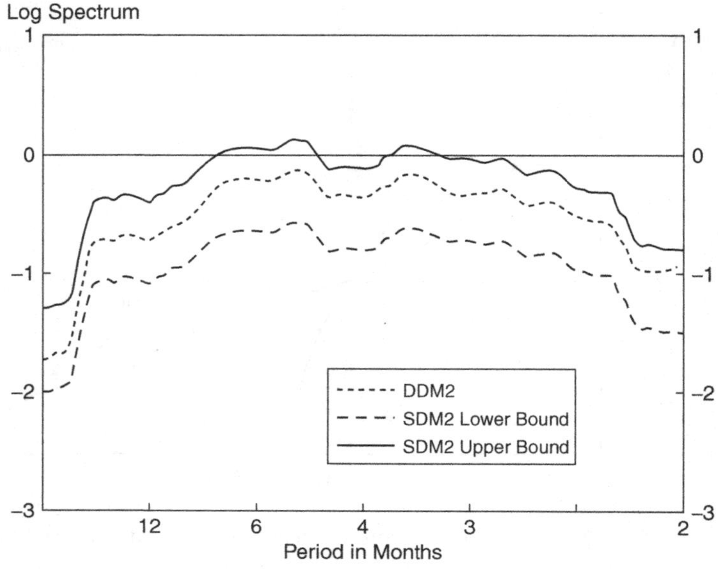

Fig. 24. Confidence Region for Supply Side Spectrum: log spectrum of DDM2 and confidence band for log spectrum of SDM2.

But to put this into context, that paper also displays plots in the time domain for simple sum M3, the supply side M3 Divisia index (SDM3), and the demand side M3 Divisia index (DDM3) over the same time period used in producing the frequency domain comparisons. See Figure 26 for those reprinted plots. Notice that it takes over a decade for the difference between the demand side and supply side Divisia index to get wider than a pencil point, but the divergence between simple sum and either Divisia aggregate begins immediately and is cumulative. In short, the error in using the simple sum monetary aggregates is overwhelmingly greater than the usually entirely negligible difference between the demand and supply side Divisia monetary aggregates. Furthermore, in recent years reserve requirements have been low and largely offset by sweeps, and it is the intent of the Federal Reserve eventually to begin paying interest on required reserves, so the difference between the demand and supply

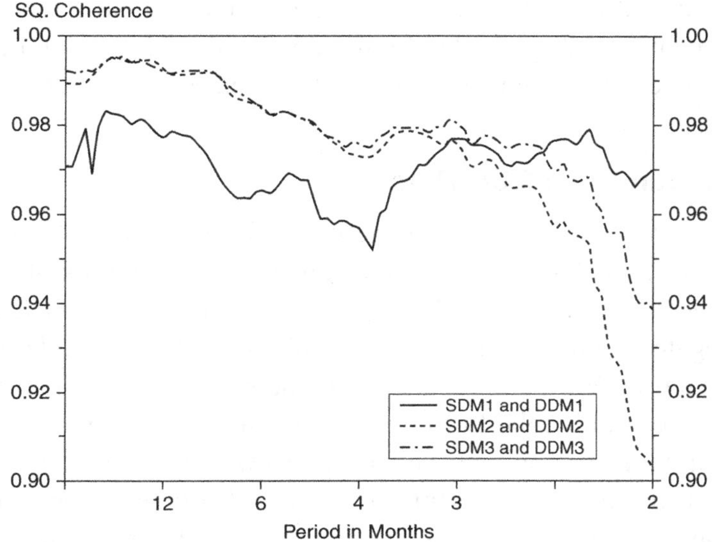

Fig. 25. Squared coherence between Divisia demand and supply side Divisia.

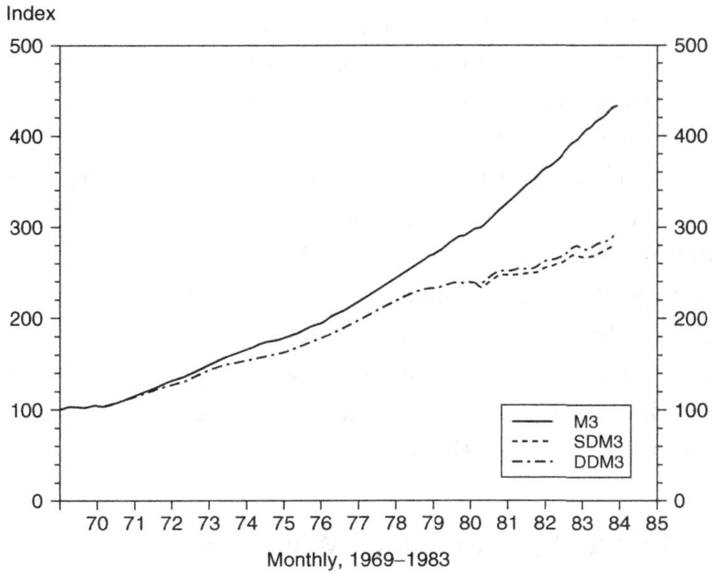

Fig. 26. Simple sum, Divisia demand, and Divisia supply.

side Divisia monetary aggregates now is much smaller than during the time period displayed in Figure 26, and eventually will be a zero difference, when interest is paid on required reserves in the future.

1.10. European ECB Data

This survey concentrates on the experience in the US, where the theory of monetary aggregation originated. But the Bank of England and the European Central Bank now also have Divisia monetary aggregates, as have many central banks — often available only for internal use. While the Bank of England makes its Divisia monetary aggregates public, the ECB does not (sadly not uncommon at many central banks throughout the world). However an economist on the staff of the ECB in Frankfurt provided to William Barnett the plots displayed in Figure 27 (without any implicit or explicit official authorization of publication from the ECB). The date was based upon the multilateral Divisia monetary aggregation theory produced for the ECB by Barnett (2007). While there is nothing "official" about Figure 27, the cross plots of velocity against an interest rate in that figure are interesting. Note the stable relationship, closely resembling that for the US displayed in Figure 6. Since the back data encompasses periods during which many non-euro currencies existed, and since even today many Europeans hold financial assets denominated in foreign currencies, such as the British pound, the multilateral approach produced by Barnett (2007) needs to be extended to the case of risky contemporaneous rates of return on money market assets, because of exchange rate risk. The theory on that extension, which could be incorporated into multilateral aggregation, is now available from Barnett and Wu (2005).

1.11. The Most Recent Data: Would You Believe This?

The most recent research on this subject is Barnett, Chauvet, and Tierney (2009) described in our introductory section 1 above. It is a

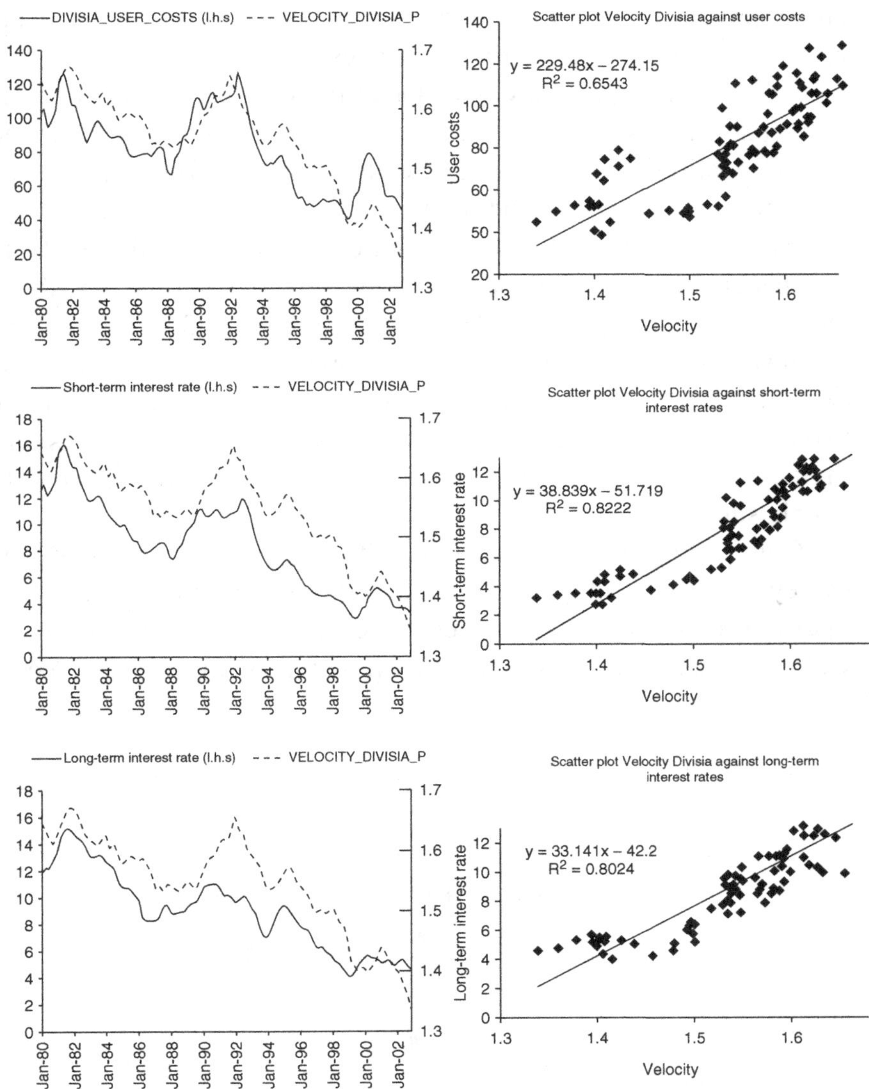

Fig. 27. ECB mondetary velocity.

latent factor Markov switching approach that separates out common dynamics from idiosyncratic terms. The dynamic factor measures the common cyclical movements underlying the observable variables. The idiosyncratic term captures movements peculiar to each index.

The approach is used to provide pairwise comparisons of Divisia versus simple-sum monetary aggregates quarterly from 1960:2 to 2005:4. In that paper, they introduced the connection between the state-space time-series approach to assessing measurement error and the aggregation theoretic concept, with emphasis upon the relevancy to monetary aggregation and monetary policy.

We have provided below as Figure 28 one of the figures from that paper. The figure displays the idiosyncratic terms specific to Divisia M3 and simple sum M3. Compare Divisia M3's idiosyncratic downward spikes in Figure 28 with simple sum M3's idiosyncratic behavior and then compare the relative predictive ability of the two extracted idiosyncratic terms with respect to NBER recessions. Figure 28 speaks for itself. Divisia is much to be preferred to simple sum.

Considering this most recent results along with the many others surveyed in this paper, and the relevant theory, based solidly on microeconomic aggregation theory, you might find it to be worthwhile comparing the results in this literature with the most recent

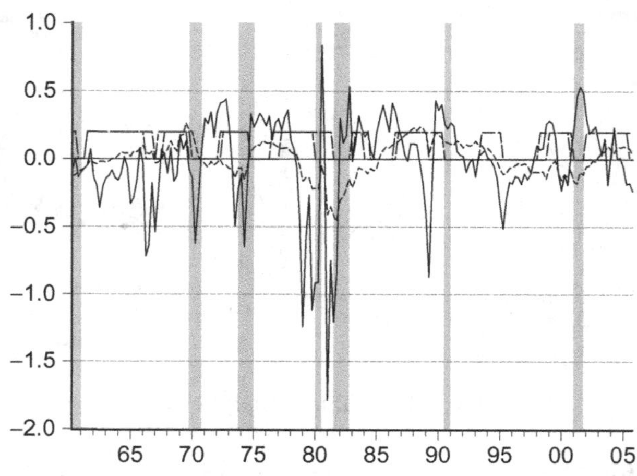

Fig. 28. Idiosyncratic terms for M3 (Dashed Line) and for Divisia M3 growth (Solid Line), High Interest Rate Phases and High Inflation Phases (- -), and NBER Recessions (shaded area).

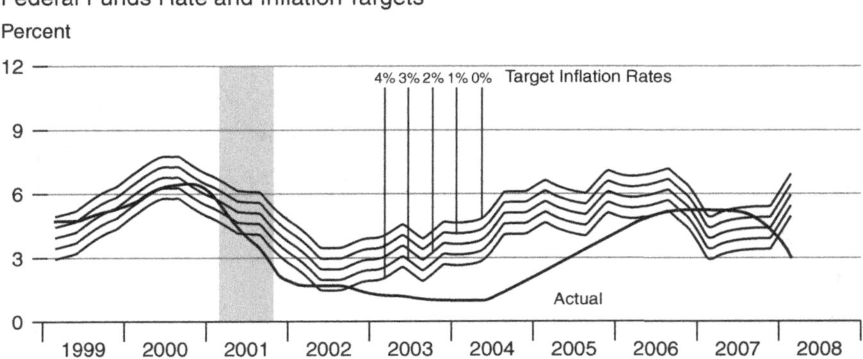

Fig. 29. Taylor rule federal funds rate.

behavior of the Taylor rule, which does not use money at all. Figure 29 is reproduced from the St. Louis Federal Reserve Bank's publication, *Monetary Trends*. That figure displays the range of the target for the federal funds rate produced from the Taylor rule along with the actual interest rate over that time period, where the actual funds rate is the dark solid line. Notice that the actual interest rate was off target for more than three successive years. Perhaps we now have a real paradox: the evident instability of the Taylor rule.

As documented in this survey, monetary policy and monetary research has been plagued by extremely bad monetary aggregates data, resulting from simple sum aggregation, that has been disreputable to professional aggregation and index number theorist for over a half century. In addition, we have shown that the puzzles that have arisen since the early 1970s were produced by simple sum aggregation and would go away, if reputable index number formulas were used, such as Divisia. With so much history and evidence and so much research documenting the data problems, it might be assumed that central banks would now be taking much care to provide high quality data that is consistent with economic theory.

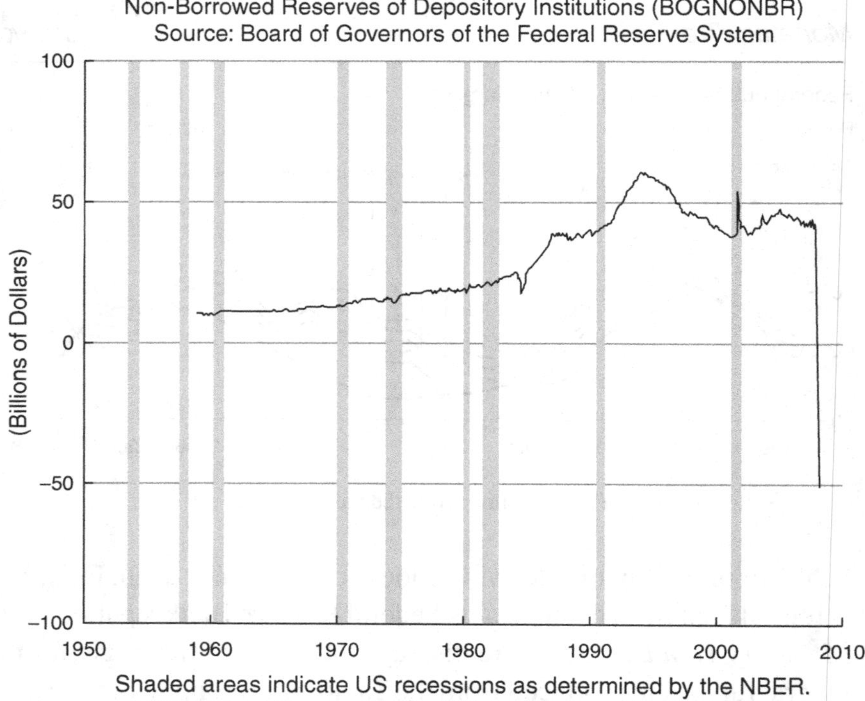

Fig. 30. Nonborrowed reserves.

If that is what you would expect, then look at Figure 30, which was downloaded from the St. Louis Federal Reserve Bank web site and is produced from official Federal Reserve Board data in Washington, DC. Recall that during Volcker's "Monetarist Experiment" period, the instrument of policy was nonborrowed reserves. Also recall from his quotation in section 3 above, that he recently has been highly critical of Federal Reserve policy. Hence it is interesting to look at Figure 30, which displays official recent data on nonborrowed reserves from the Federal Reserve Board.

Total reserves are the sum of borrowed reserves and nonborrowed reserves. Nonborrowed reserves are those reserves that were not borrowed, while borrowed reserves are those reserves that were borrowed. Clearly everything included in borrowed reserves must be reserves, and everything contained in nonborrowed reserves must be reserves. Hence it is impossible for either borrowed reserves or nonborrowed reserves to exceed total reserves. A negative value for either borrowed reserves or nonborrowed reserves would be an oxymoron.

Now look at Figure 30. Observe that nonborrowed reserves recently have crashed to about minus 50 billion dollars. The Federal Reserve's explanation is that they are including the new auction borrowing from the Federal Reserve in nonborrowed reserves, even though they need not be reserves at all. Hence according to this terrible "data," the instrument of monetary policy during Volcker's Monetarist Experiment period now has been driven to a very negative value, as is impossible by the definition of nonborrowed reserves.

1.12. Conclusion

The most advantageous direction for extension of the literature on financial aggregation theory is extension to multilateral monetary aggregation with risky interest yields resulting from exchange rate risk. In this paper we have surveyed the modern literature on financial aggregation and index number theory. We have shown that most of the puzzles and paradoxes that have evolved in the monetary economics literature were produced by the disreputable simple sum monetary aggregates provided officially by central banks, and are resolved by use of aggregation theoretic monetary aggregates. We argue that official central bank data throughout the world has mostly not gotten better, despite the existence of better data internal to those banks for their own use. As a result, researchers should be very cautious about the use of official central bank data in research. We document the fact that the profession has repeatedly been misled by bad central bank monetary data over the past half century. Many commonly held views need to be rethought, since many such views were based upon atheoretical data.

Appendix

MILTON FRIEDMAN

A Case of Bad Good News

President Reagan, politicians of all political persuasions, journalists specializing in economics, Wall Street, the business community—all these and many more are hailing the recent economic statistics showing rapid growth in output and employment as very good news indeed.

One group of economists—the monetarists—are a conspicuous exception. We were also an exception to what I labeled in February as "misleading unanimity" among economic forecasters (NEWSWEEK, Feb. 7, 1983). Almost to a person economic forecasters were predicting a slow and sluggish recovery. We predicted that "1983 will be a year of rapid and vigorous economic growth."

Monetary Explosion: That judgment was based on two considerations: the length and severity of the recession that ended in December 1982, and the monetary explosion that was then in process—a rise in M_1 at the annual rate of 15 percent from July 1982 to January 1983. It seemed to us that "this monetary explosion assures vigorous economic growth in the coming months"—but also that "unfortunately, if it continues much longer, it will also produce a renewed acceleration of inflation and a sharp rise in interest rates." The monetary explosion did produce vigorous growth. Unfortunately, it also did continue—at the annual rate of more than 14 percent from January to July. Interest rates have already risen sharply. Inflation has not yet accelerated. That will come next year, since it generally takes about two years for monetary acceleration to work its way through to inflation.

The "good news," that output grew at the annual rate of nearly 9 percent in the second quarter of this year and may equal that record in the third quarter, is really bad news—the sign of an overheated economy headed for trouble. We do not need another sharp but brief expansion—like 1980 to 1981—followed by a relapse into recession. We need moderate growth at a rate that can be maintained for a long time along with continued reduction in inflation.

The only way to maintain anything like the recent hectic pace of real growth would be to keep the monetary explosion going. But even if the Fed has learned nothing from experience, the market has—as its recent reactions to money-growth figures demonstrate. If the monetary explosion continued, both interest rates and inflation would react much more promptly than in the past. Both would head toward the sky. That reaction would make it nearly impossible for the Fed to continue the monetary explosion. However reluctantly, it will have to step on the brakes—as it already has apparently started to do.

> The monetary explosion leaves no satisfactory way out of our present situation.

The monetary explosion from July 1982 to July 1983 leaves no satisfactory way out of our present situation. The Fed's stepping on the brakes will appear to have no immediate effect. Rapid recovery will continue under the impetus of earlier monetary growth. With its historical shortsightedness, the Fed will be tempted to step still harder on the brake—just as the failure of rapid monetary growth in late 1982 to generate immediate recovery led it to keep its collective foot on the accelerator much too long. The result is bound to be renewed stagflation—recession accompanied by rising inflation and high interest rates.

Recession and the Election: The only real uncertainty is when the recession will begin. That will depend partly on the pattern of monetary growth over coming months, partly on other developments that cannot now be foreseen. Monetarists have always emphasized that the time delay between monetary change and economic change is not only long but also highly variable. Indeed, that is why we are so skeptical about the kind of monetary "fine-tuning" that the Fed has engaged in and why we favor steady monetary growth.

The precise timing of the recession will largely determine the political climate of election year 1984. Both President Reagan's supporters and his opponents are acting as if they expect recent favorable economic developments to continue through 1984—as evidenced by the search on the part of both for other issues to stress. They will be right if the recession does not begin before the third quarter of 1984. But if the recession should begin in the first or second quarter of 1984—as is entirely possible—the situation will be very different. In that case the election campaign would be conducted in an environment of declining output, rising unemployment, rising inflation and high interest rates—hardly an environment favorable to an incumbent.

84 NEWSWEEK/SEPTEMBER 26, 1983

Fig. A1. Milton Friedman, *Newsweek*, Sept 26, 1983.

Faces
Behind The Figures

Edited by John R. Dorfman

What explosion?

If you were measuring the nation's vehicle supply, you wouldn't give equal weight to roller skates and locomotives. But that, in effect, is what the Federal Reserve Board does in measuring the money supply, says William Barnett, an economist at the University of Texas (Austin).

The Fed has realized, Barnett says, that M1 excludes too many forms of money, such as the new money market accounts at banks. But the higher aggregates like M2 and M3, he says, suffer greatly from the "skates and locomotives" problem. Some of their components are much more liquid than others.

How can the Fed control money if it can't adequately define it? You have heard the question before. Barnett thinks he has the answer: Divisia aggregates, named after the late French statistician François Divisia, who published a famous paper on the subject in 1925. In Barnett's Divisia formula, the changes in the supply of various forms of money are weighted according to how liquid each form is. Checking accounts, for example, get more weight than certificates of deposit. To get his weighting factors, Barnett looks at the opportunity cost of holding such low-yield assets as checking accounts and passbook savings accounts. When you give up yield, his model figures, you are probably getting liquidity in exchange.

Crunching Divisia numbers leads Barnett to two conclusions. One is that the Fed was much tighter than it intended to be during the period from late 1979 through mid-1982. For example, in 1982, M2, measured the usual way, was up 9.4%. But Divisia M2 was up only 7.8%.

The other conclusion is that people have been panicking unnecessarily about money supply growth this year. The new bank money funds and the super NOW accounts have been sucking in money that was formerly held in other forms, and other types of asset shuffling also have occurred. But the Divisia aggregates are rising at a rate not much different from last year's, Barnett says. Thus, the "apparent explosion" can be viewed as a statistical blip.

Economist William Barnett
A new set of "M" numbers?

Is anybody listening? Yes, says Barnett, who was a research economist for the Fed for eight years until 1981. Some Fed members, including Governor Henry Wallich, regularly peruse his numbers. Such economists as Paul Samuelson, James Tobin and Milton Friedman also receive the Divisia numbers monthly. It's only a matter of time, he figures, before the Fed will go to Divisia aggregates as its official guide. "They've run out of other alternatives," says Barnett, "and are looking at this very seriously."—J.R.D.

States' rights?

As the sovereign state of South Carolina sees it, there is a provision written into the Tax Equity & Fiscal Responsibility Act (TEFRA) of 1982 that amounts to an unconstitutional effort by Washington to abrogate what remains of state powers. TEFRA mandates that bonds sold by states after July 1, 1983 be issued in registered (not bearer) form. If a state breaks this rule, the interest on the bonds can be taxed by the IRS.

That requirement galls Grady L. Patterson Jr., 59, South Carolina's

South Carolina Treasurer Grady L. Patterson Jr
Can one level of government tax another?

FORBES, SEPTEMBER 26, 1983

Fig. A2. William Barnett, *Forbes*, Sept 26, 1983.

2

The Exact Theoretical Rational Expectations Monetary Aggregate[1]

William A. Barnett, Melvin J. Hinich and Piyu Yue

In aggregation theory, index numbers are judged relative to their ability to track the exact aggregator functions nested within the economy's structure. Within the monetary sector, Barnett, Liu, and Jensen (1997) compared two statistical index numbers: the Divisia monetary aggregate and the simple sum monetary aggregate. They produced those comparisons using simulated data. In this paper, we again compare those two statistical index numbers with the exact rational expectations monetary aggregate, but we use actual data. Since we are not using simulated data, we estimate the parameters of the Euler equations and thereby of the nested monetary aggregator function using generalized method of moments. We explore the tracking errors of the two index numbers relative to the estimated exact aggregate. We investigate the circumstances under which risk aversion increases tracking error. We also use polyspectral methods to test for the existence of remaining nonlinear structure in the residual tracking errors.

2.1. Introduction

In microeconomic aggregation theory, index numbers are judged relative to their ability to track the exact aggregator functions

[1]Reprinted with permission from *Macroeconomic Dynamics* (2000), "The Exact Theoretical Rational Expectations Monetary Aggregate" by William A. Barnett, Melvin J. Hinich, and Piyu Yue, vol. 4, no. 2, June, pp. 197–221. Copyright © 2009 Cambridge University Press. Barnett's research was partially supported by NSF grant SES 9223557.

nested within the economy's structure. Relative to that criterion within the economy's monetary sector, Barnett, Liu, and Jensen (1997) compared two statistical index numbers: the Divisia monetary aggregate (with and without CCAPM adjustment for risk) and the simple sum monetary aggregate. Barnett, Liu, and Jensen (1997) produced those comparisons using simulated data at various settings of the parameters of an Euler equations model of monetary assets demand. In this paper, we similarly compare the two statistical index numbers with the exact rational expectations monetary aggregate, but we use actual data. Since we are not using simulated data, we need to estimate the parameters of the Euler equations and thereby of the nested monetary aggregator function. We do so using generalized method of moments. We then plot the time paths of the resulting estimated exact aggregate and the two approximating statistical index numbers.

We also compare the dynamic behavior of the two statistical index numbers with the dynamic behavior of the estimated exact aggregator function in the frequency domain using polyspectral methods. In particular, we investigate the ability of the two statistical indexes to extract the nonlinear structure from the estimated exact aggregate's time series. In addition to using Hinich's well know asymptotic bispectrum test, we bootstrap his test statistic to acquire a finite sample inference. The objective is to determine whether there exists any unexplained residual nonlinear structure in the tracking errors of the two statistical index numbers.

This line of research in monetary economics began with Barnett (1980) in the perfect certainty case. A long list of published papers and books have been motivated by Barnett's original perfect certainty model, based upon consumer demand theory. While the applications of the perfect certainty approach are far more extensive than those of the recent extensions to a stochastic environment, there is in place a small but growing literature on Euler equation estimation of nested aggregator functions over monetary assets. That extended literature began with Poterba and Rotemberg (1987) and Barnett,

Hinich, and Yue (1991) for consumer demand. Analogous research, in both the perfect certainty and risk cases, has recently been applied to manufacturing firms that demand monetary services and financial intermediaries that produce monetary services. A collection of many of the most important papers on this subject for all three categories of economic agents, with unifying discussion, can be found in Barnett and Serletis (2000).[2]

According to the "Barnett critique," as defined by Chrystal and MacDonald (1994, p. 76), an internal inconsistency exists between the microeconomics used to model private-sector structure and the aggregator functions implicitly used to produce the monetary aggregate data supplied by most central banks. This internal inconsistency can do considerable damage to inferences about private-sector behavior, when central bank monetary aggregate data are used. Chrystal and MacDonald (1994, p. 76) have observed the following regarding "the problems with tests of money in the economy in recent years . . . Rather than a problem associated with the Lucas crituque, it could instead be a problem stemming from the 'Barnett Critique.'" In fact, Barnett-critique issues have been used to cast doubt upon many widely held views in monetary economics, as emphasized by Barnett, Fisher, and Serletis (1992), Belongia (1996), Chrystal and MacDonald (1994), and Barnett and Serletis (2000). Based upon this rapidly growing line of research, Chrystal and MacDonald (1994, p. 108) conclude — in our opinion correctly — that "rejections of the role of money based upon flawed money measures are themselves easy to reject."

---

[2]For a survey limited to the consumer demand side, see Barnett, Fisher, and Serletis (1992). See Belongia (1996) and Belongia and Chalfant (1989) for some empirical results. For a presentation of the theory in the perfect certainty case for consumers, manufacturing firms, and financial intermediaries, see Barnett (1987). For international results on Divisia monetary aggregation, see Belongia and Binner (2000).

In the current paper, we compare the behavior of the exact monetary aggregate with that of the statistical index number approximations under risk, but only for consumers. Comparable results for manufacturing firms and financial intermediaries already have been published in Barnett and Zhou (1994a) and Barnett, Kirova, and Pasupathy (1995), but without frequency domain tests of successful extraction of nonlinear dynamics from the tracking errors. The data used in this paper are those supplied in Barnett, Hinich, and Yue (1991), to assure comparability with the results in that paper. In one case, we explore robustness to increased sample size, by extending the sample to include the most recently available data.

2.2. Consumer Demand for Monetary Assets

In this section we formulate a representative consumer's stochastic decision problem over consumer goods and monetary assets. The consumer's decisions are made in discrete time over a finite planning horizon for the time intervals, $t, t+1, \ldots, s, \ldots, t+T$, where t is the current time period and $t+T$ is the terminal planning period. The variables used in defining the consumer's decision are as follows:

$\mathbf{x}_s =$ n dimensional vector of real consumption of goods and services during period s,

$\mathbf{p}_s =$ n dimensional vector of goods and services prices and of durable goods rental prices during period s,

$\mathbf{a}_s =$ k dimensional vector of real balances of monetary assets during period s,

$\boldsymbol{\rho}_s =$ k dimensional vector of nominal holding period yields of monetary assets,

$A_s =$ holdings of the benchmark asset during period s,

$R_s =$ the one-period holding yield on the benchmark asset during period s,

$I_s =$ the sum of all other sources of income during period s,

$p_s^* = p_s^*(\mathbf{p}_s) =$ the true cost of living index.

Define Y to be a compact subset of the $n + k + 2$ dimensional nonnegative orthant. The consumer's consumption possibility set, $S(s)$, for $s \in \{t, \ldots, t+T\}$ is:

$$S(s) = \left\{ (\mathbf{a}_s, \mathbf{x}_s, A_s) \in Y: \sum_{i=1}^{n} p_{is}x_{is} \right.$$

$$= + \sum_{i=1}^{k} [(1 + \rho_{i,s-1})p^*_{s-1}a_{i,s-1} - p^*_s a_{is}]$$

$$\left. + \; (1 + R_{s-1})p^*_{s-1}A_{s-1} - p^*_s A_s + I_s \right\}. \tag{2.1}$$

Under the assumption of rational expectations, the distribution of random variables is known to the consumer. Since current period interest rates are not paid until the end of the period, they may be contemporaneously unknown to the consumer. Nevertheless, observe that during period t the only interest rates that enter into $S(t)$ are interest rates paid during period $t - 1$, which are known at the start of period t. Similarly $\mathbf{p}_t$ and p^*_t are determined and known to the consumer at the start of period t. Hence $(\mathbf{a}_t, \mathbf{x}_t, A_t)$ can be chosen deterministically in a manner that assures that $(\mathbf{a}_t, \mathbf{x}_t, A_t) \in S(t)$ with certainty. However, that is not possible for $s > t$, since at the beginning of time period t, when the intertemporal decision is solved, the constraint sets $S(s)$ for $s > t$ are random sets. Hence for $s > t$, the values of $(\mathbf{a}_s, \mathbf{x}_s, A_s)$ must be selected as stochastic process.

The benchmark asset A_s provides no services other than its yield R_s. As a result, the benchmark asset does not enter the consumer's intertemporal utility function except in the last instant of the planning horizon.[3] The asset is held only as a means of accumulating wealth

---

[3]A nonzero probability must exist that the holding period return, R_s, on the benchmark asset will exceed that of any other asset during period s, since no other motivation for holding the benchmark asset exists within the consumer's decision problem, as defined below. In fact, since the variance of the distribution of R_s is

to endow the next planning horizons. The consumer's intertemporal utility function is

$$U = U(\mathbf{a}_t, \ldots, \mathbf{a}_s, \ldots, \mathbf{a}_{t+T}; \mathbf{x}_t, \ldots, \mathbf{x}_s, \ldots, \mathbf{x}_{t+T}; A_{t+T}),$$

where U is assumed to be intertemporally additively (strongly) separable, such that

$$\begin{aligned} U &= u(\mathbf{a}_t, \mathbf{x}_t) + \left(\frac{1}{1+\xi}\right) u(\mathbf{a}_{t+1}, \mathbf{x}_{t+1}) \\ &\quad + \cdots + \left(\frac{1}{1+\xi}\right)^{T-1} u(\mathbf{a}_{t+T-1}, \mathbf{x}_{t+T-1}) \\ &\quad + \left(\frac{1}{1+\xi}\right)^{T} u(\mathbf{a}_{t+T}, \mathbf{x}_{t+T}, A_{t+T}) \\ &= \sum_{s=t}^{t+T-1} \left(\frac{1}{1+\xi}\right)^{s-t} u(\mathbf{a}_s, \mathbf{x}_s) \\ &\quad + \left(\frac{1}{1+\xi}\right)^{T} u_T(\mathbf{a}_{t+T}, \mathbf{x}_{t+T}, A_{t+T}), \end{aligned} \tag{2.2}$$

and the consumer's subjective rate of time preference, ξ, is assumed to be constant.[4] The single period utility functions, u and u_T, are assumed to be increasing and strictly quasiconcave.

Given the price and interest rate processes, the consumer selects the deterministic point $(\mathbf{a}_t, \mathbf{x}_t, A_t)$ and the stochastic processes $(\mathbf{a}_s, \mathbf{x}_s, A_s), s = t+1, \ldots, t+T$, to maximize the expected value of U over the planning horizon, subject to the sequence of choice

likely to be high relative to that of r_{is} for any i, we should expect the mean of R_s to exceed that of any element of $\mathbf{r}_s$.

[4]Although money may not exist in the elementary utility function, there exists a derived utility function that contains money, so long as money has positive value in equilibrium. See, e.g., Arrow and Hahn (1971), Phlips and Spinnewyn (1982), and Feenstra (1986). We implicitly are using that derived utility function.

set constraints. Formally, the consumer's decision problem is the following.

Problem 1: Choose the deterministic point $(\mathbf{a}_t, \mathbf{x}_t, A_t)$ and the stochastic process $(\mathbf{a}_s, \mathbf{x}_s, A_s)$, $s = t+1, \ldots, t+T$, to maximize

$$u(\mathbf{a}_t, \mathbf{x}_t) + E_t \left[\sum_{s=t+1}^{t+T-1} \left(\frac{1}{1+\xi} \right)^{s-t} u(\mathbf{a}_s, \mathbf{x}_s) + \left(\frac{1}{1+\xi} \right)^{T} u_T(\mathbf{a}_{t+T}, \mathbf{x}_{t+T}, A_{t+T}) \right] \quad (2.3)$$

subject to $(\mathbf{a}_s, \mathbf{x}_s, A_s) \in S(s)$ for $s = t, \ldots, t+T$.

We use E_t to designate the expectations operator conditionally upon the information that exists at time t.

In the infinite planning horizon case, the decision problem becomes:

Problem 2: Choose the deterministic point $(\mathbf{a}_t, \mathbf{x}_t, A_t)$ and the stochastic process $(\mathbf{a}_s, \mathbf{x}_s, A_s)$, $s = t+1, \ldots, \infty$, to maximize

$$u(\mathbf{a}_t, \mathbf{x}_t) + E_t \left[\sum_{s=t+1}^{\infty} \left(\frac{1}{1+\xi} \right)^{s-t} u(\mathbf{a}_s, \mathbf{x}_s) \right] \quad (2.4)$$

subject to $(\mathbf{a}_s, \mathbf{x}_s, A_s) \in S(s)$ for $s \geq t$, and also subject to

$$E_t \left(\frac{1}{1+\xi} \right)^{s-t} A_s \xrightarrow[s \to \infty]{} 0.$$

The latter constraint rules out perpetual borrowing at the benchmark rate of return, R_t.

2.3. Existence of a Monetary Aggregate for the Consumer

In order to assure the existence of a monetary aggregate for the consumer, we partition the vector of monetary asset quantities, $\mathbf{a}_s$, such that $\mathbf{a}_s = (\mathbf{m}_s, \mathbf{h}_s)$. We correspondingly partition the vector of interest rates of those assets, $\boldsymbol{\rho}_s$, such that $\boldsymbol{\rho}_s = (\mathbf{r}_s, \mathbf{i}_s)$. We then assume that the utility function, u, is blockwise weakly separable in $\mathbf{m}_s$ and in $\mathbf{x}_s$ for some such partition of $\mathbf{a}_s$. Hence there exists a monetary aggregator ("category utility") function, M, and consumer goods aggregator function, X, and a utility function, u^*, such that

$$u(\mathbf{a}_s, \mathbf{x}_s) = u^*(M(\mathbf{m}_s), \mathbf{h}_s, X(\mathbf{x}_s)). \tag{2.5}$$

We assume that the terminal period utility function in the finite planning horizon case is correspondingly weakly separable, such that $u_T(\mathbf{a}_s, \mathbf{x}_s, A_s) = u_T^*(M(\mathbf{m}_s), \mathbf{h}_s, X(\mathbf{x}_s), A_s)$.

Then it follows that the exact monetary aggregate, measuring the welfare acquired from consuming the services of $\mathbf{m}_s$, is

$$M_s = M(\mathbf{m}_s). \tag{2.6}$$

We define the dimension of $\mathbf{m}_s$ to be k_1, and the dimension of $\mathbf{h}_s$ to be k_2, so that $k = k_1 + k_2$.

It is clear that equation (2.6) does define the exact monetary aggregate in the welfare sense, since M_s measures the consumer's subjective evaluation of the services that he receives from holding $\mathbf{m}_s$. However it also can be shown that equation (2.6) defines the exact monetary aggregate in the aggregation theoretic sense. In particular, the stochastic process $M_s, s \geq t$, contains all of the information about $\mathbf{m}_s$ that is needed by the consumer to solve the rest of his decision problem. This conclusion is based upon the following theorem, which we call the consumer's aggregation theorem.

Let

$$D_s = I_s + \sum_{i=1}^{k_1} [(1 + r_{i,s-1})p_{s-1}^* m_{i,s-1} - p_s^* m_{is}],$$

and let

$$\Delta(s) = \left\{ (\mathbf{h}_s, \mathbf{x}_s, A_s) \in Y \colon \sum_{i=1}^{n} p_{is} x_{is} \right.$$

$$= + \sum_{i=1}^{k_2} [(1 + i_{i,s-1}) p^*_{s-1} h_{i,s-1} - p^*_s h_{is}]$$

$$\left. + (1 + R_{s-1}) p^*_{s-1} A_{s-1} - p^*_s A_s + D_s \right\}. \tag{2.7}$$

Let the deterministic point $(\mathbf{a}^*_t, \mathbf{x}^*_t, A^*_t)$ and the stochastic process $(\mathbf{a}^*_s, \mathbf{x}^*_s, A^*_s)$, $s \geq t + 1$, solve Problem 1 (or Problem 2, if $T = \infty$). Consider the following decision problems, which are conditional upon prior knowledge of the aggregate process $M^*_s = M(\mathbf{m}^*_s)$, although not upon the component processes $\mathbf{m}^*_s$.

Problem 1a: Choose the deterministic point $(\mathbf{h}_t, \mathbf{x}_t, A_t)$ and the stochastic process $(\mathbf{h}_s, \mathbf{x}_s, A_s)$, $s = t + 1, \ldots, t + T$, to maximize

$$u^*(M^*_t, \mathbf{h}_t, \mathbf{x}_t) + E_t \left[\sum_{s=t+1}^{t+T-1} \left(\frac{1}{1+\xi} \right)^{s-t} u^*(M^*_s, \mathbf{h}_s, \mathbf{x}_s) \right.$$

$$\left. + \left(\frac{1}{1+\xi} \right)^T u^*_T(M^*_T, \mathbf{h}_s, \mathbf{x}_s, A_s) \right] \tag{2.8}$$

subject to $(\mathbf{h}_s, \mathbf{x}_s, A_s) \in \Delta(s)$ for $s = t, \ldots, t + T$, with the process M^*_s given for $s \geq t$.

Problem 2a: Choose the deterministic point $(\mathbf{h}_t, \mathbf{x}_t, A_t)$ and the stochastic process $(\mathbf{h}_s, \mathbf{x}_s, A_s)$, $s = t + 1, \ldots, \infty$, to maximize

$$u^*(M^*_t, \mathbf{h}_t, \mathbf{x}_t) + E_t \left[\sum_{s=t+1}^{\infty} \left(\frac{1}{1+\xi} \right)^{s-t} u^*(M^*_s, \mathbf{h}_s, \mathbf{x}_s) \right] \tag{2.9}$$

subject to $(\mathbf{h}_s, \mathbf{x}_s, A_s) \in \Delta(s)$ for $s \geq t$, and also subject to

$$E_t \left(\frac{1}{1+\xi} \right)^{s-t} A_s \xrightarrow[s \to \infty]{} 0,$$

with the process M^*_s given for $s \geq t$.

Theorem 1 (Consumer's Aggregation Theorem): Let the deterministic point $(\mathbf{m}_t, \mathbf{h}_t, \mathbf{x}_t, A_t)$ and the stochastic process $(\mathbf{m}_s, \mathbf{h}_s, \mathbf{x}_s, A_s)$, $s = t+1, \ldots, t+T$, solve Problem 1. Then the deterministic point $(\mathbf{h}_t, \mathbf{x}_t, A_t)$ and the stochastic process $(\mathbf{h}_s, \mathbf{x}_s, A_s)$, $s = t+1, \ldots, t+T$, will solve Problem 1a conditionally upon $M_s^* = M(\mathbf{m}_s)$ for $s = t, \ldots, t+T$. Similarly let the deterministic point $(\mathbf{m}_t, \mathbf{h}_t, \mathbf{x}_t, A_t)$ and the stochastic process $(\mathbf{m}_s, \mathbf{h}_s, \mathbf{x}_s, A_s)$, $s \geq t+1$ solve Problem 2. Then the deterministic point $(\mathbf{h}_t, \mathbf{x}_t, A_t)$ and the stochastic process $(\mathbf{h}_s, \mathbf{x}_s, A_s)$, $s \geq t+1$ will solve Problem 2a conditionally upon $M_s^* = M(\mathbf{m}_s)$ for $s \geq t$.

Clearly this aggregation theorem, proved in the appendix of Barnett, Liu, and Jensen (1997), applies not only when M_s is produced by voluntary behavior, but also when the M_s process is exogenously imposed upon the consumer, as through a perfectly inelastic supply function for M_s, set by central bank policy. In that case, Problems 1a and 2a describe optimal behavior by the consumer in the remaining variables. Since $(\mathbf{h}_s, \mathbf{x}_s, A_s)$ are not assumed to be weakly separable from M_s, the information about M_s is needed in the solution of Problems 1a and 2a for the processes $(\mathbf{h}_s, \mathbf{x}_s, A_s)$. For example, the marginal rate of substitution between labor and goods may depend upon the value of M_s. Alternatively information about the simple sum aggregate over the components of $\mathbf{m}_s$ is of no use in solving either Problem 1a or 2a unless the monetary aggregator function M happens to be a simple sum. In other words, the simple sum aggregate contains useful information about behavior only if the components of $\mathbf{m}_s$ are perfect substitutes in identical ratios (linear aggregation with *equal* coefficients).

2.4. The Solution Procedure

Using Bellman's principle, we can derive the first order conditions for solving Problems 1 and 2. Under the somewhat more restrictive conditions assumed by Poterba and Rotemberg (1987), the first order conditions derived below reduce to those acquired by Poterba and Rotemberg.

We concentrate on the infinite planning horizon Problem 2, rather than on the finite planning horizon Problem 2, since the contingency plan functions ("feedback rules") that solve Problem 1 are time dependent in the finite planning horizon case, but not in the infinite planning horizon case. In the infinite planning horizon case, time enters only through the variables that enter those equations as arguments, rather than through time shifting of the functions themselves.

We begin by solving the budget constraint in equation (2.1) for the quantity of an arbitrary consumer good, x_{js}, and we then use the resulting rearranged constraint to eliminate x_{js} from the intertemporal utility function in Problem 2 for all $s \geq t$. For notational simplicity, we let $j = 1$. Let $\mathbf{z}_{1s} = (\mathbf{a}_s, A_s)$. To apply Bellman's method, we must define the control and state variables. Define the control variables during period s to be $\mathbf{z}_s = (\mathbf{z}_{1s}, x_{2s}, \ldots, x_{ns})$. We define the state variables during period s to be $(\mathbf{ß}_{1s}, \boldsymbol{ø}_s)$, where the price and income state variables are $\boldsymbol{ø}_s = ((p_{2s}, \ldots, p_{ns}), p_s^*, p_{s-1}^*, R_{s-1}, \boldsymbol{\rho}_{s-1}, I_s)/p_{1s}$, and where $\mathbf{ß}_{1s} = (\mathbf{a}_{s-1}, A_{s-1})$.

Having eliminated the budget constraint by substitution as described above, Problem 2 can be rewritten as follows:

Problem 2b: Choose the deterministic point $\mathbf{z}_t$ and the stochastic process $\mathbf{z}_s$, $s = t + 1, \ldots, \infty$, to maximize

$$u(\mathbf{z}_t, \mathbf{ß}_t) + E_t\left[\sum_{s=t+1}^{\infty}\left(\frac{1}{1+\xi}\right)^{s-t} u(\mathbf{z}_s, \mathbf{ß}_s)\right] \tag{2.10}$$

subject to

$$\mathbf{ß}_{1,s+1} = \mathbf{z}_{1s} \tag{2.11}$$

and

$$E_t\left(\frac{1}{1+\xi}\right)^{s-t} A_s \xrightarrow[s\to\infty]{} 0, \tag{2.12}$$

with $\mathbf{ß}_t$ given.

Equation (2.11) are the transition equations, $\mathbf{ß}_{s+1} = \mathbf{g}(\mathbf{z}_s, \mathbf{ß}_s)$, providing the evolution of future state variables as functions of the controls and the current state. We assume that the $\boldsymbol{ø}_s$ process is Markovian. Applying the Benveniste and Scheinkman equations, we can acquire the Euler equations for the control variables.

The Euler equations which will be of the most use to us below are those for monetary assets. Replacing $X(\mathbf{x}_t)$ by c_t in u, those Euler equations become:

$$E_t\left[\frac{\partial u}{\partial m_{it}} - \rho\frac{p_t^*(R_t - r_{it})}{p_{t+1}^*}\frac{\partial u}{\partial c_{t+1}}\right] = 0 \tag{2.13a}$$

for $i = 1, \ldots, k_1$, where $c_t = X(\mathbf{x}_t)$ is the exact quantity aggregate over $\mathbf{x}_t$ and p_t^* is its dual exact price aggregate.[5] Similarly we can acquire the Euler equation for the consumer goods aggregate c_t, rather than for each of its components. The resulting Euler equation for c_t is

$$E_t\left[\frac{\partial u}{\partial c_t} - \rho\frac{p_t^*(1 + R_t)}{p_{t+1}^*}\frac{\partial u}{\partial c_{t+1}}\right] = 0 \tag{2.13b}$$

2.5. Monetary Policy

Having the Bellman solution at hand, we are in a position to give further consideration to the policy implications of monetary aggregation through the Theoretical aggregate. Hence we now return to Theorem 1 and Problem 2a. Clearly the Bellman equation for Problem 2a can be written in a form analogous to that of the Bellman equation produced by Problem 2. The only changes are that the controls now are $(\mathbf{h}_s, x_{2s}, \ldots, x_{ns}, A_s)$, $s = t, \ldots, \infty$, while the state variables are $(\mathbf{h}_{s-1}, A_{s-1}, \boldsymbol{ø}_s, M_s^*)$, where $\boldsymbol{ø}_s$ is the vector of price and income state variables defined earlier. Hence the solution contingency

[5]Assuming that X is linearly homogeneous, the exact price aggregator function is the unit cost function.

plans solving Problem 2a are of the form:

$$(\mathbf{h}_s, x_{2s}, \ldots, x_{ns}, A_s) = \mathbf{f}(\mathbf{h}_{s-1}, A_{s-1}, \boldsymbol{\emptyset}_s, M_s^*), \tag{2.14}$$

where all of the controls and state variables are deterministic for $s = t$.

The appearance of M_s^* as a state variable has interesting policy implications. Clearly if M_s^* is used as an indicator in the conduct of monetary policy, the monetary aggregate will indeed contain information about $(\mathbf{h}_s, x_{2s}, \ldots, x_{ns}, A_s)$ and thereby about the final targets of monetary policy both in goods and labor markets. Alternatively suppose that policy instruments, such as the monetary base, are used to target the equilibrium path of M_s^* as an intermediate target of policy. Assuming that the instruments are used in a manner that is not time inconsistent, as for example through an open loop policy, the equilibrium stochastic process for M_s^* can be influenced by policy. Under our assumption of rational expectations, economic agents will know about the policy rule and hence about the targeted equilibrium process for M_s^*. The consumer then can solve Problem 2a to acquire the optimal solution for the remaining variables conditionally upon the targeted process for M_s^*.

We see that only M_s^* can play these roles, if policy operates through a monetary target or indicator. The simple sum aggregate, which does not appear as a control in **f**, can serve neither role. In fact the only information from the monetary asset portfolio, $\mathbf{m}_s^*$, that is useful in solving Problem 2a is $M_s^* = M(\mathbf{m}_s^*)$, since $\mathbf{m}_s^*$ enters the contingency plans **f** only through M.

At this point, we have completed our theoretical analysis of demand for money in a risky environment. We now can use GMM estimation to estimate the parameters of first order conditions under a particular specification for tastes. We then can compute the estimated theoretical monetary aggregate and proceed to investigate the quality of currently available statistical index numbers in tracking the monetary service flow. But we first determine the applicability of existing index number theory under the assumptions of our exact aggregation theory.

2.6. The Risk Neutral Case

In the perfect certainty case, nonparametric index number theory is highly developed and is applicable to monetary aggregation. In the perfect certainty case, Barnett (1978, 1980) proved that the nominal user cost of the services of m_{it} is π_{it}, where

$$\pi_{it} = p_t^* \frac{R_t - r_{it}}{1 + R_t} \tag{2.15}$$

The corresponding real user cost is π_{it}/p^*. In the risk neutral case, the user cost formulas are the same as in the perfect certainty case, but with the interest rates replaced by their expected values. It can be shown that the solution value of the exact monetary aggregate $M(\mathbf{m}_t)$ can be tracked without error in continuous time (see, e.g., Barnett (1983)) by the Divisia index:

$$d \log M_t = \sum_{i=1}^{k_1} s_{it} d \log m_{it}, \tag{2.16}$$

where the user cost evaluated expenditure shares are $s_{it} = \pi_{it} m_{it} / \sum_{i=1}^{k_1} \pi_{jt} m_{jt}$. The flawless tracking ability of the index in the risk neutral case holds regardless of the form of the unknown aggregator function, M.

However, under risk aversion the ability of equation (2.16) to track $M(\mathbf{m}_t)$ is compromised. We investigate the magnitude of that error below by econometrically estimating $M(\mathbf{m}_t)$.

2.7. A Generalization

The fact that the Divisia index tracks exactly under perfect certainty or risk neutrality is well know. However, we show in this section that neither perfect certainty nor risk neutrality are needed for exact tracking of the Divisia index. Only contemporaneous prices and interest rates need be known. Future interest rates and prices need not be known, and risk averse behavior relative to those stochastic processes need not be excluded. The proof is as follows.

Assume that R_t, p_t^*, and $\mathbf{r}_t$ are known at time t, although their future values are stochastic. Then the Euler equations (2.13a) for $\mathbf{m}_t$ are

$$\frac{\partial u}{\partial m_{it}} - \rho p_t^*(R_t - r_{it})E_t\left[\frac{1}{p_{t+1}^*}\frac{\partial u}{\partial c_{t+1}}\right] = 0 \qquad (2.17)$$

for $i = 1, \ldots, k_1$. Similarly the Euler equation (2.13b) for aggregate consumption of goods, c_t, becomes

$$\frac{\partial u}{\partial c_t} - \rho p_t^*(1 + R_t)E_t\left[\frac{1}{p_{t+1}^*}\frac{\partial u}{\partial c_{t+1}}\right] = 0 \qquad (2.18)$$

Eliminating $E_t\left[\frac{1}{p_{t+1}^*}\frac{\partial u}{\partial c_{t+1}}\right]$ between (2.17) and (2.18), we acquire

$$\frac{\partial u}{\partial m_{it}} = \frac{R_t - r_{it}}{1 + R_t}\frac{\partial u}{\partial c_t} \qquad (2.19)$$

But by the assumption of weak separability of u in $\mathbf{m}_t$, we have

$$\frac{\partial u}{\partial m_{it}} = \frac{\partial u}{\partial M_t}\frac{\partial M}{\partial m_{it}} \qquad (2.20)$$

where $M_t = M(\mathbf{m}_t)$ is the exact monetary aggregate that we seek to track.

Substituting (2.19) into (2.20) and using (2.15), we find that

$$\frac{\partial M}{\partial m_{it}} = \pi_{it}\frac{\partial u/\partial c_t}{\partial u/\partial M_t} \qquad (2.21)$$

Now substitute (2.21) into the total differential of M to acquire

$$dM(\mathbf{m}_t) = \frac{\partial u/\partial c_t}{\partial u/\partial M_t} \sum_{i=1}^{k_1} \pi_{it} dm_{it}. \tag{2.22}$$

But since M is assumed to be linearly homogeneous, we have Euler's equation for linearly homogeneous functions. Substituting (2.21) into Euler's equation, we have

$$M(\mathbf{m}_t) = \frac{\partial u/\partial c_t}{\partial u/\partial M_t} \sum_{j=1}^{k_1} \pi_{jt} m_{jt} \tag{2.23}$$

Dividing (2.22) by (2.23), we acquire (2.16), which is the Divisia index. Hence the exact tracking property of the Divisia index is not compromised by uncertainty regarding future interest rates and prices or by risk aversion.

Nevertheless, this assumption is not trivial, as emphasized by Poterba and Rotemberg (1987), since current period interest rates are not paid until the end of the current period. In fact current period interest rates are not assumed contemporaneously known in our Euler equations (2.13a) and (2.13b). Barnett, Liu, and Jensen (1997) have derived the consumption CAPM beta risk adjustment to interest rates that removes the tracking error of the Divisia index under risk aversion. With that adjustment inserted in the user cost prices, Barnett, Liu, and Jensen (1997) proved that the Divisia index again tracks the aggregator function exactly in continuous time, regardless of the degree of risk aversion. But with the current controversies regarding CCAPM and the associated "equity premium puzzle," no central banks currently are using risk adjusted interest rates. In the current paper, we therefore do not include the risk adjusted Divisia index among the statistical index numbers that we compare for their ability to track the GMM estimated theoretical aggregator function.

2.8. Data and Specification

We conduct our comparisons at two levels of monetary aggregation: $M1$ and $M2$. In order to simplify the illustration, we accept a common clustering of $M2$ components without first testing for weak separability. We first set $\mathbf{m}_s$ equal to those components of $M1$ found by Belongia and Chalfant (1989) to be weakly separable.[6] We refer to the resulting aggregates over those components to be $M1$ aggregates. We then repeat our analysis with $\mathbf{m}_s$ set equal to the components of $M2$, but with those components clustered into three groups with prior aggregation within groups, so that $\mathbf{m}_s$ contains three aggregated elements. Hence we implicitly assume that $\mathbf{a}_s$ is partitioned in accordance with a recursively nested two level separable blocking, such that the components of our $M1$ aggregate are separable within the components of our $M2$ aggregate, which in turn are separable within $\mathbf{a}_s$. Considering the little that is known about testing for separability in the risk averse case, the clustering that we have chosen without explicit separability testing is hardly the last word on that subject.

We now select a specification for the function u satisfying our weak separability assumption, and we estimate the parameters by GMM. In that estimation, the data that we use is the monthly monetary component data available in Fayyad (1986) for January 1969 to March 1985.[7] In our estimation of the parameters of tastes, we use that data in per capita real balances form. We begin by defining $\mathbf{m}_s$ to contain two components: currency and demand deposits,

---

[6]On testing for weak separability, also see Swofford and Whitney (1987).

[7]Although component data is available for more recent months, we decided to use the data supplied in the appendix of Fayyad (1986) to assure comparability with Barnett, Hinich, and Yue (1991), who also published that data along with results which are worth comparing with those in this paper. But in our frequency domain analysis, we use that data only when comparison with Barnett, Hinich, and Yue (1991) is relevant. Otherwise we use updated data now maintained and published by the St. Louis Federal Reserve Bank. That data can be found in St. Louis Federal Reserve Bank's data web site, FRED.

which Belongia and Chalfant (1989) found to be blockwise weakly separable, at least under risk neutrality, from other goods and assets.[8] In the utility function, $u^*(M(\mathbf{m}_s), \mathbf{h}_s, \mathbf{x}_s)$, we assume a further higher level of nested blockwise strong separability, such that

$$u(\mathbf{m}_s, \mathbf{h}_s, \mathbf{x}_s) = V(M(\mathbf{m}_s), X_s) + H(\mathbf{h}_s), \tag{2.24}$$

where $X_s = X(\mathbf{x}_s)$ is the exact quantity aggregate over consumer goods.[9] The utility function that we specify and estimate is the category utility function $V(M(\mathbf{m}_s), X_s)$.[10]

Since the variables in $V(M(\mathbf{m}_s), X_s)$ are disjoint from those in $H(\mathbf{h}_s)$, we can restrict the original decision to be defined in terms of the utility function $V(M(\mathbf{m}_s), X_s)$ in the following manner, without altering the solution for the variables $(\mathbf{m}_s, X_s)$. We redefine the utility function in Problem 2 to be

$$V(M(\mathbf{m}_t), X_t) + E_t\left[\sum_{s=t+1}^{\infty}\left(\frac{1}{1+\xi}\right)^{s-t} V(M(\mathbf{m}_s), X_s)\right]. \tag{2.25}$$

The utility function in Problem 1 can be restricted in the analogous manner. The budget constraint in either case is simplified in the following manner. All terms containing the variables $(\mathbf{h}_s, \mathbf{h}_{s-1})$ are

[8] See Barnett, William A., Melvin Hinich, and Piyu Yue (1991) regarding the need to test for weak separability and for further details regarding the data.

[9] Formally, we assume that $\mathbf{x}_s$ is in a weakly separable block within u, with linearly homogeneous category utility function $X(\mathbf{x}_s)$. The true cost of living index $p_s^* = p^*(\mathbf{p}_s)$ is the unit cost function dual to the quantity aggregator function, X_s. As described earlier, we approximate the true cost of living index by the Fisher ideal index.

We are able to appeal to perfect certainty aggregation theory in this case, since current period prices, unlike current period interest rates, are known in the current period. Hence two stage budgeting over consumer goods is possible, and thereby perfect certainty aggregation and index number theory are applicable to consumer goods.

[10] The strong separability assumption is largely for expository convenience. Weak separability of the form $u(\mathbf{m}_{1s}, \mathbf{m}_{2s}, L_s, \mathbf{x}_s) = U[V(M(\mathbf{m}_{1s}), X_s), \mathbf{m}_{2s}, L_s]$ would be sufficient to assure the existence of the function $V(M(\mathbf{m}_{1s}), X_s)$ that we use below.

absorbed into the "other income" variable, I_s, with $(\mathbf{h}_s, \mathbf{h}_{s-1})$ replaced by their stochastic processes solving the complete unrestricted decision (Problem 1 or 2).

The budget constraint then becomes:

$$\Bigg\{(\mathbf{m}_s, X_s, A_s) \in H\colon p_s^* X_s$$
$$= + \sum_{i=1}^{k_1} [(1 + r_{i,s-1}) p_{s-1}^* m_{i,s-1} - p_s^* m_{is}]$$
$$+ \ (1 + R_{s-1}) p_{s-1}^* A_{s-1} - p_s^* A_s + I_s \Bigg\}. \qquad (2.26)$$

In short, with $M1$ components we estimate a three goods model, including two monetary components and the aggregate quantity of consumer goods, X_s. With $M2$ components we estimate a four goods model, including three aggregated monetary components and the aggregate quantity of consumer goods, X_s. We now define our specification for V.[11]

We assume constant proportional risk aversion, such that the utility function $V = V(M(\mathbf{m}_s), X_s)$ is of the form

$$V(M(\mathbf{m}_s), X_s) = \frac{1}{\sigma}[J(X_s, M_s)]^\sigma \qquad (2.27)$$

for some function, J, where $M_s = M(\mathbf{m}_s)$ is the Theoretical monetary aggregate we seek to estimate. We then assume that the function J

[11]We use the same aggregator function specifications used by Poterba and Rotemberg (1987), although we believe that at a later stage of this research the aggregator functions should be replaced by those of the highly flexible seminonparametric AIM (asymptotically ideal model) specification. See, e.g., Barnett, Geweke, and Wolfe (1991a, b) and Barnett, Geweke, and Yue (1991).

has the Cobb-Douglas form

$$J(X_s, M_s) = X_s^{\beta} M_s^{1-\beta} \tag{2.28}$$

Finally we assume that the monetary aggregator function, $M(\mathbf{m}_s)$, has the CES (constant elasticity of substitution) form

$$M_s = \left(\sum_{i=1}^{k_1} \delta_i m_{si} \right)^{1/\nu} \tag{2.29}$$

with $\sum_{i=1}^{n} \delta_i = 1$, where $n = 2$ for $M1$ and $n = 3$ for $M2$.

Substituting (2.29) into (2.28), and then substituting the result into (2.27), we get

$$V(M(\mathbf{m}_s), X_s) = \frac{1}{\sigma} \left[X_s^{\beta} \left(\sum_{i=1}^{k_1} \delta_i m_{si} \right)^{(1-\beta)/\nu} \right]^{\sigma}. \tag{2.30}$$

Denoting the rate of subjective time discount by $\rho = 1/(1+\xi)$ and substituting (2.30) into (2.25), we get the complete intertemporal expected utility function

$$E_t(U) = \frac{1}{\sigma} \left[X_t^{\beta} \left(\sum_{i=1}^{k_1} \delta_i m_{ti} \right)^{(1-\beta)/\nu} \right]^{\sigma} + E_t \left[\sum_{s=t+1}^{\infty} \rho^{s-t} \frac{1}{\sigma} \left[X_s^{\beta} \left(\sum_{i=1}^{k_1} \delta_i m_{si} \right)^{(1-\beta)/\nu} \right]^{\sigma} \right]. \tag{2.31}$$

The parameters to be estimated are ρ, σ, β, $\{\delta_i\}$, and ν. The constraints imposed on those parameters are

$$\sum_{i=1}^{k_1} \delta_i = 1, \quad 0 < \beta \leq 1, \quad \text{and} \quad 0 < \delta_i \leq 1.$$

All consumption and asset quantity data are real per capita. We approximate the benchmark rate, R_s, by the maximum holding period yield across all assets in Fayyad's (1986) tables during period s.

The particular asset which produced that rate of return need not be the same for all s, since our measurement of R_s produces a proxy for the rate of return on some very illiquid asset (such as human capital in a world without slavery), on which we may have no monthly data.

2.9. Estimation

We use Hansen and Singleton's (1982) generalized method of moments estimator to estimate the parameters of the Euler equations, (2.13a) and (2.13b). In accordance with Hansen and Singleton's estimator, we iterate on the weighting matrix until convergence. The Hansen and Singleton GMM estimator requires the selection of instrumental variables. When estimating the Theoretical $M1$ aggregate, we use the following five instruments: Z_1 = constant = 10, $Z_2 = X_{s-1} - X_s$, $Z_3 = (m_{s+1,1} - m_{s1}) + (m_{s+1,2} - m_{s2})$, $Z_4 = m_{s-1,1} + m_{s-1,2}$, and $Z_5 = R_{s-1}$.

The sample size in Fayyad (1986) is 195 which covers monthly periods from January of 1969 to March of 1985. In order to impose the constraints on the parameters, we transform the parameters in the following manner:

$$\sum_{i=1}^{k_1} \rho = B_1, \quad \sigma = B_2, \quad \beta = cos^2 B_3, \quad \delta = \cos^2 B_4, \quad \nu = B_5,$$

and we estimate the new parameters B_1, B_2, B_3, and B_4. The GMM estimator converged at its fourth stage. The resulting parameter estimates are as in Table 1.[12] Using these parameter estimates and the component data, the estimated theoretical $M1$ monetary aggregate, $M_s = M(\mathbf{m}_s)$, was computed at each observation. We also computed

[12]The t-ratios should be interpreted with caution, since the use of transformations of parameters to impose inequality constraints biases conventional methods of estimating standard errors. As a result, we supply no standard errors or t-ratios for the original untransformed parameters.

Table 1. GMM Estimates of Parameters of $M1$ Theoretical Aggregator Function Nested within Consumer Demand Model.

	Inside Aggregator		Outside Aggregator		
Estimated Parameter	B_1	B_2	B_3	B_4	B_5
Estimate	0.9168	−0.3329	7.6018	42.717	0.6800
t-ratio	62.489	−3.726	19.171	10.424	2.3769
Derived Parameter	ρ	α	β	δ	ν
Implied Estimate	0.9168	−0.3329	0.9825	0.5398	0.6800

the Divisia quantity index and the simple sum index over the same components.

This procedure then was repeated with the $M2$ data. The components of $M2$ were clustered into three groups, and asset quantities within the groups were aggregated by simple summation to produce three aggregated components over which we then aggregate by the three methods. For details of the prior clustering of components, see Table 4.1 in Barnett, Hinich, and Yue (1991).

In order to impose the constraints on the parameters, we transform them as follows

$$\rho = B_1, \quad \sigma = B_2, \quad \beta = \cos^2 B_3, \quad \delta_1 = \cos^2 B_5,$$
$$\delta_2 = \sin^2 B_5 \sin^2 B_6, \quad \nu = B_4.$$

The GMM estimation converged at the third stage. The resulting parameter estimates are provided in Table 2.

Table 2. GMM Estimates of Parameters of $M2$ Theoretical Aggregator Function Nested within Consumer Demand Model.

	Inside Aggregator			Outside Aggregator		
Estimated Parameter	B_1	B_2	B_3	B_4	B_5	B_6
Estimate	0.8975	−0.2669	0.2173	0.8426	0.8198	0.9177
t-ratio	43.9094	−3.3072	13.1376	1.9011	17.6566	14.6081
Derived Parameter	ρ	σ	β	ν	δ_1	δ_2
Implied Estimate	0.8975	−0.2669	0.9535	0.8426	0.4656	0.3371

Using these parameter estimates and the component data, the estimated theoretical $M2$ monetary aggregate, $M_s = M(\mathbf{m}_s)$, was computed at each observation. We also computed the Divisia quantity index and the simple sum index over the same components. In Figure 1, the nominal per capita monetary indices are supplied for the three methods of aggregation at both the $M1$ and $M2$ levels of aggregation.

The properties of the three aggregates at each level of aggregation are easily seen by inspecting Figure 1. At both levels of aggregation, the Divisia index tracked the estimated Theoretical aggregate more closely than did the simple sum monetary aggregate. At the $M1$ level, Divisia $M1$ tracks the estimated Theoretical aggregate rather well throughout the sample period. At the $M2$ level, the growth rates of the Divisia and estimated Theoretical aggregates diverged from each other from September 1982 through April 1983, with the growth rate of the estimated Theoretical aggregate being consistently higher

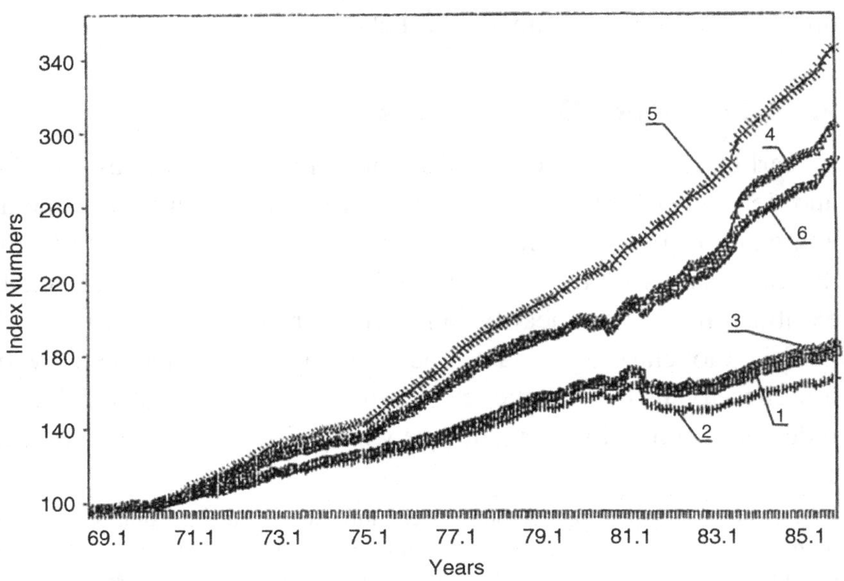

Fig. 1. Levels of nominal per capita $M1$ and $M2$ monetary indices (1, $M1$ theoretic; 2, $M1$ simple sum; 3, $M1$ Divisia; 4, $M2$ theoretic; 5, $M2$ simple sum; 6, $M2$ Divisia).

than that of the Divisia aggregate throughout that time period. This phenomenon opened a gap between the plots of the levels of the two series. However, the two paths tracked parallel to each other after the eight months of diverging growth rates, since the growth rates of the two series returned to being very similar after April 1983.

The source of the divergence from September 1982 through April 1983 probably can be found in the unusual circumstances that existed in money markets. Many innovations in money markets evolved during that period, such as the introduction of super-NOW accounts and money-market deposit accounts at commercial banks.[13] There also was more than the usual degree of uncertainty regarding monetary policy, since that period immediately followed the termination of the Federal Reserve's "monetarist experiment," and the targets of monetary policy immediately following the termination of that experiment were unclear. In short, we find that the Divisia monetary aggregates would have benefited from Barnett, Liu, and Jensen's (1997) risk adjustment only during that one period of unusually high risk in money markets.

2.10. Frequency Domain Tests

In earlier research, Barnett, Gallant, Hinich, Jungeilges, Kaplan, and Jensen (1995) detected nonlinearity in the Divisia monetary aggregate time series. In this paper, we seek to determine whether the time series of the estimated Theoretical monetary aggregates exhibit similar nonlinearity, and whether the nonlinearity in the Divisia monetary aggregate stochastic process is induced by the nonlinearity in the Theoretical aggregate process that the Divisia index is tracking. In particular, we wish to investigate whether there

[13]In particular, superNow accounts were introduced during January 1983 and money market deposit accounts were introduced during December 1982. The period during which the growth rate of the estimated Theoretic $M2$ aggregate diverged from the Divisia and simple sum $M2$ aggregates was September 1982 through April 1983.

exists any remaining nonlinear structure in the difference between the Divisia and estimated Theoretical monetary aggregate. We use this test as a form of residual analysis to explore the dynamic properties of the Divisia index as an approximation to the Theoretical aggregate.

The mathematical theory relating the normalized squared skewness function to linearity and Gaussianity has been used to derive testing procedures by Hinich (1982) and Rao and Gabr (1980). The procedure used in this paper is the one derived in Hinich (1982). Details of the Hinich test are also discussed in Hinich and Patterson (1985, 1989) and Ashley, Hinich, and Patterson (1986).

There are an infinite number of polyspectra, where the order of the polyspectra are determined by the number of frequencies in their Fourier transform. The bispectrum, having two frequencies (its "bifrequencies"), is the second order polyspectrum. The Hinich test is based upon the skewness function, which is the normalized bispectrum, normalized by division by the product of the ordinary power spectra of the two individual frequencies and their sum.

The conventional methods of bispectrum estimation are reviewed in Nikias and Raghuveer (1987). The bispectrum can be estimated consistently from a finite sample $\{x(1), \ldots, x(N)\}$ by the following procedure. Segment the record of N observations into K (non-overlapped) blocks of L observations each, where L is called the block-length.[14] The parameter $K/N = 1/L$, is the resolution bandwidth.[15] For $k = 1, \ldots, K$, define the bi-periodogram for the bifrequency pair (f_i, f_j) as

$$G_k(f_i, f_j) = \frac{1}{L} X_k(f_i) X_k(f_j) X_k^*(f_i + f_j),$$

[14] Melvin Hinich, in personal correspondence, has suggested that the block-length be set to insure that $\ln(L)/\ln(N) \approx .4$. Consistency of the estimators requires that the parameter $e = \ln(L)/\ln(N) < .5$.

[15] If the last frame is incomplete, it is dropped from the calculation of the estimator.

where $X_k(f) = \sum_{n=(k-1)L+1}^{kL} x(n) \exp[-i2\pi fn/N]$ and where X_k^* denotes the complex conjugate of X_k.

A consistent and asymptotically normal estimator of the bispectrum is

$$\hat{B}_{xxx}(f_i, f_j) = \frac{1}{K} \sum_{k=1}^{K} G_k(f_i, f_j),$$

where $2f_i + f_j < N$ and $0 < f_j < f_i < N$, and $f_i = i/L$ $(i = 1, 2, \ldots, L)$. See Hinich and Messer (1995) for details on the estimator.[16] This type of estimator is analogous to the direct estimator of the power spectrum described in Welch (1967) and Groves and Hannan (1968), in which the data record is segmented into frames, and periodograms are computed frame by frame, and then averaged at each frequency.

The lowest order polyspectrum, having only one frequency, is the ordinary power spectrum. The power spectrum estimator is

$$\hat{P}_{xx}(f_i) = \frac{1}{K} \sum_{k=1}^{K} I_k(f_i),$$

where the periodogram is defined as $I_k(f_i) = \frac{1}{2\pi L} X_k(f_i) X_k^*(f_i)$, $k = 1, 2, \ldots, K$.[17] In the bispectrum case, bi-periodograms are computed frame by frame and then averaged at each frequency pair. It is the final averaging step which leads to consistency of the estimator in both cases. The variance is reduced by averaging over more frames, but at a cost of reduced resolution.[18]

We estimate the bispectrum over a range of values for the block length, L, in accordance with a suggestion of Stokes (1991). The

[16]For highly kurtotic stochastic processes, Hinich and Messer (1995) state that the use of the asymptotic distribution may not be warranted.

[17]We employ a trapezoidal taper to reduce side lobe distortion. Some modification of these formulas is therefore required.

[18]Koopmans (1974) called this tradeoff the Grenander uncertainty principle. For a discussion of power spectral estimation, see Kay and Marple (1981).

suggested range of block lengths is $(N/3)^{1/2}$ to $(N)^{1/2}$, which, for our sample size ($N = 396$), corresponds to a range of block lengths between 12 and 19. See Stokes (1991) for an example using a well known gas data model. The setting $L = 12$, corresponds to $N^{.42}$ and is the closest to Hinich's suggestion of $N^{.4}$.

The Hinich test for nonlinearity produces a test statistic Z, which is distributed asymptotically as the standard normal under the null hypothesis of constant skewness. Linear stochastic processes have constant skewness for all pairs of frequencies. The test corresponds to a test of flatness of the bispectrum against variations in the frequency pair. If the bispectrum is not flat, the power of clashes between frequency pairs depends upon the frequency pair. If that power is not only independent of the frequency pair, but is always zero, then the process has satisfied a necessary condition for Gaussianity, which is a special case of linearity. The conditions for linearity and Gaussianity would not only be necessary but also sufficient, if the conditions also applied to all higher order polyspectra. The Hinich Gaussianity test produces a test statistic G, which is asymptotically standard normal under the null of zero skewness, which corresponds to flatness of the bispectrum at zero power. Both the linearity and Gaussianity tests are one sided, and the null is rejected if the test statistics are large.

The Hinich test is extremely conservative. If the stochastic processes $x(t)$ is linear, then all of its polyspectra of order greater than or equal to two are independent of the frequency n-tuples, $(f_1, f_2, \ldots, f_n)$, for all $n \geq 2$. But the Hinich test is based only on the bispectrum having $n = 2$. A rejection of its null would be a strong result, because the null includes all linear processes and some nonlinear processes. Consequently, the Hinich test cannot confirm linearity. It only can reject or fail to reject it. In principle, we could test for nonlinearities using polyspectra of higher order than the bispectrum, but estimation of even the trispectrum is not feasible for common sample sizes of economic data sets.

The conservatism of the Hinich test has been reflected in empirical studies. For example, Barnett, Gallant, Hinich, Jungeilges,

Kaplan, and Jensen (1997) find that the Hinich test was much less likely to reject its null than other competing tests, such as the BDS test (Brock, Dechert, Scheinkman, and LeBaron (1996)). In addition, Hong (1996) notes that the third order cumulants of an ARCH (autoregressive conditional heteroskedastic) process can be identically zero, in which case the bispectrum test would fail to reject linearity. Barnett, Gallant, Hinich, Jungeilgies, Kaplan, and Jensen (1997) demonstrate that empirically the Hinich test has low power against ARCH. In fact ARCH is linear in the mean, and Ashley, Hinich, and Patterson (1986) have shown that the Hinich nonlinearity test does have substantial power (at reasonable sample sizes) against many commonly considered forms of nonlinear serial dependence.

The Hinich test has been applied previously in economic analysis. Hinich and Patterson (1989) examine trade by trade stock market data for evidence of nonlinearity. Barnett, Gallant, Hinich, Jungeilges, Kaplan, and Jensen (1995) find that Divisia monetary aggregate growth rate data exhibit deep nonlinearity at the $M1$ level of aggregation. The value of the asymptotic Z statistic for Divisia $M1$ in their test was 21.66, far exceeding customary rejection levels of 2 or 3. Considering the conservative nature of the test, this rejection of linearity is dramatic.

2.11. Frequency Domain Results

With the same monthly nominal per capita growth rate data used by Barnett, Gallant, Hinich, Jungeilges, Kaplan, and Jensen (1995) and by Barnett, Hinich, and Yue (1991), we run the same bispectrum tests for nonlinearity, but for the difference between the growth rate of the Divisia monetary aggregate and its corresponding GMM estimated Theoretical monetary aggregate. At the $M1$ level of aggregation, the Hinich asymptotic Z statistic for testing nonlinearity of that tracking error is 1.322. Hence we cannot reject linearity of the residual process for the Divisia approximation. We conclude that the strong evidence of nonlinearity found in the Divisia monetary aggregate $M1$ data by Barnett, Gallant, Hinich, Jungeilges, Kaplan, and Jensen (1995) was induced by the stochastic process of the exact Theoretical monetary aggregate that is tracked by the corresponding Divisia monetary aggregate.

At the $M2$ level, Barnett, Gallant, Hinich, Jungeilges, Kaplan, and Jensen (1995) found little evidence of nonlinearity in the Divisia monetary aggregate's stochastic process. The Hinich asymptotic Z statistic was 1.542, and hence they could not reject linearity. At that level of aggregation, we similarly find little evidence of nonlinearity in the residual process. The Hinich Z statistic for the difference in growth rates between the Divisia and estimated Theoretical $M2$ aggregate is 1.426. Hence there was little nonlinear structure for Divisia to remove from the Theoretical aggregate's time series at the $M2$ level, and little nonlinear structure is evident in the tracking errors.

Since sample size is important in the Hinich test, we decided to determine whether nonlinearity would become evident in Divisia $M2$ when the data is updated to include the latest observations reported by the Federal Reserve Bank of St. Louis. We repeated the Hinich test with the full available sample size of monthly Divisia $M2$ data. The sample is from January 1959 through October 1999 and is seasonally adjusted. We converted it to per capita form by division by noninstitutional population and transformed to growth rates. We ran the Hinich test for nonlinearity with that data, both with and without deflation to real balances using the consumer price index as the deflator. In addition to computing Hinich's asymptotic Z statistic to test for linearity, we also bootstrapped his test statistic to acquire a finite sample inference.

The bootstrap method used was to resample the data 300 times and compute the Z statistic for each resample. The 300 Z statistics are then sorted, and the 95%, 96%, 97%, 98%, 99%, 99.5%, and 99.9% quantiles are computed. The level of the 95% quantile is the threshold to use for the Z statistic, if one wants to achieve a 5% size for the test based on the resampling method.

For the per capita real growth rate data, the asymptotic Z statistic was 0.26 and the 95% quantile of the bootstrapped Z was 1.19. With the per capita real nominal growth rate data, the asymptotic Z statistic was 0.96 and the 95% quantile of the bootstrapped Z was 1.01. Hence there is even less evidence of statistically significant nonlinearity in the Divisia $M2$ data in the large sample than in the original smaller sample using the Hinich asymptotic Z statistic.

Nevertheless, it is interesting to inspect the estimated bispectrum. That three dimensional surface can contain information about the frequency pairs at which nonlinear interactions might exist, even if the inference about general nonlinearity is statistically insignificant. Recall that the test seeks to detect deviations from flatness of the skewness function (the normalized bispectrum). The skewness function is the square of the absolute value of the bispectrum divided by the product of the spectra of the bifrequencies and their sum.

Rather than plotting the skewness values, we plot the normal cumulative distribution of the skewness multiplied by a scale factor to make skewness have a chi square distribution with two degrees-of-freedom, using the mean non-centrality parameter for each bifrequency pair. Again the theory is developed for a large sample, but simulations have shown that the results are conservative. Thus the values plotted are the probabilities of obtaining such a value of the skewness at that bicorrelation under the null of linearity. In Figure 2 we display the skewness function plotted against the two periods (inversely related to the two frequencies) for the per capita real growth rate Divisia $M2$ data. The view is looking down from above, and the color code designates height.[19] Although the true bispectrum and normalized skewness function are smooth functions,

[19]The axes are the periods of the two frequencies, varying from 12 down to 2. The vertical axis (not displayed in the figure) is scaled identically to the horizontal axis, and also varies from 12 down to 2 as the vertical axis rises in the figure. The height of the estimated skewness function above the frequency pair plane is identified by the color code.

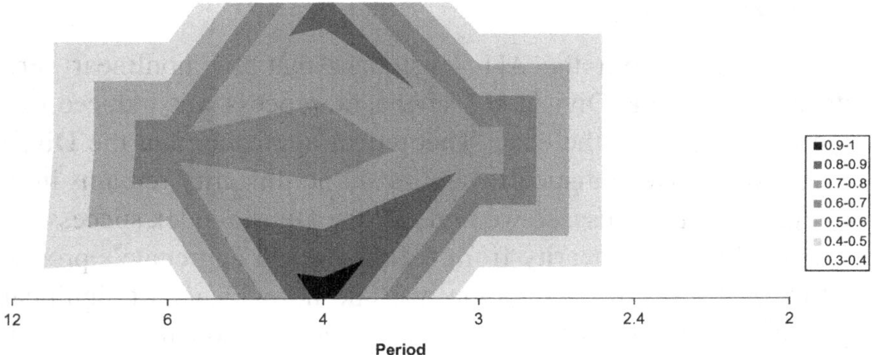

Fig. 2. Estimated normalized bispectrum level surfaces for real per capita Divisia M2.

Hinich's test uses discrete bifrequencies in accordance with the sampling procedure described above. With this extended sample, we used a resolution bandwidth in monthly time units of 12 months, which produces nine bifrequencies. Figure 2 displays level surfaces corresponding to the tops of the boxes produced in estimating the bispectrum and skewness functions from the finite samples.

It was evident from the plots of the nominal and real per capita Divisia $M2$ data that the estimated skewness function is not flat versus frequency (or period) pairs. The (4 month, 4 month) bifrequency for the nominal data has a probability value of 0.971. If we believe that the use of asymptotic theory is valid, then the probability of obtaining such a result for one of the nine bifrequencies is 2.9%. This result suggests that there is some nonlinear structure remaining in that data, although in the test of general nonlinearity we cannot reject the null of linearity. We do not supply that plot, but we do supply the corresponding plot for the deflated real data. Figure 2 was produced from that deflated real data. Inspection of Figure 2 suggests that deflation to real balances filtered out whatever little nonlinearity existed in the nominal data. In particular, in Figure 2 we see that the largest probability value for the real data is 0.944 for the (12 month, 4 month) bifrequency.

2.12. Conclusions

We conclude from the $M1$ level data that the nonlinear serial dependence in the Divisia $M1$ stochastic process was induced from the nonlinearity in the exact Theoretical aggregate that the Divisia index tracks. No statistically significant nonlinearity remains in the tracking error process, so we find that the Divisia index successfully extracted the nonlinearity from the theoretical aggregate's process. At the $M1$ level of aggregation, we find no evidence of significant gains from the use of the risk adjusted Divisia monetary aggregate, so our frequency domain tests are based upon the tracking ability of the unadjusted Divisia $M1$ index.

At the $M2$ level, we find that the use of the CCAPM beta adjusted Divisia monetary aggregate would be advantageous only during a brief period of a few months. That period was one during which the level of risk in the financial sector of the economy was unusually high. Risk aversion does not seem to be a significant problem for the unadjusted Divisia monetary aggregates, except at broad levels of aggregation during periods of unusually high risk.

3

On User Costs of Risky Monetary Assets[1]

William A. Barnett and Shu Wu

We extend the monetary-asset user-cost risk adjustment of Barnett, Liu, and Jensen (1997) and their risk-adjusted Divisia monetary aggregates to the case of multiple non-monetary assets and intertemporal non-separability. Our model can generate potentially larger and more accurate CCAPM user-cost risk adjustments than those found in Barnett, Liu, and Jensen (1997). We show that the risk adjustment to a monetary asset's user cost can be measured easily by its *beta*. We show that any risky non-monetary asset can be used as the benchmark asset, if its rate of return is adjusted in accordance with our formula. These extensions could be especially useful, when own rates of return are subject to exchange rate risk, as in Barnett (2003).

3.1. Introduction

Barnett (1978, 1980, 1997) produced the microeconomic theory of monetary aggregation under perfect certainty, derived the formula for the user cost of monetary assets, and originated the Divisia monetary aggregates to track the theory's quantity and price aggregator functions nonparametrically. The monetary aggregation theory was extended to risk by Barnett (1995) and Barnett, Hinich, and Yue (2000). In producing the Divisia index approximations to the theory's aggregator functions under risk, Barnett, Liu, and Jensen (1997) and Barnett and Liu (2000) showed that a risk adjustment term should be

[1]Reprinted from *Annals of Finance* (2005), "On User Costs of Risky Monetary Assets" by William A. Barnett and Shu Wu, vol. 1, no. 1, January, pp. 35–50; with kind permission of Springer Science+Business Media.

added to the certainty-equivalent user cost in a consumption-based capital asset pricing model (CCAPM). The risk adjustment depends upon the covariance between the rates of return on monetary assets and the growth rate of consumption. Using the components of the usual Federal Reserve System monetary aggregates, Barnett, Liu, and Jensen (1997) showed, however, that the CCAPM risk adjustment is slight and the gain from replacing the unadjusted Divisia index with the extended index is usually small. An overview of the relevant literature is provided in Barnett and Serletis (2000).

The small adjustments are mainly due to the very low contemporaneous covariance between asset returns and the growth rate of consumption. Under the standard power utility function and a reasonable value of the risk-aversion coefficient, the low contemporaneous covariance between asset returns and consumption growth implies that the impact of risk on the user cost of monetary assets is very small. This finding is closely related to those in the well-established literature on the equity premium puzzle [see, e.g., Mehra and Prescott (1985)], in which it is shown that consumption-based asset pricing models with the standard power utility function usually fail to reconcile the observed large equity premium with the low covariance between the equity return and consumption growth. Many different approaches have been pursued in the literature to explain the equity premium puzzle. One successful approach is the use of more general utility functions, such as those with intertemporal non-separability. For example, Campbell and Cochrane (1999) showed that, in an otherwise standard consumption-based asset pricing model, intertemporal non-separability induced by habit formation can produce large time-varying risk premia similar in magnitude to those observed in the data. This suggests that the CCAPM adjustment to the certainty-equivalent monetary-asset user costs can similarly be larger under a more general utility function than those used in Barnett, Liu, and Jensen (1997), who assumed a standard time-separable power utility function.

In this paper, we extend the results in Barnett, Liu, and Jensen (1997) to the case of intertemporal non-separability. We show that the basic result of Barnett, Liu, and Jensen (1997) still holds under a more general utility function. But by allowing intertemporal non-separability, our model can lead to substantial, and we believe accurate, CCAPM risk adjustment, even with a reasonable setting of the risk-aversion coefficient. We believe that the resulting correction is accurate, since the full impact of asset returns on consumption is not contemporaneous, but rather spread over time, as would result from intertemporal non-separability of tastes. This fact has been well established in the finance literature regarding non-monetary assets, and, as we shall see below, the risk adjustment to the rates of return on non-monetary assets plays an important role within the computation of risk adjustments for monetary assets. Hence, even if intertemporal separability from consumption were a reasonable assumption for monetary assets, the established intertemporal non-separability of non-monetary assets from consumption would contaminate the results on monetary assets, under Barnett, Liu, and Jensen's (1997) assumption of the conventional fully intertemporally-separable CCAPM.

We also extend the model in Barnett, Liu, and Jensen (1997) to include multiple risky non-monetary assets, which are the assets that provide no liquidity services, other than their rates of return. This extension is important for two reasons. First, it was shown by Barnett (2003) that the same risk-free benchmark rate cannot be imputed to multiple countries, except under strong assumptions on convergence across the countries. In the literature on optimal currency areas and monetary aggregation over countries within a monetary union, multiple risk-free benchmark assets can be necessary. Even within a single country that is subject to regional regulations and taxation, Barnett's (2003) convergence assumptions for the existence of a unique risk-free benchmark rate may not hold. Under those circumstances, Barnett (2003) has shown that the theory, under perfect certainty, requires multiple benchmark rates of return and the imputation of an additional regional or country subscript to all monetary asset quantities and rates of return, to differentiate assets and rates of return by region or country. Second, the need to compute a unique risk-free benchmark rate of return, when theoretically relevant, presents difficult empirical and measurement problems. We rarely observe the theoretical risk-free asset (in real terms) in financial markets, and hence the risk-free benchmark rate of return is inherently an unobserved variable that, at best, has been proxied. But we show that the relationship between the user cost of a monetary asset and a risky "benchmark" asset's rate of return holds for an arbitrary pair of a monetary and a risky non-monetary asset. Because of this fundamental extension, our results on risk adjustment do not depend upon the existence of a unique risk free rate or the ability to measure such a rate. This important extension remains relevant, even if all monetary asset rates of return are subject to low risk, since relevant candidates for the benchmark asset may all have risky rates of return.

In the asset pricing literature, one of the most popular models is the Capital Asset Pricing Model (CAPM) developed by Sharpe (1964) and Lintner (1965), among others. In CAPM, the risk premium on an individual asset is determined by the covariance of its excess rate of return with that of the market portfolio, or equivalently its *beta*. The advantage of CAPM is that it circumvents the issue of unobservable marginal utility, and the *beta* can easily be estimated. We show in this paper that there also exists a similar *beta* that relates the user cost of an individual monetary asset to the user cost of the consumer's wealth portfolio.

The rest of the paper is organized as follows. In the next section, we specify the representative consumer's intertemporal optimization problem. The main results are contained in Section 3, while Section 4 concludes.

3.2. Consumer's Optimization Problem

We use a setup similar to that in Barnett, Liu, and Jensen (1997). We assume that the representative consumer has an intertemporally non-separable general utility function, $U(\mathbf{m}_t, c_t, c_{t-1}, \ldots, c_{t-n})$, defined over current and past consumption and a vector of L current-period monetary assets, $\mathbf{m}_t = (m_{1,t}, m_{2,t}, \ldots, m_{L,t})'$. The consumer's holdings of non-monetary assets, $\mathbf{k}_t = (k_{1,t}, k_{2,t}, \ldots, k_{K,t})'$, do not enter the utility function, since those assets are assumed to produce no services other than their investment rate of return. To ensure the existence of a monetary aggregate, we further assume that there exists a linearly homogenous aggregator function, $M(\,\cdot\,)$, such that U can be written in the form

$$U(\mathbf{m}_t, c_t, c_{t-1}, \ldots, c_{t-n}) = V(M(\mathbf{m}_t), c_t, c_{t-1}, \ldots, c_{t-n}). \quad (3.1)$$

Given initial wealth, W_t, the consumer seeks to maximize her expected lifetime utility function,

$$E_t \sum_{s=0}^{\infty} \beta^s U(\mathbf{m}_{t+s}, c_{t+s}, c_{t+s-1}, \ldots, c_{t+s-n}), \quad (3.2)$$

subject to the following budget constraints,

$$W_t = p_t^* c_t + \sum_{i=1}^{L} p_t^* m_{i,t} + \sum_{j=1}^{K} p_t^* k_{j,t} = p_t^* c_t + p_t^* A_t \quad (3.3)$$

and

$$W_{t+1} = \sum_{i=1}^{L} R_{i,t+1} p_t^* m_{i,t} + \sum_{j=1}^{K} \tilde{R}_{j,t+1} p_t^* k_{j,t} + Y_{t+1}, \quad (3.4)$$

where $\beta \in (0, 1)$ is the consumer's subjective discount factor, p_t^* is the true cost-of-living index, and $A_t = \sum_{i=1}^{L} m_{i,t} + \sum_{j=1}^{K} k_{j,t}$ is the real value of the asset portfolio. Non-monetary asset j is defined to provide no services other than its gross rate of return, $\tilde{R}_{j,t+1}$, between periods t and $t+1$. Monetary asset i, having quantity $m_{i,t}$, has a gross rate of return $R_{i,t+1}$ between periods t and $t+1$, and does provide monetary services. At the beginning of each period, the consumer allocates her wealth among consumption, c_t, investment in the monetary assets, $\mathbf{m}_t$, and investment in the non-monetary assets, $\mathbf{k}_t$. The consumer's income from any other sources, received at the beginning of period $t+1$, is Y_{t+1}. If any of that income's source is labor income, then we assume that leisure is weakly separable from consumption of goods and holding of monetary assets, so that the function U exists and the decision exists, as a conditional decision problem. The consumer also is subject to the transversality condition

$$\lim_{s\to\infty} \beta^s p_t^* A_{t+s} = 0. \tag{3.5}$$

The equivalency of the two constraints (3.3) and (3.4) with the single constraint used in Barnett (1980) and Barnett, Liu, and Jensen (1997) is easily seen by substituting equation (3.3) for period $t+1$ into equation (3.4) and solving for $p_t^* c_t$.

Define the value function of the consumer's optimization problem to be $H_t = H(W_t, c_{t-1}, \ldots, c_{t-n})$. Assuming the solution to the decision problem exists, we then have the Bellman equation

$$H_t = \underset{(c_t,\mathbf{m}_t,\mathbf{k}_t)}{Sup} \; E_t\{U(\mathbf{m}_t, c_t, c_{t-1}, \ldots, c_{t-n}) + \beta H_{t+1}\}, \tag{3.6}$$

where the maximization is subject to the budget constraints, (3.3) and (3.4).

The first order conditions can be obtained as

$$\lambda_t = \beta E_t\left[\lambda_{t+1}\tilde{R}_{j,t+1}p_t^* / p_{t+1}^*\right] \tag{3.7}$$

and

$$\partial U_t / \partial m_{i,t} = \lambda_t - \beta E_t\left[\lambda_{t+1}R_{i,t+1}p_t^* / p_{t+1}^*\right], \tag{3.8}$$

where $U_t = U(\mathbf{m}_t, c_t, c_{t-1}, \ldots, c_{t-n})$ and $\lambda_t = E_t(\partial U_t / \partial c_t + \beta \partial U_{t+1} / \partial c_t + \cdots + \beta^n \partial U_{t+n} / \partial c_t)$. Note that λ_t is the expected present value of the marginal utility of consumption, c_t. In the standard case in which the instantaneous utility function is time-separable, λ_t reduces to $\partial U(\mathbf{m}_t, c_t) / \partial c_t$.

3.3. Risk-adjusted User Cost of Monetary Assets

3.3.1. *The Theory*

As in Barnett, Liu, and Jensen (1997), we define the contemporaneous real user-cost price of the services of monetary asset i to be the ratio of the marginal utility of the monetary asset and the marginal utility of consumption, so that

$$\pi_{i,t} = \frac{\frac{\partial U_t}{\partial m_{i,t}}}{E_t\left(\frac{\partial U_t}{\partial c_t} + \beta\frac{\partial U_{t+1}}{\partial c_t} + \cdots + \beta^n\frac{\partial U_{t+n}}{\partial c_t}\right)} = \frac{\frac{\partial U_t}{\partial m_{i,t}}}{\lambda_t}. \tag{3.9}$$

We denote the vector of L monetary asset user costs by $\boldsymbol{\pi}_t = (\pi_{1,t}, \pi_{2,t}, \ldots, \pi_{L,t})'$. With the user costs defined above, we can show that the solution value of the exact monetary aggregate, $M(\mathbf{m}_t)$, can be tracked accurately in continuous time by the generalized Divisia index, as proved in the perfect certainty special case by Barnett (1980).

Proposition 1. *Let* $s_{i,t} = \frac{\pi_{i,t}m_{i,t}}{\sum_{l=1}^{L}\pi_{l,t}m_{l,t}}$ *be the user-cost-evaluated expenditure share. Under the weak-separability assumption,* (3.1), *we have for any linearly homogenous monetary aggregator function,* $M(\cdot)$, *that*

$$d\log M_t = \sum_{i=1}^{L} s_{i,t}d\log m_{i,t}, \tag{3.10}$$

where $M_t = M(\mathbf{m}_t)$.

Proof. Under the assumption of weak-separability, we have

$$\frac{\partial U_t}{\partial m_{i,t}} = \frac{\partial V_t}{\partial M_t}\frac{\partial M_t}{\partial m_{i,t}}, \tag{3.11}$$

where $V_t = V(M(\mathbf{m}_t), c_t, c_{t-1}, \ldots, c_{t-n})$. By the definition in (3.9) and equation (3.11), it then follows that

$$\frac{\partial M_t}{\partial m_{i,t}} = \pi_{i,t}\left(\lambda_t \middle/ \frac{\partial V_t}{\partial M_t}\right). \tag{3.12}$$

Taking the total differential of $M_t = M(\mathbf{m}_t)$ and using the result in (3.12), we obtain

$$dM_t = \left(\lambda_t \Big/ \frac{\partial V_t}{\partial M_t}\right) \sum_{i=1}^{L} \pi_{i,t} dm_{i,t}$$

$$= \left(\lambda_t \Big/ \frac{\partial V_t}{\partial M_t}\right) \sum_{i=1}^{L} \pi_{i,t} m_{i,t} d \log m_{i,t}. \qquad (3.13)$$

On the other hand, because of the linear homogeneity of $M_t = M(\mathbf{m}_t)$, it follows from (3.12) that

$$M_t = \sum_{i=1}^{L} \frac{\partial M_t}{\partial m_{i,t}} m_{i,t} = \left(\lambda_t \Big/ \frac{\partial V_t}{\partial M_t}\right) \sum_{i=1}^{L} \pi_{i,t} m_{i,t}. \qquad (3.14)$$

The proposition therefore follows by dividing (3.13) by (3.14). ■

The exact price aggregate dual, $\Pi_\tau = \Pi(\boldsymbol{\pi}_t)$, to the monetary quantity aggregator function, $M_t = M(\mathbf{m}_t)$, is easily computed from factor reversal, $\Pi(\boldsymbol{\pi}_t)M(\mathbf{m}_t) = \sum_{i=1}^{L} \pi_{it} m_{it}$, so that

$$\Pi(\boldsymbol{\pi}_t) = \frac{\sum_{i=1}^{L} \pi_{it} m_{it}}{M(\mathbf{m}_t)}.$$

In continuous time, the user cost price dual can be tracked without error by the Divisia user cost price index

$$d \log \Pi_t = \sum_{i=1}^{L} s_{i,t} d \log \pi_{i,t}.$$

To get a more convenient expression for the user cost, $\pi_{i,t}$, we define the pricing kernel to be

$$Q_{t+1} = \beta \lambda_{t+1} / \lambda_t. \qquad (3.15)$$

Recall that λ_t is the present value of the marginal utility of consumption at time t. Hence Q_{t+1} measures the marginal utility growth from t to $t + 1$. For example, if the utility function (3.1) is time-separable, we have that $Q_{t+1} = \beta \frac{\partial U(\mathbf{m}_{t+1}, c_{t+1}) / \partial c_{t+1}}{\partial U(\mathbf{m}_t, c_t) / \partial c_t}$, which is the subjectively discounted marginal rate of substitution between consumption this period and consumption next period. Clearly Q_{t+1} is positive, as required of marginal rates of substitution.

While the introduction of a pricing kernel is well understood in finance, the intent also should be no surprise to experts in index number theory either. The way in which statistical index numbers, depending upon prices and quantities, track quantity aggregator functions, containing no prices, is through the substitution of first order conditions to replace marginal utilities by functions of relevant prices. This substitution is particularly well known in the famous derivation of the Divisia index by Francois Divisia (1925). In our case, the intent, as applied below, is to replace Q_{t+1} by a function of relevant determinants of its value in asset market equilibrium. If we use the approximation that characterizes CAPM, then the pricing kernel, Q_{t+1}, would be a linear function of the rate of return on the consumer's asset portfolio, A_t.

Using (3.9) and (3.15), the first order conditions (3.7) and (3.8) can alternatively be written as

$$0 = 1 - E_t(Q_{t+1}\tilde{r}_{j,t+1}), \tag{3.16}$$

$$\pi_{i,t} = 1 - E_t(Q_{t+1}r_{i,t+1}), \tag{3.17}$$

where $\tilde{r}_{j,t+1} = \tilde{R}_{j,t+1}p_t^* / p_{t+1}^*$ is the real gross rate of return on non-monetary asset, $k_{j,t}$, and $r_{i,t+1} = R_{i,t+1}p_t^* / p_{t+t}^*$ is the real gross rate of return on monetary asset, $m_{i,t}$, which provides the consumer with liquidity service.

Equations (3.16) and (3.17) impose restrictions on asset returns. Equation (3.16) applies to the returns on all risky non-monetary assets, $k_{j,t}$ ($j = 1, \ldots, K$), in the usual manner. For monetary assets, equation (3.17) implies that the "deviation" from the usual Euler equation measures the user cost of that monetary asset. To obtain good measures of the user costs of monetary assets, the non-monetary asset pricing within the asset portfolio's pricing kernel, Q_{t+1}, should be as accurate as possible. Otherwise, we would attribute any non-monetary asset pricing errors to the monetary asset user costs in (3.17), as pointed out by Marshall (1997). From the above Euler equations, we can obtain the following proposition.

Proposition 2. *Given the real rate of return, $r_{i,t+1}$, on a monetary asset and the real rate of return, $\tilde{r}_{j,t+1}$, on an arbitrary non-monetary asset, the risk-adjusted real user-cost price of the services of the monetary asset can be obtained as*

$$\pi_{i,t} = \frac{(1+\omega_{i,t})E_t\tilde{r}_{j,t+1} - (1+\omega_{j,t})E_t r_{i,t+1}}{E_t\tilde{r}_{j,t+1}}, \tag{3.18}$$

where

$$\omega_{i,t} = -Cov_t(Q_{t+1}, r_{i,t+1}) \tag{3.19}$$

and

$$\omega_{j,t} = -Cov_t(Q_{t+1}, \tilde{r}_{j,t+1}). \tag{3.20}$$

Proof. From the Euler equation (3.16), we have

$$1 = E_t Q_{t+1} E_t\tilde{r}_{j,t+1} + Cov_t(Q_{t+1}, \tilde{r}_{j,t+1}), \tag{3.21}$$

and similarly from the Euler equation (3.17), we have

$$\pi_{i,t} = 1 - E_t Q_{t+1} E_t r_{i,t+1} - Cov_t(Q_{t+1}, r_{i,t+1}). \tag{3.22}$$

Note that (3.21) implies that

$$E_t Q_{t+1} = \frac{1 - Cov_t(Q_{t+1}, \tilde{r}_{j,t+1})}{E_t\tilde{r}_{j,t+1}}. \tag{3.23}$$

Hence Proposition 2 follows by substituting $E_t Q_{t+1}$ into (3.22). ■

Proposition 2 relates the user cost of a monetary asset to the rates of return on financial assets, which need not be risk free. It applies to an arbitrary pair of monetary and non-monetary assets. In fact, observe that the left hand side of equation (3.18) has no j subscript, even though there are j subscripts on the right hand side. The left hand side of (3.18) is invariant to the choice of non-monetary asset used on the right hand side, as a result of equation (3.23), which holds for all j, regardless of i. This result suggests that we can choose an arbitrary non-monetary financial asset as the "benchmark" asset in calculating the user costs of the financial assets that provide monetary services, so long as we correctly compute the covariance, $\omega_{j,t}$, of the return on the non-monetary asset with the pricing kernel.

Practical considerations in estimating that covariance could tend to discourage use of multiple benchmark assets. In particular, a biased estimate of $\omega_{j,t}$ for a non-monetary asset j would similarly bias the user costs of all monetary assets, if that non-monetary asset were used as the benchmark asset in computing all monetary asset user costs. Alternatively, if a different non-monetary financial assets were used as the benchmark assets for each monetary asset, errors in measuring $\omega_{j,t}$ for different j's could bias relative user costs of monetary assets.

Nevertheless, in theory it is not necessary to use the same benchmark asset j for the computation of the user cost of each monetary asset i. In particular, we have the following corollary.

Corollary 1. *Under uncertainty we can choose any non-monetary asset as the "benchmark" asset, when computing the risk-adjusted user-cost prices of the services of monetary assets.*

Notice that Proposition 2 doesn't require existence of a risk-free non-monetary asset (in real-terms). Since we rarely observe the rate of return on such an entirely illiquid asset in financial markets, our proposition generalizes the main result in Barnett, Liu, and Jensen (1997) in a very useful manner. Although a unique risk-free totally illiquid investment, having no secondary market, may exist in theory, Corollary 1 frees us from the need to seek a proxy for its inherently unobservable rate of return.

If we were to impose the further assumption of perfect certainty on top of the other assumptions we have made above, there would be only one benchmark asset, and all of our results would reduce, as a special case, to those of Barnett (1978, 1980). Without risk and with no monetary services provided by benchmark assets, arbitrage would assure that there could be only one benchmark asset.

To see the intuition of Proposition 2, assume that one of the non-monetary assets is risk-free with *gross* real interest rate of r_t^f at time t. Further, as proven by Barnett (1978), the certainty-equivalent user cost, $\pi_{i,t}^e$, of a monetary asset $m_{i,t}$ is

$$\pi_{i,t}^e = \frac{r_t^f - E_t r_{i,t+1}}{r_t^f}. \tag{3.24}$$

From equation (3.16), the first order condition for r_t^f is

$$1 = E_t(Q_{t+1} r_t^f). \tag{3.25}$$

Hence we have, from the nonrandomness of r_t^f, that

$$E_t Q_{t+1} = \frac{1}{r_t^f}. \tag{3.26}$$

Replacing $E_t Q_{t+1}$ in (3.17) with $\frac{1}{r_t^f}$, we then have

$$\pi_{i,t} = \frac{r_t^f - E_t r_{i,t+1}}{r_t^f} + \omega_{i,t} = \pi_{i,t}^e + \omega_{i,t}, \tag{3.27}$$

where $\omega_{i,t} = -Cov_t(Q_{t+1}, r_{i,t+1})$. Therefore, $\pi_{i,t}$ could be larger or smaller than the certainty-equivalent user cost, $\pi_{i,t}^e$, depending on the sign of the covariance between $r_{i,t+1}$ and Q_{t+1}. When the return on a monetary asset is positively correlated with the pricing kernel, Q_{t+1}, and thereby negatively correlated with the rate of return on the full portfolio of monetary and non-monetary assets, the monetary asset's user cost will be adjusted downwards from the certainty-equivalent user cost. Such assets offer a hedge against aggregate risk by paying off when the full asset portfolio's rate of return is low. In contrast, when the return on a monetary asset is negatively correlated with the pricing kernel, Q_{t+1}, and thereby positively correlated with the rate of return on the full asset portfolio, the asset's user cost will be adjusted upwards from the certainty-equivalent user cost, since such assets tend to pay off when the asset porfolio's rate of return is high. Such assets are very risky.

To calculate the risk adjustment, we need to compute the covariance between the asset return $r_{i,t+1}$ and the pricing kernel Q_{t+1}, which is unobservable. Consumption-based asset pricing models allow us to relate Q_{t+1} to consumption growth through a specific utility function. But most utility functions have been shown not to be able to reconcile the aggregate consumption data with the observed stock returns and the interest rate. Kocherlakota (1996) provides an excellent survey on the equity premium puzzle literature. In fact the empirical results from Barnett, Liu, and Jensen (1997) show that the consumption risk adjustments for the user costs of monetary assets are small in many cases under the standard utility function with moderate risk aversion.

With more general utility functions than used in previous empirical studies on monetary aggregation, we can use the theory in this paper to extend the existing empirical studies on the user costs of risky monetary assets, and thereby on the induced risk-adjusted Divisia monetary quantity and user cost aggregates. Campbell and Cochrane (1999), among others, have shown that a habit-formation-based utility function with reasonable risk-aversion coefficient could produce large time-varying risk premia, similar in magnitude to those observed in the data. The risk-adjustment for the user costs of monetary assets is intimately related to the determination of risk premia. As a result, there is reason to believe that intertemporally non-separable utility functions, such as the one in Campbell and Cochrane (1999), can produce larger risk adjustments to the certainty-equivalent user costs than the small adjustments found in Barnett, Liu, and Jensen (1997). The results could be particularly dramatic in open economy applications in which rates of return are subject to exchange rate risk. We are currently conducting an empirical study to implement the theoretical model proposed in this paper.

There is a particularly important reason to use more general and flexible utility functions in computing the user costs of risky monetary assets. As discussed above, to obtain good measures of the user costs of monetary assets, we need to choose the pricing kernel, and hence the utility function, such that the pricing of non-monetary assets within the kernel is as accurate as possible. Otherwise, the user costs of monetary assets would be contaminated by the pricing errors. Since standard utility functions are known to lead to erroneous estimates of non-monetary-asset risk premia, the risk adjustments to the users cost of monetary assets with those utility functions are likely to be much less accurate than those with utility functions that have better empirical performance in matching the observed non-monetary-asset risk premia.

3.3.2. *Approximation to the Theory*

All of the consumption-based asset pricing models require us to make explicit assumptions about investors' utility functions. An alternative approach, which is commonly practiced in finance, is to approximate Q_{t+1} by some simple function of observable macroeconomic factors that are believed to be closely related to investors' marginal utility growth. For example, the well-known CAPM [Sharpe (1964) and Lintner (1965)] approximates Q_{t+1} by a linear function of the rate of return on the market portfolio. Then the rate of return on any individual asset is linked to its covariance with the market rate of return. Fama and French (1992) include two additional factors, firm size and book-to-market value, and show that the three-factor model is able to capture the cross-sectional variation in average stock returns. Using stock returns, Chen, Roll, and Ross (1986) and Lamont (2000) try to identify macroeconomic variables as priced risk factors. Cochrane (2000) provides detailed discussion on the approximation of the pricing kernel Q_{t+1}.

We show that there also exists a similar CAPM-type relationship among user costs of risky monetary assets, under the assumption that

Q_{t+1} is a linear function of the rate of return on a well-diversified wealth portfolio. We believe that this simple specification of the pricing kernel, based upon a long standing tradition in finance, is a reasonable first step in the extension of Barnett, Liu, and Jensen (1997) to the case of intertemporal nonseparability. In the finance literature, the CAPM specification of the pricing kernel results from a special case of a linear factor-model decomposition of the first order conditions, (3.16) and (3.17), under the assumption of quadratic utility or Gaussianity. Deeper specifications of the pricing kernel, as being proposed now in finance, might prove similarly advantageous in future extensions of our research.

Specifically, define $r_{A,t+1}$ to be the share-weighted rate of return on the consumer's asset portfolio, including both the monetary assets, $m_{i,t}$ $(i = 1, \ldots, L)$, and the non-monetary assets, $k_{j,t}$ $(j = 1, \ldots, K)$. Then the traditional CAPM approximation to Q_{t+1} mentioned above is of the form $Q_{t+1} = a_t - b_t r_{A,t+1}$, where a_t, and b_t can be time dependent.

Let $\phi_{i,t}$ and $\varphi_{j,t}$ denote the share of $m_{i,t}$ and $k_{j,t}$, respectively, in the portfolio's stock value, so that

$$\phi_{i,t} = \frac{m_{i,t}}{\sum_{l=1}^{L} m_{l,t} + \sum_{j=1}^{K} k_{j,t}} = \frac{m_{i,t}}{A_t}$$

and

$$\varphi_{j,t} = \frac{k_{j,t}}{\sum_{l=1}^{L} m_{l,t} + \sum_{i=1}^{K} k_{i,t}} = \frac{k_{j,t}}{A_t}.$$

Then, by construction, $r_{A,t+1} = \sum_{i=1}^{L} \phi_{i,t} r_{i,t+1} + \sum_{j=1}^{K} \varphi_{j,t} \tilde{r}_{j,t+1}$, where

$$\sum_{i=1}^{L} \phi_{i,t} + \sum_{j=1}^{K} \varphi_{j,t} = 1. \tag{3.28}$$

Multiplying (3.24) by $\varphi_{j,t}$ and (3.25) by $\phi_{i,t}$, we have

$$0 = \varphi_{j,t} - E_t(Q_{t+1}\varphi_{j,t}\tilde{r}_{j,t+1}) \tag{3.29}$$

and

$$\phi_{i,t}\pi_{i,t} = \phi_{i,t} - E_t(Q_{t+1}\phi_{i,t}r_{i,t+1}). \tag{3.30}$$

Summing (3.29) over j and (3.30) over i, adding the two summed equations together, and using the definition of $r_{A,t+1}$, we get

$$\sum_{i=1}^{L} \phi_{i,t}\pi_{i,t} = 1 - E_t(Q_{t+1}r_{A,t+1}). \tag{3.31}$$

Let $\Pi_{A,t} = \sum_{i=1}^{L} \phi_{i,t}\pi_{i,t} + \sum_{j=1}^{K} \varphi_{i,t}\tilde{\pi}_{j,t}$, where $\tilde{\pi}_{j,t}$ is the user cost of non-monetary asset j. We define $\Pi_{A,t}$ to be the user cost of the consumer's asset wealth portfolio. But the user cost, $\tilde{\pi}_{j,t}$, of every non-monetary asset is simply 0, as shown in (3.16), so equivalently $\Pi_{A,t} = \sum_{i=1}^{L} \phi_{i,t}\pi_{i,t}$. The reason is that consumers do not pay a price, in terms of foregone interest, for the monetary services of non-monetary assets, since they provide no monetary services and provide only their investment rate of return. We can show that our definition of $\Pi_{A,t}$ is consistent with Fisher's factor reversal test, as follows.

Result: *The pair* $(A_t, \Pi_{A,t})$ *satisfies factor reversal, defined by*:

$$\Pi_{A,t}A_t = \sum_{i=1}^{L} \pi_{i,t}m_{i,t} + \sum_{j=1}^{K} \tilde{\pi}_{j,t}k_{j,t}.$$

Since we know that $\tilde{\pi}_{j,t} = 0$ for all j, factor reversal equivalently can be written as

$$\Pi_{A,t}A_t = \sum_{i=1}^{L} \pi_{i,t}m_{i,t}.$$

The proof of the result is straightforward.

Proof. By the definition of $\phi_{i,t}$, we have $m_{i,t} = \phi_{i,t}A_t$. Hence, we have

$$\sum_{i=1}^{L} \pi_{i,t} m_{i,t} = \sum_{i=1}^{L} \pi_{i,t}\phi_{i,t}A_t$$
$$= A_t \sum_{i=1}^{L} \pi_{i,t}\phi_{i,t} = A_t \Pi_{A,t},$$

which is our result. ■

Observe that the wealth portfolio is different from the monetary services aggregate, $M(\mathbf{m}_t)$. The portfolio weights in the asset wealth stock are the market-value-based shares, while the growth rate weights in the monetary services flow aggregate are the user-cost-evaluated shares.

Suppose one of the non-monetary assets is (locally) risk-free with gross real interest rate r_t^f. By substituting equation (3.24) for $\pi_{i,t}$ into the definition of $\Pi_{A,t}$, using the definition of $r_{A,t+1}$, and letting $r_t^f = E\tilde{r}_{j,t+1}$ for all j, it follows that the certainty equivalent user cost of the asset wealth portfolio is $\Pi_{A,t}^e = \frac{r_t^f - E_t r_{A,t+1}}{r_t^f}$. We now can prove the following proposition.

Proposition 3. *If one of the non-monetary assets is (locally) risk-free with gross real interest rate r_t^f, and if $Q_{t+1} = a_t - b_t r_{A,t+1}$, where $r_{A,t+1}$ is the gross real rate of return on the consumer's wealth portfolio, then the user cost of any monetary asset i is given by*

$$\pi_{i,t} - \pi_{i,t}^e = \beta_{i,t}(\Pi_{A,t} - \Pi_{A,t}^e), \tag{3.32}$$

where $\pi_{i,t}$ and $\Pi_{A,t}$ are the user costs of asset i and of the asset wealth portfolio, respectively, and $\pi_{i,t}^e = \frac{r_t^f - E_t r_{i,t+1}}{r_t^f}$ and $\Pi_{A,t}^e = \frac{r_t^f - E_t r_{A,t+1}}{r_t^f}$ are the certainty-equivalent user costs of asset i and the asset wealth portfolio, respectively. The "beta" of asset i in equation (3.32) *is* *given by*

$$\beta_{i,t} = \frac{Cov_t(r_{A,t+1}, r_{i,t+1})}{Var_t(r_{A,t+1})}. \tag{3.33}$$

Proof. From (3.31) and the definition of $\Pi_{A,t}$, we have for the wealth portfolio that

$$\Pi_{A,t} = 1 - E_t Q_{t+1} E_t r_{A,t+1} - Cov_t(Q_{t+1}, r_{A,t+1}). \tag{3.34}$$

Given the risk-free rate r_t^f, we have that $E_t Q_{t+1} = \frac{1}{r_t^f}$ from equation (3.26). Hence

$$\begin{aligned} \Pi_{A,t} &= 1 - \frac{E_t r_{A,t+1}}{r_t^f} - Cov_t(Q_{t+1}, r_{A,t+1}) \\ &= \Pi_{A,t}^e - Cov_t(Q_{t+1}, r_{A,t+1}). \end{aligned} \tag{3.35}$$

Using the assumption that $Q_{t+1} = a_t - b_t r_{A,t+1}$, so that $Cov_t(Q_{t+1}, r_{A,t+1}) = -b_t Var_t(r_{A,t+1})$, it follows that

$$\Pi_{A,t} = \Pi_{A,t}^e + b_t Var_t(r_{A,t+1}). \tag{3.36}$$

On the other hand, for any asset i we have from (3.27) and $Q_{t+1} = a_t - b_t r_{A,t+1}$ that

$$\pi_{i,t} = \pi_{i,t}^e - Cov_t(Q_{t+1}, r_{i,t+1}) = \pi_{i,t}^e + b_t Cov_t(r_{A,t+1}, r_{i,t+1}). \tag{3.37}$$

Hence, from equations (3.36) and (3.37), we can conclude that

$$\frac{\pi_{i,t} - \pi_{i,t}^e}{\Pi_{A,t} - \Pi_{A,t}^e} = \frac{Cov_t(r_{A,t+1}, r_{i,t+1})}{Var_t(r_{A,t+1})}, \tag{3.38}$$

and the proposition follows. ■

In the approximation, $Q_{t+1} = a_t - b_t r_{A,t+1}$, to the theoretical pricing kernel, Q_{t+1}, the reason for the minus sign is similar to the reason for the minus signs before the own rates of return within monetary asset user costs: the intent in the finance literature is to measure a "price," not a rate of return. In particular, with the minus sign in front of b_t and with b_t positive, we can interpret b_t in equations (3.36) and

(3.37) as a "price" of risk. This interpretation can be seen from the fact that b_t then measures the amount of risk premium added to the left hand side per unit of covariance (in (3.37)) or variance (in (3.36)). Also recall that the pricing kernel itself, as a subjectively-discounted marginal rate of substitution, should be positive. Hence the signs of a_t and b_t must both be positive, and a_t must be sufficiently large so that the pricing kernel is positive for all observed values of $r_{A,t+1}$.

Proposition 3 is very similar to the standard CAPM formula for asset returns. In CAPM theory, the expected excess rate of return, $E_t r_{i,t+1} - r_t^f$, on an individual asset is determined by its covariance with the excess rate of return on the market portfolio, $E_t r_{M,t+1} - r_t^f$, in accordance with

$$E_t r_{i,t+1} - r_t^f = \beta_{i,t}(E_t r_{M,t+1} - r_t^f), \tag{3.39}$$

where $\beta_{i,t} = \frac{Cov_t(r_{i,t+1} - r_t^f, r_{M,t+1} - r_t^f)}{Var_t(r_{M,t+1} - r_t^f)}$.

This result implies that asset i's risk premium depends on its market portfolio risk exposure, which is measured by the *beta* of this asset. Our proposition shows that the risk adjustment to the certainty equivalent user cost of asset i is determined in that manner as well. The larger the *beta*, through risk exposure to the wealth portfolio, the larger the risk adjustment. User costs will be adjusted upwards for those monetary assets whose rates of return are positively correlated with the return on the wealth portfolio, and conversely for those monetary assets whose returns are negatively correlated with the wealth portfolio. In particular, if we find that $\beta_{i,t}$ is very small for all the monetary assets under consideration, then the risk adjustment to the user cost is also very small. In that case, the unadjusted Divisia monetary index would be a good proxy for the extended index in Barnett, Liu, and Jensen (1997).

Notice that Proposition 3 is a conditional version of CAPM with time-varying risk premia. Lettau and Ludvigson (2001) have shown that a conditional version of CAPM performs much better empirically in explaining the cross section of asset returns, than the unconditional

CAPM. In fact, the unconditional CAPM is usually rejected in empirical tests. See, e.g., Breeden, Gibbons, and Litzenberger (1989) and Campbell (1996).

3.4. Concluding Remarks

Simple sum monetary aggregates treat monetary assets with different rates of return as perfect substitutes. Barnett (1978, 1980) showed that the Divisia index, with user cost prices, is a more appropriate measure for monetary services, and derived the formula for the user cost of monetary asset services in the absence of uncertainty. Barnett, Liu, and Jensen (1997) extended the Divisia monetary quantity index to the case of uncertain returns and risk aversion. For risky monetary assets, however, the magnitude of the risk adjustment to the certainty equivalent user cost is unclear. Using a standard time-separable power utility function, Barnett, Liu, and Jensen (1997) showed that the difference between the unadjusted Divisia index and the index extended for risk is usually small. However, this result could be a consequence of the same problem that causes the equity premium puzzle in the asset pricing literature. The consumption-based asset pricing model with more general utility functions, most notably those that are intertemporally non-separable, can reproduce the large and time-varying risk premium observed in the data. We believe that similarly extended asset pricing models will provide larger and *more accurate* CCAPM adjustment to the user costs of monetary assets than those found in Barnett, Liu, and Jensen (1997). The current paper extends the basic result in Barnett, Liu, and Jensen (1997) in that manner.

How big the risk adjustment should be is an empirical issue. We show in this paper that for any individual monetary asset, the risk adjustment to its certainty equivalent user cost can be measured by its *beta*, which depends on the covariance between the rate of return on the monetary asset and on the wealth portfolio of the consumer. This result is analogous to the standard Capital Asset Pricing Model

(CAPM). In practice, if the *beta* is found to be very small, then the certainty equivalent user cost would be a good approximation to the true user cost price of the monetary asset services under uncertainty. In that special case, the unadjusted Divisia index could still be used for monetary aggregation. We are currently conducting research on the empirical implications of the models proposed in this paper. Relevant modeling and inference methodology are available in Barnett and Binner (2004).

Another extension of the current paper could be to introduce heterogeneous investors, as considered for the case of perfect certainty by Barnett (2003). This extension can be of particular importance in multicountry or multiregional applications, in which regional or country-specific heterogeneity cannot be ignored. In such cases regional or national subscripts must be introduced to differentiate goods and assets by location. With the possibility of regulatory and taxation differences across the heterogeneous groups, arbitrage cannot be assumed to remove the possibility of multiple benchmark assets, even under perfect certainty, except under special assumptions on institutional convergence. See Barnett (2004) regarding those assumptions.

4

The Discounted Economic Stock of Money with VAR Forecasting[1]

William A. Barnett, Unja Chae and John W. Keating

We measure the economic capital stock of money implied by the Divisia monetary aggregate service flow, in a manner consistent with asset pricing theory. Based on Barnett's (1991) definition of the economic stock of money, we estimate the expected discounted flow of expenditure on the services of monetary assets, where expenditure on monetary services is evaluated at the user costs of the monetary components. We use forecasts based on martingale expectations, asymmetric vector autoregressive expectations, and the Bayesian vector autoregressive expectations. We find the resulting capital-stock index to be surprisingly robust to the modeling of expectations.

4.1. Introduction

Empirical research in monetary economics commonly has used official central bank measures of aggregate money supply. Conventionally, central banks have measured the official monetary aggregates by adding up the nominal quantities of components included in the monetary aggregates. The resulting monetary aggregate is called the simple sum aggregate or simple sum index (SSI). But the SSI has long been questioned as a measure of money stock, because of its

[1]Reprinted from *Annals of Finance* (2006), "The Discounted Economic Stock of Money with VAR Forecasting" by William A. Barnett, Unja Chae, and John W. Keating, vol. 2, no. 2, July, pp. 229–258; with kind permission of Springer Science+Business Media.

disconnect from microeconomic aggregation and index number theory. The simple sum aggregate implicitly assumes that all monetary components are perfect substitutes, with all monetary components having equal linear weights. Since monetary assets began yielding interest over half a century ago, with different interest rates paid on different monetary assets, perfect substitutability among monetary assets with equal weights has become an unrealistic assumption.

A theoretically appropriate alternative to the simple sum aggregate is the Divisia monetary aggregate derived by Barnett (1980). By taking into account the different user-cost prices of monetary components, the Divisia monetary aggregate permits imperfect substitutability among monetary assets and reflects the properly weighted contributions of all monetary components to the economy's flow of monetary services. However, the Divisia aggregate measures monetary service flows, not monetary stock. While most variables in economic theory are flows, monetary stock is needed for some purposes. For instance, the wealth variable in intertemporal Fisherine wealth constraints should be entered as money stock. Similarly Pigou "real-balance" wealth-effects of monetary policy require stock explanatory-variables. The objective of this paper is to measure money stock in a manner consistent with the aggregation-theoretic foundations of the Divisia service-flow aggregate. We compute the first theory-based economic stock of money not requiring the assumption of martingale expectations.

Barnett (1991) showed that the monetary stock implied by the Divisia flow aggregate is the expected discounted monetary-service-flow expenditure, with expenditure on monetary services being evaluated at user-cost prices. Following Barnett, we call the money stock implied by the Divisia monetary service flow — the "economic stock of money." In addition to its direct derivation from microeconomic theory, the economic monetary stock (ESM hereafter) has several attractive properties. First, the ESM is consistent with asset pricing theory. In particular, the formula for ESM is consistent with valuation of a cash-flow generating asset by discounting the flow to present value. Second, the economic monetary stock provides a general capital stock formula that nests the simple sum index and the currency equivalent (CE) index (of Rotemberg (1991) and Rotemberg, *et al.* (1995)) as special cases. In particular, under the assumption of martingale expectations, the ESM index reduces to the CE index (Barnett (1991)). With the additional assumption of zero return-yield rates for all monetary assets, CE reduces to the simple sum index.

The assumptions of zero yield rates and martingale expectations are both highly implausible. We make neither of those assumptions. We compute the ESM using forecasts of the future variables in the formula. Our forecasts are based upon an asymmetric vector autoregressive model (AVAR) and a Bayesian vector autoregressive model (BVAR). For purposes of comparison, we also compute the ESM using actual realized future data within sample. This paper compares the estimated ESM with the simple sum index (SSI) and the CE index. We thereby investigate the measurement biases inherent in the SSI and the CE index. Our use of VAR forecasting is part of our measurement procedure, rather than a means of judging policy relevance. Our approach is aggregation-theoretic rather than policy-focused. But VAR comparisons of Divisia and simple sum monetary aggregation for policy purposes do exist. See Schunk (2001).

Use of the economically correct measure for monetary stock can improve the quality of empirical research on wealth effects caused by changes in the expected monetary service flow induced by policy shifts.

4.2. Microfoundations of Consumer Demand for Money

4.2.1. *Overview*

In this section we review the theoretical foundations for a representative consumer's money demand under perfect foresight in accordance with Barnett (1980). We first define the variables for period s, where t is the current period, and T is the length of the planning horizon for

$t \leq s \leq t+T$:

$\mathbf{c}_s$ = vector of per capita planned consumption of goods and services,
$\mathbf{p}_s$ = vector of goods and services expected prices and of durable goods expected rental prices,
p_s^* = the true cost of living index,
$\mathbf{m}_s$ = vector of planned real balances of monetary assets with components m_{is} $(i = 1, 2, \ldots, n)$,
r_{is} = the expected nominal holding period yield on monetary asset i,
L_s = planned labor supply,
w_s = the expected wage rate,
B_s = planned holdings of the benchmark asset,
R_s = the expected nominal holding-period yield on the benchmark asset,
I_s = all other sources of income.

The benchmark asset is defined to be a pure investment asset providing financial yield R_s but no liquidity or other services. A representative economic agent holds the asset solely as a means of accumulating and of transferring wealth among periods. Thus under risk neutrality (Barnett (1995), section 3), the benchmark rate R_s will be the maximum expected holding-period yield in the economy in period s.

During period t, let the representative consumer's intertemporal utility function, $\mathcal{U}_t$, be weakly separable in the block of each period's consumption of goods and monetary assets, so that an exact monetary aggregator function, u, exists:

$$\mathcal{U}_t = \mathcal{U}(u(\mathbf{m}_t), u_{t+1}(\mathbf{m}_{t+1}), \ldots, u_{t+T}(\mathbf{m}_{t+T}); \\ v(\mathbf{c}_t), v_{t+1}(\mathbf{c}_{t+1}), \ldots, v_t(\mathbf{c}_{t+T}); B_{t+T}). \tag{4.1}$$

The function u is assumed to be linearly homogeneous, which is a sufficient condition in aggregation theory for u to serve simultaneously as the monetary asset category utility function and the monetary asset quantity aggregator function. Dual to the category utility function, $v_s(\mathbf{c}_s)$, of non-monetary goods and services, there exists true cost of living index, $p_s^* = p_s^*(\mathbf{p}_s)$, which can be used to deflate nominal values to real values during period s.

Maximization of intertemporal utility is subject to the following budget constraints for $s = t, \ldots, t+T$:

$$\mathbf{p}_s'\mathbf{c}_s = w_s L_s + \sum_{i=1}^{n} \left[(1 + r_{i,s-1})p_{s-1}^* m_{i,s-1} - p_s^* m_{is}\right] + \left[(1 + R_{s-1})p_{s-1}^* B_{s-1} - p_s^* B_s\right] + I_s \tag{4.2}$$

4.2.2. *User Cost of Money*

Money is a durable good. The cost of using the services of a durable good or asset during one period is the user cost price or rental price. Barnett (1978, 1980) derived the user cost price of the services of monetary assets by recursively combining the $T+1$ multi-period budget constraints, equation (4.2), into the single discounted Fisherine wealth constraint,

$$\begin{aligned}\sum_{s=t}^{t+T}\left(\frac{\mathbf{p}_s'}{\rho_s}\right)\mathbf{c}_s &+ \sum_{s=t}^{t+T}\sum_{i=1}^{n}\left[\frac{p_s^*}{\rho_s} - \frac{p_s^*(1 + r_{is})}{\rho_{s+1}}\right] m_{is} \\ &+ \sum_{i=1}^{n}\frac{p_{s+T}^*\left(1 + r_{i,t+T}\right)}{\rho_{t+T+1}} m_{i,t+T} + \frac{p_{s+T}^*}{\rho_{s+T}} B_{t+T} \\ &= \sum_{s=t}^{t+T}\left(\frac{w_s}{\rho_s}\right) L_s + \sum_{i=1}^{n}(1 + r_{i,t-1})p_{t-1}^* m_{i,t-1} \\ &\quad +(1 + R_{t-1})B_{t-1}p_{t-1}^*.\end{aligned} \tag{4.3}$$

From that factorization of the intertemporal constraint, we see that the forward user cost of the services of the monetary asset m_i in period s is

$$\psi_{is} = \frac{p_s^*}{\rho_s} - \frac{p_s^*(1 + r_{is})}{\rho_{s+1}}, \tag{4.4}$$

where the discount rate for period s is

$$\rho_s = \begin{cases} 1 & for\ s = t \\ \Pi_{u=t}^{s-1}(1 + R_u) & for\ s > t \end{cases}. \tag{4.5}$$

As a result, the current period nominal user cost of monetary asset m_i is

$$\psi_{it} = p_t^* \frac{R_t - r_{it}}{1 + R_t}, \tag{4.6}$$

while the corresponding real user cost of monetary asset m_i is $\psi_{it}^r = \psi_{it}/p_t^*$.

4.3. Economic Aggregation and Index Number Theory

Let $\boldsymbol{\psi}_t = (\psi_{1t}, \ldots, \psi_{nt})\prime$, and define total current period expenditure on monetary services during period t to be $(TE)_t = \boldsymbol{\psi}_t' \mathbf{m}_t^*$, where $\mathbf{m}_t^*$ is the optimized value of $\mathbf{m}_t$ from maximizing (4.1) subject to (4.2). Then the exact monetary aggregate, $M_t = M(\mathbf{m}_t^*) = u(\mathbf{m}_t^*)$, can be tracked without error by the Divisia index (Barnett (1983)) in the continuous time analog to ((4.1), (4.2)):

$$\frac{d\ \log\ M_t}{dt} = \sum_{i=1}^{n} w_{it} \frac{d\ \log\ m_{it}^*}{dt}, \tag{4.7}$$

where $w_{it} = \frac{\psi_{it} m_{it}^*}{(TE)_t}$ is the i'th asset's share in expenditure on all monetary assets' service flows at instant of time t.

In discrete time, the Törnqvist second order approximation to the Divisia index is

$$\log\ M_t - \log\ M_{t-1} = \sum_{i=1}^{n} \bar{w}_{it}(\log\ m_{it}^* - \log\ m_{i,t-1}^*), \tag{4.8}$$

where $\bar{w}_{it} = (w_{it} + w_{i,t-1})/2$. Equation (4.8) defines the discrete time "Divisia monetary aggregate," which measures the aggregate monetary service flow during period t. This Törnqvist approximation, (4.8), to the continuous time Divisia index, (4.7), is in the class of superlative index numbers defined by Diewert (1976) to provide a chained quadratic approximation to the continuous time index.

4.3.1. *Definition of the Economic Stock of Money under Perfect Foresight*

The economic stock of money (ESM), as defined by Barnett (1991) under perfect foresight, follows immediately from the manner in which monetary assets are found to enter the derived wealth constraint, (4.3). As a result, the formula for the economic stock of money under perfect foresight is

$$V_t = \sum_{s=t}^{\infty} \sum_{i=1}^{n} \left[\frac{p_s^*}{\rho_s} - \frac{p_s^*(1 + r_{is})}{\rho_{s+1}} \right] m_{is}. \tag{4.9}$$

The economic stock of money is thereby found to be the discounted present value of expenditure flow on the services of all monetary assets, with each asset priced at its user cost. Let M_{is} be the nominal balance of monetary asset i in period s, so that $M_{is} = p_s^* m_{is}$. Using definition (4.5), V_t becomes

$$V_t = \sum_{s=t}^{\infty} \sum_{i=1}^{n} \left[\frac{R_s - r_{is}}{\prod_{u=t}^{s} (1 + R_u)} \right] M_{is}. \tag{4.10}$$

A mathematically equivalent alternative form of (4.10) can be derived from quantity and user cost flow aggregates, discounted to present value. Dual to any exact quantity flow aggregate, there exists a unique price aggregate. The price aggregate equals the minimum cost of consuming one unit of the quantity aggregate. Let $\psi_t = \psi(\boldsymbol{\psi}_t)$ be the nominal user cost aggregate that is dual to the exact, real monetary quantity aggregate, M_t. By Fisher's factor reversal, the product of the quantity and user cost price aggregate must equal expenditure on the components, so that

$$(TE)_s = \sum_{i=1}^{n} m_{is}\psi_{is} = M(\mathbf{m}_s)\Psi(\boldsymbol{\psi}_s), \tag{4.11}$$

where $(TE)_s$ is total nominal expenditure on the monetary services of all monetary components. Alternatively, instead of using real quantities and nominal user costs, we can use nominal quantities and real user costs to acquire

$$(TE)_s = \sum_{i=1}^{n} M_{is}\psi_{is}^r = M(\mathbf{M}_s)\Psi(\boldsymbol{\psi}_s^r), \tag{4.12}$$

where $\psi_{is}^r = \psi_{is}/p_s^* = \frac{R_s - r_{is}}{1+R_s}$ is the real user cost of monetary asset i in period s, $\mathbf{M}_s = (M_{1s}, \ldots, M_{ns})$ is the vector of nominal balances, and $\boldsymbol{\psi}_s^r = (\psi_{1s}^r, \ldots, \psi_{ns}^r)'$ is the vector of real user costs. Since M is the aggregator function, $M(\mathbf{M}_s)$ is aggregate nominal balances and is a scalar.

Therefore, V_t can be rewritten as follows:

$$\begin{aligned} V_t &= \sum_{s=t}^{\infty} \sum_{i=1}^{n} \left[\left(M_{is} \frac{R_s - r_{is}}{1+R_s} \right) \frac{1}{\rho_s} \right] = \sum_{s=t}^{\infty} \left[M(\mathbf{m}_s)\Psi(\boldsymbol{\psi}_s) \frac{1}{\rho_s} \right] \\ &= \sum_{s=t}^{\infty} \frac{(TE)_s}{\rho_s}. \end{aligned} \tag{4.13}$$

Note that equation (4.13) provides a connection between the Divisia aggregate flow index, $M(\mathbf{m}_s)$, and the discounted money stock, V_t. Also observe that the formula contains a time-varying discount rate.

4.3.2. *Extension to Risk*

All of the theory reviewed above assumes perfect foresight. It has been shown by Barnett (1995) and Barnett, *et al.* (1997) that all of the results on user costs and on Divisia aggregation, including (4.4), (4.6), (4.7), and (4.8), carry over to risk neutrality, so long as all random interest rates and prices are replaced by their expectations. Under risk aversion, a beta-type correction for risk aversion is shown in Barnett (1997) to appear in those formulas. Those derivations did not use the discounted Fisherine wealth constraint, (4.3), but rather were produced from the Euler equations that solve the stochastic dynamic programming problem of maximizing expected intertemporally-separable utility, subject to the sequence of random flow of funds constraints, (4.2).[2] Barnett and Wu (2005) have extended those results to intertemporal nonseparability. In this paper, we assume risk neutrality. We introduce the expectations operator, E_t, to designate expectations conditional upon all information available at current period t.

In accordance with consumption-based capital asset pricing theory (see, e.g., Blanchard and Fischer (1989), p. 292), the general formula for the economic capital stock of money under risk becomes

$$V_t = E_t\left[\sum_{s=t}^{\infty} \xi_s (TE)_s\right], \tag{4.14}$$

where ξ_s is the subjectively-discounted intertemporal rate of substitution between consumption of goods in current period t and in future period s. In general, ξ_s is random and can be correlated with current and future values of $(TE)_s$. Assuming maximization of expected intertemporal utility subject to the sequence of flow of funds equations (4.2), Barnett (1995) and Barnett *et al.* (1997) have derived the relevant Euler equations for ξ_s under intertemporal separability. If we further assume risk neutrality, as in Blanchard (1989),

[2]Under risk, equation (4.3) is a state-contingent random constraint. Neither (4.3) nor its expectation is used in Bellman's method for solving and is not useful in producing the extension to risk aversion in Barnett (1995) of Barnett (1997).

p. 294, it follows that

$$V_t = E_t\left[\sum_{s=t}^{\infty}\frac{(TE)_s}{\rho_s}\right], \tag{4.15}$$

which becomes (4.13) under perfect foresight.

4.3.3. *CE and Simple Sum Indexes as Special Cases of the ESM*

4.3.3.1. *The CE Index*

Rotemberg (1991) and Rotemberg, *et al.* (1995) introduced the currency equivalent index (CE index),

$$V_t^{CE} = \sum_{i=1}^{n}\left[\frac{(R_t - r_{it})}{R_t}\right] M_{it}, \tag{4.16}$$

as a flow index under assumptions stronger than needed to derive the Divisia monetary flow index. But Barnett (1991) proved that the CE index can be interpreted to be a stock index, rather than a flow index. In particular, he showed that the CE index is a special case of the ESM, (4.15), under the assumption of martingale expectations in addition to the assumption of risk neutrality used in deriving (4.15) from (4.14).

Following Barnett's proof, assume M_{it}, r_{it}, and R_t follow martingale processes. Then we can see from (4.10), under risk neutrality, that equation (4.15) can be written as

$$V_t = \sum_{i=1}^{n}\sum_{s=t}^{\infty}\left[\frac{R_t - r_{it}}{(1+R_t)^{s-t+1}}\right] M_{it}, \tag{4.17}$$

so that

$$V_t = \sum_{i=1}^{n}\left[\frac{(R_t - r_{it})}{R_t}\right] M_{it} = V_t^{CE}. \tag{4.18}$$

This shows the CE index is a special case of the economic stock of money, when the conditional expectation of the future value of each variable is equal to its current value.

From equation (4.17) under martingale expectations, we furthermore can show that the CE index is proportional to the Divisia current-period monetary flow aggregate, as follows:

$$V_t^{CE} = \sum_{s=t}^{\infty}\sum_{i=1}^{n}\left[\left(\frac{R_t - r_{it}}{(1+R_t)}M_{it}\right)\frac{1}{(1+R_t)^{s-t}}\right]$$
$$= \sum_{s=t}^{\infty}\frac{M(\mathbf{m}_t)\Psi(\boldsymbol{\psi}_t)}{(1+R_t)^{s-t}} = \sum_{s=t}^{\infty}\frac{(TE)_t}{(1+R_t)^{s-t}}. \tag{4.19}$$

4.3.3.2. *The SSI Index*

We define the simple sum aggregate, V_t^{SSI}, by

$$V_t^{SSI} = \sum_{i=1}^{n} M_{it}. \tag{4.20}$$

As a flow index, this index requires that all monetary components are perfect substitutes, so that linear aggregation is possible, and furthermore that the coefficients in the resulting linear quantity aggregator function are equal for all components. But we also can acquire that index as a stock index under the assumption of martingale expectations, since it then follows that

$$V_t^{SSI} = \sum_{i=1}^{n}\left[\frac{(R_t - r_{it})}{R_t}\right]M_{it} + \sum_{i=1}^{n}\left[\frac{r_{it}}{R_t}\right]M_{it} = V^{CE} + IY, \tag{4.21}$$

where $IY = \sum_{i=1}^{n}\left[\frac{r_{it}}{R_t}\right]M_{it}$ is the discounted investment yield part of the simple sum aggregate and V^{CE} is the discounted monetary service flow part.

Hence the simple sum monetary aggregate, treated as a stock index, is the stock of a joint product, consisting of a discounted monetary service flow and a discounted investment yield flow. For the SSI to be a valid as money stock measure, all monetary assets must yield no interest. Clearly investment yield cannot be viewed as a monetary service, or the entire capital stock of the country would have to be counted as part of the money stock. The simple sum monetary aggregates confound together the discounted monetary service flow and the non-monetary investment-motivated yield. The simple sum aggregates will overestimate the actual monetary stock by the amount of the discounted non-monetary services. Furthermore, the magnitude of the simple sum aggregates' upward bias will increase, as more interest-bearing monetary assets are introduced into the monetary aggregates.

Under martingale expectations and the assumption that all monetary assets yield zero interest, it follows that:

$$V_t = V_t^{CE} = V_t^{SSI}. \tag{4.22}$$

In short, the ESM is the general formula for measuring money stock and fully nests the CE and the SSI as special cases. As financial innovation and deregulation of financial intermediation have progressed, the assumption that all monetary assets yield zero interest rates has become increasingly unrealistic.

4.4. Measurement of the Economic Stock of Money

The previous section showed that the economic monetary stock provides a general capital stock formula nesting the currency equivalent (CE) index and the simple sum index as special cases. Each of these results requires martingale expectations, and the simple sum result further requires that every monetary asset pay a nominal return of zero. This section shows how the ESM can be computed without making either of those restrictive assumptions. Although we make the simplifying assumption of risk neutrality in this paper, equation (4.15) remains analytically and empirically challenging. We propose three methods of approximating V_t. The first two linearize the function in terms of expected future variables and the third imposes a set of convenient covariance restrictions.

4.4.1. *Method 1: Linearizing Around Current Values*

The first method uses a first-order Taylor series expansion of V_t around current values to produce a linear approximation in the future benchmark rates, R_s, and future total monetary-services expenditures, $(TE)_s$. This procedure converts the non-linear expectations equation into a linear expression that is easier to evaluate.

First, it is convenient to rewrite V_t as:

$$V_t = E_t \sum_{s=t}^{\infty} \left[\frac{(TE)_s}{\rho_s} \right] = (TE)_t + E_t \sum_{s=t+1}^{\infty} \left[\frac{(TE)_s}{\rho_s} \right].$$

Then taking the first-order Taylor series expansion around current values of TE and R, we obtain:

$$\begin{aligned} V_t &= (TE)_t + E_t \sum_{s=t+1}^{\infty} \left[\frac{(TE)_t}{(1+R_t)^{s-t}} + \frac{1}{(1+R_t)^{s-t}} \{(TE)_s - (TE)_t\} \right. \\ &\quad \left. - \sum_{u=t}^{s-1} \frac{(TE)_t}{(1+R_t)^{s-t+1}} (R_u - R_t) \right] \\ &= (TE)_t + \sum_{s=t+1}^{\infty} \left[\frac{E_t(TE)_s}{(1+R_t)^{s-t}} - \sum_{u=t}^{s-1} \frac{(TE)_t}{(1+R_t)^{s-t+1}} (E_t R_u - R_t) \right] \end{aligned} \tag{4.23}$$

Linearizing in this fashion is equivalent to approximating V_t around the CE index.

This measure of the economic stock of money depends on uncertain future values of the benchmark rate and of expenditures on monetary services. Forecasting models must be used to calculate these future values. Instead of separately forecasting individual components and their respective interest rates, we forecast total expenditures on monetary services. This approach reduces the number of variables to forecast and reduces the number of parameters in the forecasting models.

We use vector autoregression (VAR) models to produce these forecasts. A VAR with any number of lags can be transformed into the VAR(1) form, $\mathbf{y}_t = \mathbf{A}\mathbf{y}_{t-1} + \mathbf{e}_t$, by suitably redefining the coefficient matrix, $\mathbf{A}$, the residuals, $\mathbf{e}_t$, and the vector of variables, $\mathbf{y}_t$. In this equation, the vector of variables may include current and lagged variables. Based on this VAR and the assumption that residuals are not serially correlated, the optimal forecast of $\mathbf{y}_{t+j}$, given all information at time t, is $\mathbf{A}^j\mathbf{y}_t$. Then the value of the k-th variable in vector $\mathbf{y}$ expected to occur j periods into the future is obtained by pre-multiplying $\mathbf{A}^j\mathbf{y}_t$ by a selection vector having a one in the k-th position and a zero in all other locations. Define this selection vector as $\boldsymbol{\delta}'_k$. If $(TE)_t$ is the first element in $\mathbf{y}_t$ and R_t is the second element, then expectations are given as: $E_t[(TE)_{t+j}] = \boldsymbol{\delta}'_1\mathbf{A}^j\mathbf{y}_t$ and $E_tR_{t+j} = \boldsymbol{\delta}'_2\mathbf{A}^j\mathbf{y}_t$. These expressions are used to eliminate expectation terms form (4.23). For example, the function of current and expected future monetary expenditures becomes:

$$\left[\sum_{s=t}^{\infty} \frac{E_t[(TE)_s]}{(1+R_t)^{s-t}}\right] = \sum_{s=t}^{\infty} \boldsymbol{\delta}'_1\mathbf{A}^{s-t}\mathbf{y}_t\left(\frac{1}{1+R_t}\right)^{s-t} \tag{4.24}$$

The terms involving the sum of current and expected future benchmark returns are:

$$\begin{aligned}
&\sum_{s=t+1}^{\infty}\left[\sum_{u=t}^{s-1} \frac{(TE)_t}{(1+R_t)^{s-t+1}}(E_tR_u - R_t)\right] \\
&= \sum_{s=t+1}^{\infty}\sum_{u=t}^{s-1} \frac{(TE)_t}{(1+R_t)^{s-t+1}}(\boldsymbol{\delta}'_2\mathbf{A}^{u-t}\mathbf{y}_t - R_t)
\end{aligned} \tag{4.25}$$

Combining results from equations (4.24) and (4.25), we obtain the Method 1 solution for V_t:

$$V_t = \sum_{s=t}^{\infty} \delta_1' \mathbf{A}^{s-t} \mathbf{y}_t \left(\frac{1}{1+R_t} \right)^{s-t} - \sum_{s=t+1}^{\infty} \sum_{u=t}^{s-1} \frac{TE_t}{(1+R_t)^{s-t+1}} (\delta_2' \mathbf{A}^{u-t} \mathbf{y}_t - R_t). \quad (4.26)$$

A significant difference from either the simple sum or the CE index is that this measure of V_t depends upon past, as well as current, variables and upon coefficients in the forecasting model.

4.4.2. *Method 2: Martingale Expectations for Only the Benchmark Rate*

Our second method makes the martingale assumption, but only on the benchmark rate, while continuing to use VARs to forecast total monetary expenditures. This approach lies somewhere between Method 1, which uses a VAR to forecast both variables, and the CE index, which uses only current values in forecasting both variables. Assuming $E_t R_s = R_t$ for all $s \geq t$ yields:

$$V_t = \sum_{s=t}^{\infty} \frac{E_t[(TE)_s]}{(1+R_t)^{s-t}}. \quad (4.27)$$

With this formula, V is linear in current and expected future values of TE and is calculated in equation (4.24). Note that Methods 1 and 2 yield essentially the same measure of V_t, if changes in the benchmark rate are unforecastable. If, in addition, changes in total monetary expenditures are unforecastable, then the CE index, Method 1, and Method 2 all should obtain very similar measures.

4.4.3. *Method 3: Setting Covariances to Zero*

Method 3 assumes that the covariance between $(TE)_s$ and the benchmark rate at any time is zero and all covariances between benchmark rates at different points in time are zero.[3] Then the expression for V_t becomes:

$$V_t = E_t\left[\sum_{s=t}^{\infty}\frac{(TE)_s}{\rho_s}\right] = \sum_{s=t}^{\infty}\frac{E_t[(TE)_s]}{\widehat{\rho_s}}$$

$$= (TE)_t + \sum_{s=t+1}^{\infty}\frac{\boldsymbol{\delta}_1'\mathbf{A}^{s-t}\mathbf{y}_t}{\prod_{u=t}^{s-1}(1+\boldsymbol{\delta}_2'\mathbf{A}^{u-t}\mathbf{y}_t)}, \tag{4.28}$$

where the last expression is obtained from the VAR forecasts, and where the expected discount factor is

$$\widehat{\rho_s} = \begin{cases} 1 & for\ s = t \\ \prod_{u=t}^{s-1}(1+E_tR_u) & for\ s > t. \end{cases}$$

We use a finite approximation to solve the infinite sums in each of the three methods (equations (4.24), (4.26), and (4.28)). For example, the finite sum approximation for Method 3 is

$$V_t(J) = \left[\sum_{s=t}^{j}\frac{E_t\,[(TE)_s]}{\widehat{\rho_s}}\right] \tag{4.29}$$

for any value of $J > t$. Taking the limit as J goes to infinity in equation (4.29) yields equation (4.28). Having expectations in the numerator and denominator rules out a simple closed-form solution.[4]

---

[3]The same results can be acquired from the nearly equivalent Assumption 3 of Barnett, *et al.* (1997).

[4]Note that we can obtain closed-form expressions for Methods 1 and 2, if all roots of $\mathbf{A}/(1+R_t)$ are outside the unit circle. The finite approximations to infinite sums in the paper also require that condition on roots. These finite approximations will be nearly the same as the closed form solutions, because the convergence criterion, equation (4.31), is very small.

An alternative way of writing equation (4.29) is

$$V_t(J) = V_t(J-1) + \frac{E_t\left[(TE)_J\right]}{\widehat{\rho_J}}. \tag{4.30}$$

Starting with $V_t(0) = (TE)_t$, this equation builds up the measure of V_t recursively. Our approach is to let J increase until we get the convergence, $V_t(J) - V_t(J-1) \to 0$, with the convergence criterion

$$\left|\frac{V_t(J) - V_t(J-1)}{V_t(J-1)}\right| < 10^{-7}. \tag{4.31}$$

4.5. Forecasting Models

To construct the forecasts needed for calculating each approximation to the ESM, we consider three types of vector autoregressions: unrestricted, asymmetric, and Bayesian VAR. Because of Bayesian VAR models' prior degree of success in forecasting economic data, we emphasize those results within the body of the paper, and provide results with the other two approaches in footnotes. Since robustness across forecasting methods is our primary result, rather than our advocacy of any particular forecasting model, we do view the unrestricted and asymmetric VAR results to be relevant to understanding the findings of this paper.

4.5.1. *Unrestricted VARs*

The unrestricted vector autoregressive model (UVAR) pioneered by Sims (1980) is a standard model in the literature. Sims developed the VAR approach as a tool for allowing historical data to summarize the dynamic interactions among time series variables. A hallmark feature of any UVAR is that it has the same number of lags of each variable in each equation. UVARs tend to obtain a relatively large number of statistically insignificant coefficients. As a result, there are concerns about forecasting with UVAR models. Various approaches exist for solving this overparameterization problem.

4.5.2. *Asymmetric VARs*

One way to reduce the number of parameters in the VAR is to eliminate the common lag assumption. Keating (1993, 2000), for example, developed the asymmetric VAR (AVAR), which is a VAR allowing lag lengths to vary across variables in the model. The AVAR and UVAR models share a common trait: each equation in the model has exactly the same set of explanatory variables without cross equation restrictions. Consequently, AVARs and UVARs are consistently and efficiently estimated by ordinary least squares under standard regularity conditions. However, an AVAR model is expected to have fewer insignificant coefficients, and thereby may obtain smaller out-of-sample forecast errors than the UVAR. An AVAR lag specification can be chosen by an information criterion or by any other methods capable of testing non-nested alternatives.

4.5.3. *Bayesian VARs*

Another response to overparameterization in UVAR models is the Bayesian approach of Doan, *et al.* (1984) and Litterman (1986). A Bayesian VAR (BVAR) model avoids exclusion restrictions, such as the different lag lengths permitted under the AVAR approach. Instead, BVAR models assume each VAR coefficient is drawn from a normal distribution and impose restrictions on the mean and the variance of each of those distributions.

The Minnesota (or Litterman) prior is based on the empirical evidence that most economic variables appear to have a unit root. Thus each coefficient is given a prior mean of zero, except for the coefficient on the first lag of the dependent variable in each equation. That coefficient has a mean of one. Coefficients on shorter lags are given larger prior variances than the coefficients on longer lags. This choice of prior variances is based on the reasonable assumption that recent data are likely to be more informative than older data in explaining current outcomes, so recent data should be permitted to dominate prior views about short lag parameters.

This approach also allows different priors to be imposed on different variables. For example, if a certain variable is thought to have more explanatory power than other variables, the prior variance associated with that variable would be made larger than for the other variables to permit the information in the data to dominate the prior. Flat (non-informative) priors are assumed for all deterministic variables.

4.6. Model Specification

4.6.1. *Data Description*

The models in this paper use U.S. data for total expenditure on monetary services (*TE*), the benchmark interest rate (*BENCH*), industrial production (*INDPRO*), and the consumer price index (*CPI*). Relative to the notation in section (4.1), $BENCH_t = R_t$ and $CPI_t = p_t^*$, although the latter equality is an index number theoretic approximation to the exact true cost of living index of economic theory. Data are monthly and seasonally adjusted, covering the period from 1959:1 through 2004:3. All data were obtained from the Federal Reserve Economic Database (FRED), published by the Federal Reserve Bank of St. Louis.[5] The initial choice of output and price was based on *a priori* beliefs regarding those variables most likely to help forecast interest rates and monetary-services expenditures. Those prior beliefs were then supported by statistical tests for marginal predictive content. We also considered other variables in the specification search, but those additional variables did not improve the forecasts and are therefore omitted from the final equations.

[5]At each level of aggregation, j, total expenditure on the monetary services, $(TE)_t^j$, was computed from the first equality in equation (4.12). The data source details and the list of monetary assets included at each level of aggregation can be found in Barnett (2006), which contains the details of the design and data, but not the empirical results that are in this paper.

The choice of benchmark rate can have important consequences for the ESM or the CE index. Rotemberg, *et al.* (1995) used the commercial paper rate and found that their CE index was extremely volatile. Our benchmark rate path is the upper envelope over the paths of Moody's BAA bond rate and the interest rates of all of the components of the Federal Reserve's broadest aggregate. The resulting benchmark rate is not as volatile as the commercial paper rate.

In each VAR, we control for the effects of exogenous oil supply shocks by including dummy variables for oil shock dates. We used the dates identified by Hoover, *et al.* (1994).[6] To model the dynamic response of the economy to oil price shocks, the VAR included current and seven lags of the oil shock dummy variables. To appropriately specify the forecasting models, we needed answers to several important questions. Are the data nonstationary? How many lags should the VAR models have? What values should be given to the hyperparameters that are used in constructing priors in the BVAR approach?

4.6.2. *Nonstationarity and Data Transformation*

We use standard unit root tests to answer questions about stationarity. Table 1 reports ρ-test results from augmented Dickey-Fuller regressions along with results from Phillips-Perron (PP) Z-tests.

In all but one of these cases, the test fails to reject the null hypothesis of unit root at the 10% significance level. The exception is the ADF test on total monetary expenditures for M2, but even in this case we fail to reject at the 5% level. Therefore, we conclude that each variable has a unit root. We take the log transform of all variables, except for interest rates. Based on the unit root evidence, we then take the first difference of each transformed series, when estimating UVAR and AVAR models. The BVAR models are estimated in the log

[6]Hoover and Perez's (1994) shock dates are 1969:3, 1970:12, 1974:1, 1978:3, 1979:9, and 1981:2.

Table 1. Dickey-Fuller Tests (ρ) and Phillips-Perron Tests (Z) for Unit Roots.

	Trend + Constant			Constant Only			No Constant		
Variable	lags	ρ_τ^{ADF}	$Z^{PP}(\rho_\tau)$	lags	ρ_μ^{ADF}	$Z^{PP}(\rho_\mu)$	Lags	ρ^{ADF}	$Z^{PP}(\rho)$
Log $(TE)^{m1}$	2	−5.563	−6.46	2	−1.714	−1.7694	2	0.649	0.643
Log $(TE)^{m2}$	2	−18.236	−8.535	2	−0.445	−1.873	2	1.405	0.676
Log $(TE)^{m3}$	2	−12.683	−8.996	2	0.141	−1.711	2	1.732	0.716
BENCH	8	−4.57	−5.759	8	−5.422	−6.497	8	−0.399	−0.507
log *CPI*	9	−9.657	−0.301	9	−0.666	−0.169	9	0.406	0.418
log INDPRO	3	−9.984	−7.872	3	−0.966	−1.180	3	0.312	0.329

Notes: The lag was selected using SIC information criterion.

levels, because our prior assumptions allow for possible unit roots. Since the benchmark rate is an interest rate, those levels and changes were not transformed by logarithm in any of the models.

4.6.3. *Selection of Lag Length*

Likelihood ratio tests, modified by the small-sample correction of Sims (2001), are used to select the lags in unrestricted VARs. We used that same lag length for a Bayesian VAR. We considered a maximum lag of 24 and sequentially tested for smaller lags until a test was significant at the 1 percent level. This procedure selected 13 lags. We used the Akaike (AIC) and Schwarz (SIC) information criteria to select lags in the AVAR models, while searching over all models with up to a maximum of 13 lags for each variable. With 4 variables and up to 13 lags, there were 13^4 possible AVAR specifications from which to choose. For the AVAR-M1 model at the M1 level of aggregation, the AIC chose six lags of Δ log $(TE)^{m1}$, three lag of Δ log *INDPRO*, six lags of Δ log *CPI*, and six lags of Δ *BENCH*, while for the AVAR-M2 model at the M2 level of aggregation and the AVAR-M3 model at the M3 level of aggregation, AIC selected six lags of Δ log $(TE)^{m2}$ in the AVAR-M2 model, six lags of Δ log $(TE)^{m3}$ in the AVAR-M3 model, three lags of Δ log *INDPRO*, six lags of Δ log *CPI*, and seven lags of Δ *BENCH*. The notation j designates the level of aggregation of

Mj, where $j = 1, 2, 3$. The SIC chose 1 or 2 month lags for all variables in each model. Since these lag lengths are insufficient to capture dynamics, we used only AVAR models selected by the AIC.

4.6.4. *Criterion for Evaluation of Forecasting Performance*

Forecasts are assessed using the following procedure. Estimate a VAR with the sample from 1959:1 to 1990:12 and forecast for each month up to 48 months ahead. Then add the next month's data to the sample, estimate a VAR, and forecast up to 48 periods ahead. Continue adding a month, re-estimating the VAR, and forecasting until we can no longer make the 48-month-ahead forecast, at which point we forecast ahead by as many observations as remain. Since our full sample ends in 2004:3, our sequential procedure begins forecasting a declining number of periods ahead at 2000:4, until no more forward observations remain within the sample for forecasting.

Then we use root mean squared error (RMSE) and Theil's U statistic to evaluate forecasting models. If y_{t+h} is the value of a variable at $t+h$ and $\hat{y}_{t+h}$ is the forecast of this variable at time t, then

$$RMSE\text{ (model)} = \sqrt{T_h^{-1} \sum_{t=1}^{T_h} (y_{t+h} - \hat{y}_{t+h})^2}$$

and

$$Theil\ U = \frac{\text{RMSE (model)}}{\text{RMSE (randomwalk)}} = \sqrt{\frac{\sum_{t=1}^{T_h} (y_{t+h} - \hat{y}_{t+h})^2}{\sum_{t=1}^{T_h} (y_{t+h} - y_t)^2}}, \tag{4.32}$$

where h is the forecast horizon and T_h is the total number of forecasts computed for the forecast horizon h. Theil's U statistic compares the RMSE for a model's forecast errors with the RMSE from a no-change forecast. When a U statistic is less than one, the model forecasts better than a no-change forecast. If a U statistic exceeds one, the naive no-change forecast outperforms the model. Note that a no-change forecast is analogous to the martingale expectations assumption used by Barnett (1991) to motivate the CE index as a stock index. Thus when U-statistics are less than 1, our approximations are expected to be more accurate measures of the ESM than the CE index.

4.6.5. *Specification of Priors*

In estimating the BVAR, the first step is to search for the Litterman (1986) prior's hyperparameters, γ, d, and $\mathbf{W}$, that can minimize out-of-sample forecast errors. The criterion function, $\bar{U}$, used in selecting the priors is set to be the weighted average of the Theil U statistics for one month-ahead to 24 months-ahead forecasts. The weights are the number of forecasts for each forecast horizon divided by the total number of forecasts for all forecast horizons during a given period. The hyperparameters are $\gamma =$ measure of overall tightness, $d =$ the lag decay parameter, and $\mathbf{W} = [w_{ij}]$, where $w_{ij} =$ relative tightness, defined to be the tightness on variable j in equation i relative to variable i. In the literature on this BVAR approach, the parameter γ is usually equal to the standard deviation of the parameter of the first own lag in each equation in the VAR. The parameters γ and d are scalars that are constant across equations in the specification. For more formal definitions of parameters and details of the BVAR specification, see sections 5.3 and 6.5 of Barnett, Chae, and Keating (2005).[7]

After many experiments, we decided to estimate two sets of priors by minimizing the criterion function over two different periods (1989:1–1990:12, 2000:1–2001:12). With starting periods in the range 1991:1 to 2001:12 and 2002:1 to 2004:3, respectively, we applied the priors in generating forecasts for up to 200 steps ahead.[8] The reason we select two sets of priors for two different periods

---

[7]Alternatively see Littermann (1986) regarding the "Litterman prior."

[8]Although we do not consider more than 48 step-ahead forecasts to be meaningful in comparing models, we needed more than 48 step-ahead forecasts to seek convergence of equation (4.31). We generated the 200 step ahead forecasts to assure

is that the best priors selected on the basis of a certain period may not necessarily be optimal for far beyond that period. Forecast performance is sensitive to the priors. The priors were selected by searching over the arguments $(\gamma, \mathbf{W}, d)$ to minimize the following objective function:

$$Min\ \bar{U}(\gamma, \mathbf{W}, d) = \sum_{i=1}^{2}\sum_{h=1}^{24} \alpha_h U_{ih} = \sum_{i=1}^{2} \bar{U}_i, \qquad (4.33)$$

where the $i = 1, 2$ subscript indexes the two variables, total monetary-services expenditure and benchmark rate, h is forecast step, U_{ih} is Theil's U statistic for variable i's h-step ahead forecast,$\alpha_h = \frac{k_h}{K}$ is the weight for each forecast step h, and $\bar{U}_i = \sum_{h=1}^{24} \alpha_h U_{ih}$ is the weighted average of Theil's U statistics for variable i's 1-month-ahead to 24-months-ahead forecasts during the evaluation period.[9] The variable k_h is the number of times that the h-step ahead forecast has been computed during the evaluation period, and $K = \sum_{h=1}^{24} k_h$ is the total number of times that all forecasts for 1 to 24 months ahead have been computed during the evaluation period.[10]

The criterion function (4.33) is an average of the accumulated Theil U statistics for all forecasts during the evaluation period. The

---

that we would have enough to attain convergence of (4.31). But for purposes of evaluating forecast performance, we used no more than 48 step-ahead forecasts.

[9]In principle, there could be advantages to selecting an objective function that is directly derivable from the ESM formula. But in choosing equation (4.33), we had the more modest objective of minimizing forecast errors. Regarding the limitation to 24 step-ahead forecasts for this purpose, we would have preferred to have used 48 step-ahead forecasts, but data limitations prevented us from doing so. We forecasted 1989:1–1990:12, after using data up to 1988:12 to estimate the priors. The split of the sample between observations needed for estimating the priors and observations used in forecast evaluation prevented forecast evaluation for 48 step-ahead forecasts. If we had split the sample earlier, there would not have been enough observations available for the estimation of priors.

[10]For instance, when $h = 1, 2, \ldots.., 24$, and if evaluation period is 24 months, then k_1 is 24, k_2 is 23,...., and k_{24} is 1.

number of forecasts, k_h, at each forecast step decreases, as the forecast steps become longer during the evaluation period. Hence, the number of forecast statistics for shorter-step horizons, relative to that of all step-horizons, plays a role as a weight, in computing average Theil U statistics for all forecast-step horizons in the criterion function. In constructing the criterion function, more weight is thereby put on shorter forecast steps than longer ones. Forecasts of total monetary-services expenditure and of the benchmark rate will enter the formula for the discounted economic money stock. As expected from the flow discounting, the weight on shorter forecast steps will be heavier than on longer ones, since forecasts for short horizons will have the heaviest impact in determining the discounted economic stock of money.

Our criterion function includes U statistics for only total monetary-services expenditure and the benchmark rate, instead of considering all variables in the VAR, since we are forecasting only those two variables. We start with a symmetric prior by setting the same values for relative tightness, w_{ij}, to all the off-diagonal variables of $\mathbf{W}$ with the diagonal elements normalized to equal 1.0, and then relax the prior to allow for more general interactions among the variables. The search for the optimizing hyperparameters was conducted using the genetic algorithm optimization method.

For notational convenience, we will name the models according to the level of aggregation:

UVAR-M1, UVAR-M2, and UVAR-M3 are unrestricted VAR models, with the total expenditure variable being on the services of the monetary assets that are included in M1, M2 and M3, respectively. Analogously AVAR-M1, AVAR-M2, and AVAR-M3 are the asymmetric VAR model, with the total expenditure variable being on the services of monetary assets that are included in M1, M2 and M3, respectively; while BVAR-M1, BVAR-M2, and BVAR-M3 are the Bayesian VAR model, with total expenditure being on the services of monetary assets that are included in M1, M2 and M3, respectively.

When we searched for symmetric priors by minimizing the criterion function over two different periods (1989:1–1990:12,

Table 2. Weighted Average of Theil's U under Symmetric Priors.

Period for *Min* ($\bar{U}$)	BVAR-M1 $\bar{U}_1$	BVAR-M1 $\bar{U}_2$	BVAR-M2 $\bar{U}_1$	BVAR-M2 $\bar{U}_2$	BVAR-M3 $\bar{U}_1$	BVAR-M3 $\bar{U}_2$
	$(TE)^{m1}$	BENCH	$(TE)^{m2}$	BENCH	$(TE)^{m3}$	BENCH
1989:1–1990:12	0.8405	1.07944	0.950	1.079	0.935	1.079
2000:1–2001:12	0.8900	0.78016	0.883	0.788	0.891	0.787

Table 3. Weighted Average of Theil's U under General Priors.

Period for *Min* ($\bar{U}$)	BVAR-M1 $\bar{U}_1$	BVAR-M1 $\bar{U}_2$	BVAR-M2 $\bar{U}_1$	BVAR-M2 $\bar{U}_2$	BVAR-M3 $\bar{U}_1$	BVAR-M3 $\bar{U}_2$
	$(TE)^{m1}$	BENCH	$(TE)^{m2}$	BENCH	$(TE)^{m3}$	BENCH
1989:1–1990:12	0.80442	0.89229	0.90	0.898	0.877	0.897
2000:1–2001:12	0.88178	0.75825	0.798	0.76	0.763	0.772

2000:1–2001:12), we found no symmetric prior that produced weighted average U statistics for the benchmark rate that were less than one in all three BVAR models for the period 1989:1–1990:12. Hence, we then searched for general priors to optimize the criterion function. For total monetary-services expenditure and for the benchmark rate, the best general priors[11] yield Theil U statistics that are less than one for all models. Tables 2 and 3 show how much the weighted average of Theil's U statistics, under the general prior specification, have improved, compared to that under the symmetric prior. In the tables, the weighted average $\bar{U}_i$ has subscript $i = 1$ for total expenditure and $i = 2$ for benchmark rate.

4.7. Empirical Results: Forecasting Performance and Evaluation

We generated forecast using the general priors selected in section 6.5. The accuracy of out-of-sample forecasts for 1991:1–2004:3 was

[11] We do not report the selected priors here. Interested readers can see the complete set of priors in Barnett (2006).

evaluated based on the average of Theil's U statistics for 1 to 48 month-ahead forecasts. Table A1 in the appendix reports out-of-sample forecast performance statistics for UVAR and AVAR models.[12]

Table 4 reports forecast performance for the BVAR models. We estimate BVARs with two sets of general priors for two different periods, 1991:1–2001:12 and 2002:–2004:3, respectively, since the

[12]Those performance statistics are based on the average of Theil's U statistics for 1 to 48 step-ahead forecast errors over the period 1991:1 to 2004:3. The results are also reported for sub-samples 1991:1–1995:12, 1996:1–2001:12, and 2002:1–2004:3, since forecasting performance may depend on sample period. In all three AVARs (AVAR-M1, AVAR-M2, AVAR-M3) and three UVARs (UVAR-M1, UVAR-M2, UVAR-M3), the averages of Theil U statistics for $(TE)^{m1}$, $(TE)^{m2}$, $(TE)^{m3}$ and for the benchmark rate are significantly less than one over the full sample periods and over the sub-sample periods. Hence, forecasts of total expenditure and benchmark rate based on AVARs and UVARs are more accurate than martingale no-change forecasts. Comparing performances of AVARs relative to those of UVARs in forecasting benchmark rate, with average Theil statistics of 0.737 for AVAR-M1, 0.738 for AVAR-M2, and 0.738 for AVAR-M3, we find that AVARs perform slightly better than the UVARs counterparts over all sample periods except for the third sub-period 2002:1–2004:3, during which UVAR-M1 and UVAR-M2 outperform the AVAR counterparts. In addition, the average Theil's U statistics for $(TE)^{m1}$, $(TE)^{m2}$, and $(TE)^{m3}$ from AVARs are also less than those from UVARs over most of the sample periods, but are only marginally less.

To examine forecasting performance for various forecasting horizons, we also computed the average Theil's U statistics for every additional 6 month horizon. We do not report the average Theil's U statistics for every additional 6 month horizon, but interested readers can find those statistics in Barnett (2006). The results indicate that over short horizons, AVAR-M models improve relative to the UVAR-M models. In addition, in both AVARs and UVARs, the average Theil's U statistics over the shorter horizons are greater than those over the longer horizons, so that forecasting accuracy of AVARs and UVARs improves relative to random walk forecasting model over the longer horizons.

We also report in-sample forecast statistics over 1960:2–1990:12 in table 5. In contrast with out-of-sample forecast performance, in-sample forecast statistics show that UVARs marginally outperform AVARs in terms of average Theil's U statistics for $(TE)^{m1}$, $(TE)^{m2}$, $(TE)^{m3}$, and for the benchmark rate. These in-sample results are to be expected, since AVAR is nested within UVAR as a special case.

Table 4. Out-of Sample Forecast Performance Statistics: BVAR model.

Evaluation Period	BVAR-M1 $\bar{U}_1$	$\bar{U}_2$	BVAR-M2 $\bar{U}_1$	$\bar{U}_2$	BVAR-M3 $\bar{U}_1$	$\bar{U}_2$
	$(TE)^{m1}$	BENCH	$(TE)^{m2}$	BENCH	$(TE)^{m3}$	BENCH
1991:1–2001:12	0.928	0.868	0.936	0.864	0.889	0.862
1991:1–1995:12	0.759	0.819	1.02	0.815	1.09	0.816
1996:1–2001:12	0.816	0.859	0.838	0.849	0.741	0.847
2002:1–2004:3	1.278	0.833	1.189	0.824	1.289	0.844

accuracy of the forecasts is sensitive to the specification of the priors and the optimal prior is likely to depend on sample period. The set of priors obtained by minimizing the weighted average of U values for 1989:1 to 1990:12 was used to generate forecasts for the period of 1991:1 to 2001:12, and the other set of priors obtained from 2000:1 to 2001:12 was applied to compute forecasts for the period of 2002:1 to 2004:3.[13]

Over the sample period 1991:1 to 2001:12, forecasts of $(TE)^{m1}$, $(TE)^{m2}$, and $(TE)^{m3}$ from BVARs are better than the corresponding no-change forecasts. But forecast performances for $(TE)^{m1}$ and $(TE)^{m2}$ are unimpressive, since the weighted average U statistics are not considerably less than one. Over the period 2002:1 to 2004:3, forecasts of *TEs* from the BVAR models are even worse than the no-change forecasts, with weighted average U statistics of 1.28, 1.19, and 1.29 for $(TE)^{m1}$, $(TE)^{m2}$, and $(TE)^{m3}$, respectively. On the other hand, out-of sample forecasts of the benchmark rate from BVAR-M1, BVAR-M2, and BVAR-M3 are consistently and substantially better than the no-change forecast in all sample periods.

[13]The time frame is as follows: 1959:1–1988:12: Initial estimation. 1989:1–1990:12: Specify a set of priors by minimizing criterion function over this period. 1991:1–2001:12: Generate forecasts and evaluate out-of-sample forecast performance.

2000:1–2001:12: Specify a set of priors by minimizing criterion function over this period. 2002:1–2003:12: Generate forecasts and evaluate out-of-sample forecast performance.

Table 5. Within-Sample Forecast Performance Statistics: Evaluation Period (1960:2–1990:12).

UVAR-M1		AVAR-M1		BVAR-M1	
$(TE)^{m1}$	*BENCH*	$(TE)^{m1}$	BENCH	$(TE)^{m1}$	BENCH
$\bar{U}_1$	$\bar{U}_2$	$\bar{U}_1$	$\bar{U}_2$	$\bar{U}_1$	$\bar{U}_2$
0.665	0.650	0.670	0.658	0.694	0.763
UVAR-M2		AVAR-M2		BVAR-M2	
$(TE)^{m2}$	BENCH	$(TE)^{m2}$	BENCH	$(TE)^{m2}$	BENCH
0.678	0.648	0.684	0.654	0.637	0.758
UVAR-M3		AVAR-M3		BVAR-M3	
$(TE)^{m3}$	BENCH	$(TE)^{m3}$	*BENCH*	$(TE)^{m3}$	BENCH
0.681	0.648	0.687	0.655	0.634	0.759

In the within-sample forecast performances reported in table 5, the BVARs offer a considerable improvement relative to the naive model, with average Theil U statistics of 0.69, 0.63, and 0.63 for $(TE)^{m1}, (TE)^{m2}$, and $(TE)^{m3}$ respectively. In-sample forecast of the benchmark rate from BVARs is also much better than the no-change forecast. Based on forecast performance results, we chose AVAR and BVAR to generate forecasts of total expenditure and benchmark rate.[14]

It is worthwhile to note the gains from BVAR forecasting. We have estimated BVARs in log level, and evaluated forecast performance based on Theil's U statistic. In computing the ESM, forecasts of variables in the ESM formula that outperform no-change forecasts of those variables should permit more accurate measures of ESM than available from the martingale forecast assumption implied by the CE index. To facilitate direct comparison with the CE index, we therefore compute the economic stock of money using BVAR forecasts of total expenditure and the benchmark rate.

[14]The reason that we chose AVAR over UVAR is that the AVAR models outperformed their UVAR counterparts in out-of-sample forecast. Although UVAR models marginally outperformed their AVAR counterparts at in-sample forecasting, we are more interested in out-of-sample forecast performance.

4.8. Empirical Results: Estimation of Money Stock

4.8.1. *Economic Stock of Money Computed using Actual Data*

First, we assume perfect foresight and compute the ESM using actual future data for monetary-services expenditure and the benchmark asset's rate of return. We use the formula for V_t given by equation (4.13). Although future values cannot be known ahead of time, the ESM computed using actual future data provides a useful yardstick in assessing the ESM computed using forecasted values. With actual data available through 2004:3, we were able to compute and display the economic stock of money up to 1991:9.[15] To facilitate comparisons among different money stock measures, all figures contain simple-sum aggregates and the CE aggregates, as well as the economic stock aggregates. For the CE index, we computed not only the contemporaneous CE index that uses the current weight, $\frac{R_t - r_{it}}{R_t}$, for each asset, but also the smoothed CE index. In smoothing the volatile contemporaneous CE index, Rotemberg, *et al.* (1995) used centered moving averages of the weights. Following the same smoothing procedure, we computed smoothed CE index by replacing weights of monetary assets with 13-month centered moving averages of the weights. At the start and end of the sample, when symmetric centered moving averages are not available, asymmetric uncentered moving averages of the weights were used.

Figures 1, 2, and 3 show ESM1_actual, ESM2_actual, and ESM3_actual, respectively, from 1959:1 through 1991:9, where ESM1_actual, ESM2_actual, and ESM3_actual denote the ESM computed using actual future data at each level of aggregation, while CE_mov13 denotes the CE aggregates computed using 13-month centered moving averages of the weights.

---

[15]The stopping point was determined by the convergence criterion in equation (4.31).

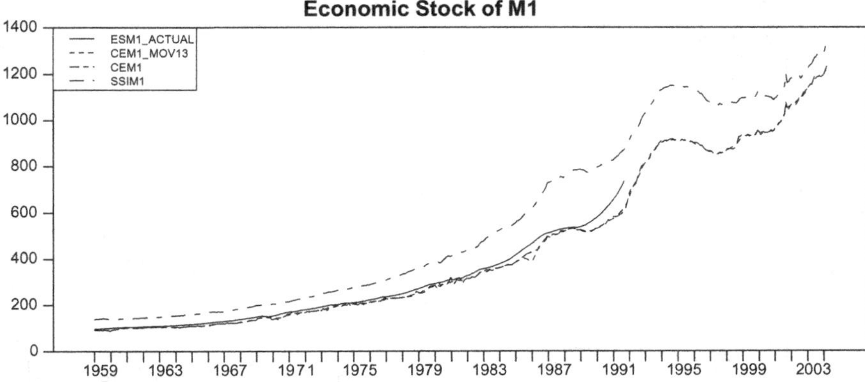

Fig. 1. Using Actual Current and Future Data.
Note: ESM1_actual: Economic stock of M1 computed using actual data.
CEM1_Mov13: Smoothed CEM1, in which weights are replaced by 13 month centered moving average.
CEM1: Contemporaneous CEM1; SSM1: Simple-sum M1.

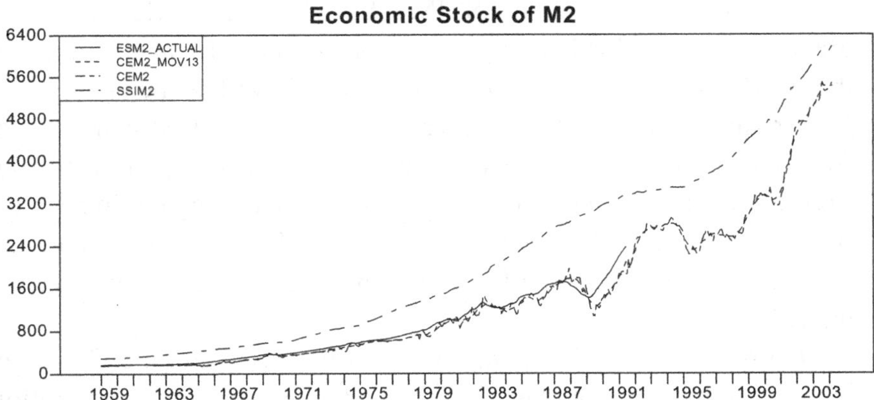

Fig. 2. Using Actual Current and Future Data.
Note: ESM2_actual: Economic stock of M2 computed using actual data.
CEM2_Mov13: Smoothed CEM2, in which weights are replaced by 13 month centered moving average.
CEM2: Contemporaneous CEM2; SSM2: Simple-sum M2.

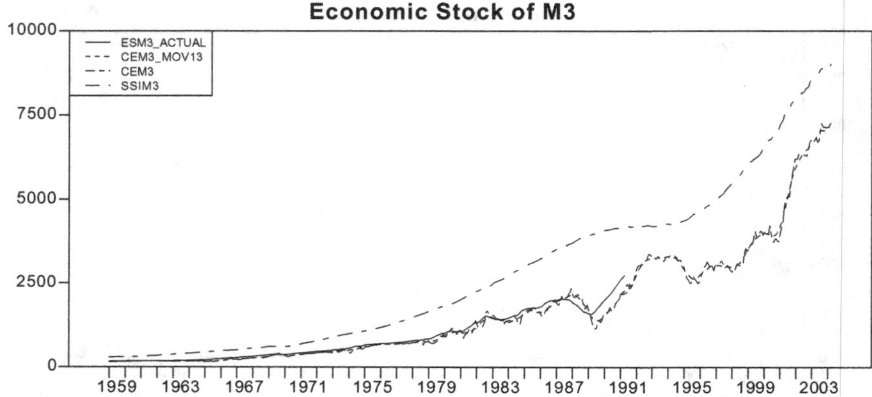

Fig. 3. Using Actual Current and Future Data.

Note: ESM3_actual: Economic stock of M3 computed using actual data.
CEM3_Mov13: Smoothed CEM3, in which weights are replaced by 13 month centered moving average.
CEM3: Contemporaneous CEM3.
SSM3: Simple-sum M3.

The figures show that the SSIM1, SSIM2, and SSIM3 are always greater than their ESM_actual counterparts. The vertical gap between the ESM and the simple sum index can be viewed as the error in the SSI arising from the SSI's failure to remove the investment motive from the discounted stock of money, as shown by equation (4.21). Figure 4 presents the size of the errors of the SSI aggregates in percent. As demonstrated by equation (4.21), the SSI fails to recognize the joint product nature of the money stock, when money yields interest.[16]

On the other hand, the gap between the ESM and the CE index represents the bias of the CE index from its implicit assumption of martingale expectations. Figures 1, 2, and 3 show that the CE index underestimates their ESM counterparts almost always, except

[16]The size of that error in SSIM1 is relatively small, but the errors increase as the level of money aggregation broadens, since the broader aggregates introduce more discounted investment-motivated yield into the simple sum stock.

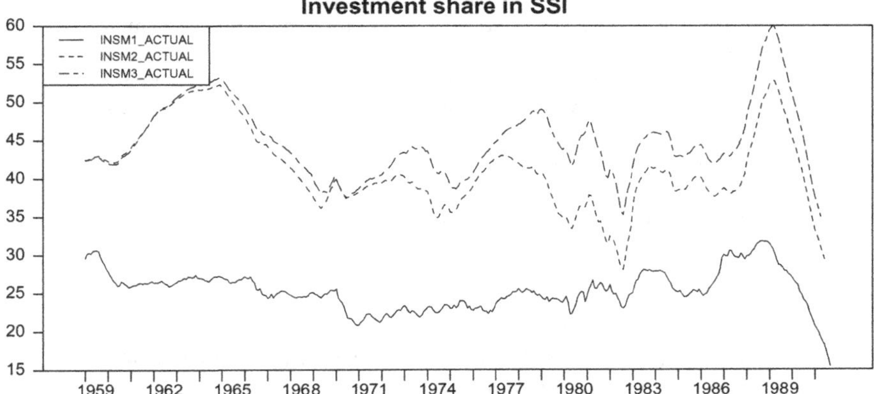

Fig. 4. Using Actual Future Data.
Note: Investment share was computed by ((SSI-V)/(SSI))*100 where V is the ESM_actual.

for CEM2 and CEM3 during the late 1980s. However, the gaps between the CE index and the ESM_actual counterparts are very small, particularly early in the sample period.

To examine quantitatively the errors in the SSI and the CE index, we decomposed the SSI, as a joint product, into its monetary services share and non-monetary services (discounted investment yield) share. Table 6 reports monetary services share percentage and investment share percentage for the SSI relative to the economic money stock and CE aggregate, which both remove the investment motive from the discounted flow.

We compute the monetary services share as 100(ESM/SSI) or 100(CE/SSI) and the investment share as 100(SSI-ESM) /SSI or 100(SSI-CE) /SSI. Monetary services share and investment share were computed by averaging 100(V/SSI) and 100(SSI-V) /SSI over the sample period, respectively. Over the sample period from 1959:1 to 1991:9, the decomposition relative to the ESM_actual suggests that the simple sum M1 index contains non-monetary services share of 25.32%, while the simple sum M2 and M3 indexes include non-monetary services of 41.3% and 44.86%, respectively. The decomposition of the SSI based on the CE index suggests that,

Table 6. Partition of Simple-Sum Aggregates into Monetary Services and Non-Monetary Services Share (Investment Share), Sample Period: 1959:1–1991:9.

V	Monetary Share of SSI	Investment Share of SSI
ESM1_actual	74.68%	25.32%
ESM2_actual	58.7%	41.3%
ESM3_actual	55.14%	44.86%
CEM1	70.32%	29.68%
CEM2	53.98%	46.02%
CEM3	50.56%	49.44%

Note: Sample Period is 1959:1–1991:9. Money stock V was computed using actual data available up to 2004:3.

over the same sample period, SSIM1, SSIM2, and SSIM3 contain investment shares of 29.68%, 46.02%, and 49.44%, respectively. These percentages are slightly greater than those implied by the ESM_actual data. We thereby find that when the CE index is used as the money stock measure, the CE aggregates underestimate economic money stock by 4.36% of SSIM1, 4.72% of SSIM2, and 4.58% of SSIM3. However, these biases in the CE index are relatively small, compared to the biases of 25.32%, 41.3%, and 44.86% contained within SSI index.

4.8.2. *Economic Stock of Money Based on BVAR Forecasts*

In the previous section, the ESM was computed assuming perfect knowledge of the future. In this section, we compute the ESM using forecasts of the benchmark rate and monetary-services expenditure. The forecasts we report in this paper were generated using the BVAR, but to investigate robustness we also used AVAR models. The models were first estimated using initial data from 1959:1 through 1990:12, and forecasts were then computed for up to 200 steps ahead. In each month from 1991:1 through 2004:3, the coefficients are updated sequentially by adding one more observation. Based on the resulting updated coefficients, a series of 200-step-ahead forecasts are computed. For the period 1959:1 to 1990:12 over which we estimated the forecasting models, we generated in-sample forecasts. For the period from 1991:1 to 2004:3, we generated out-of-sample forecasts.

For the period 2002:1 to 2004:3, the BVAR models produced less accurate forecasts for TEs than a "naive" martingale model. As a result, for that period we replaced those BVAR total-expenditure forecasts with the martingale forecast. Even in this case, the ESM should contain less error than the CE index, since we use a better forecast of the benchmark rate. The CE index uses the martingale forecast for both the TEs and the benchmark rate. To compute the ESM, we use the three methods proposed in equations (4.26), (4.27), and (4.28), which we call Methods 1, 2, and 3, respectively. The convergence criterion, used with all three methods, is provided by equation (4.31).

4.8.2.1. *ESM Computed Using Forecasts from BVAR*

Figures 5, 6, and 7 present ESM1, ESM2, and ESM3, computed using forecasts from the BVAR model with Method 1. The ESM computed using forecasts from BVAR with Method 1 is denoted by ESM_mtd1_BVAR. Figure 5 shows that ESM1_mtd1_BVAR is very close to ESM1_actual, especially in the early sample period. Observing the period after 1980, when the divergence of CEM1 from ESM1_actual begins to increase, we see that ESM1_mtd1_BVAR deviates less from ESM1_actual than the CEM1 does. However, during the same period, ESM2_mtd1_BVAR and ESM3_mtd1_BVAR are not much different from CEM2 and CEM3, in terms of their gaps with ESM2_actual and ESM3_actual, respectively.

The errors in SSI over time are measured by the investment shares in figure 8. In comparing ESM_mtd1_BVAR with the SSI index, we can observe the same patterns as those obtained in the previous section. In particular, the simple sum aggregates are biased upward. As in the previous section, the CE aggregates turned out to be almost always biased downward throughout the sample period, but the gap

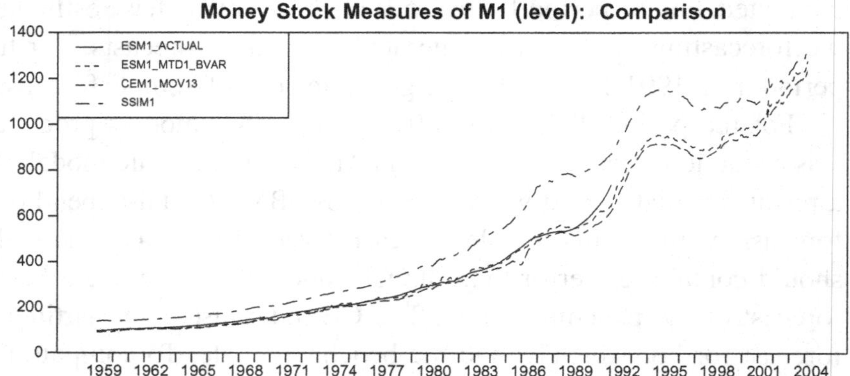

Fig. 5. Including Results with BVAR Forecasts.

Note: ESM1_actual: Economic Stock of M2 computed using actual data.
ESM1_mtd1_BVAR: Economic Stock of M1 computed using Method 1 and forecasts from BVAR.
CEM1_Mov13: smoothed CEM1 in which weights are replaced by 13 month centered moving average.
SSM1: Simple-sum M1.

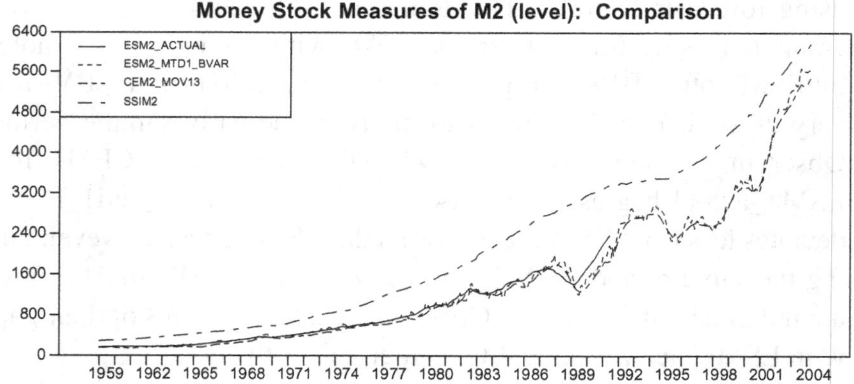

Fig. 6. Including Results with BVAR Forecasts.

Note: ESM2_actual: Economic Stock of M2 computed using actual data.
ESM2_mtd1_BVAR: Economic Stock of M2 computed using Method 1 and forecasts from BVAR.
CEM2_Mov13: smoothed CEM2 in which weights are replaced by 13 month centered moving average.
SSM2: Simple-sum M2.

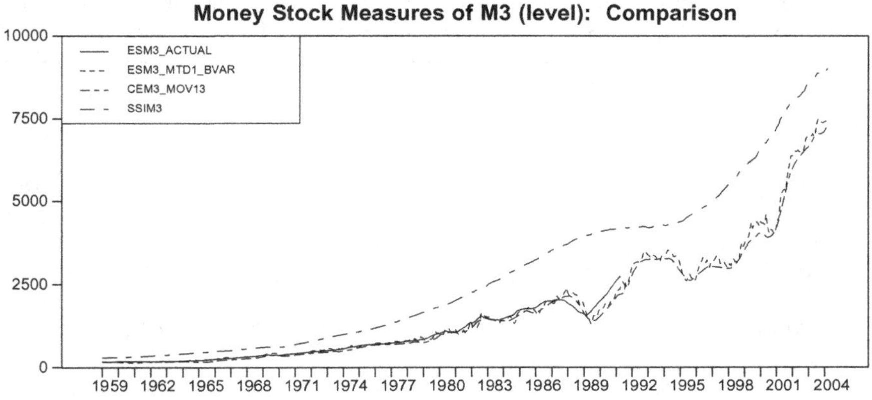

Money Stock Measures of M3 (level): Comparison

Fig. 7. Including Results with BVAR Forecasts.

Note: ESM3_actual: Economic Stock of M3 computed using actual data.
ESM3_mtd1_BVAR: Economic Stock of M3 computed using Method 1 and forecasts from BVAR.
CEM3_Mov13: smoothed CEM3 in which weights are replaced by 13 month centered moving average.
SSM3:Simple-sum M3.

between ESM_mtd1_BVAR and the CE index is small. However, ESM_mtd1_BVAR appears to be more volatile than ESM_actual or smoothed CE index. From Table 7, it is clear that the bias of SSI grows, as the level of aggregation broadens, and the sizes of the errors in the SSI based on ESM_BVAR are very close to those measured by the gap between the SSI index and the ESM using actual data.[17]

[17]Over sample periods ranging from 1960:2 to 2004:3, when the ESM is computed using forecasts from BVAR and Method 1, the simple sum M1 contains non-monetary services share of 22.76%, while the simple sum M2 and M3 indexes include non-monetary service of 37.11% and 41.26%, respectively. We first focus on the period from 1960:2 to 1991:9, during which the ESM, computed using actual future data, is available. Over this sub-sample period in Table 8, the ESM, based on forecasts from the BVAR model with Method 1, indicate that the simple sum M1 contains non-monetary services share of 26.4%, while the simple sum M2 and M3 indexes include non-monetary services of 42.12% and 45.63%, respectively. The error measures are investment shares of 25.17%, 41.21%, and 44.94%. Over the same period, the CE index indicates that SSIM1, SSIM2, and SSIM3 contain

Table 7. Partition of Simple-Sum Aggregates into Monetary Service and Non-Monetary Services Share (Investment Share), Sample Period: 1960(2)–2004(3).

	Method 1		Method 2		Method 3	
V	*VS*	*IS*	*VS*	*IS*	*VS*	*IS*
ESM1-BVAR	77.24%	22.76%	79.95%	20.05%	77.08%	22.92%
ESM2-BVAR	62.89%	37.11%	64.8%	35.2%	62.71%	37.29%
ESM3-BVAR	58.74%	41.26%	60.41%	39.59%	58.12%	41.88%
ESM1-AVAR	76.48%	23.52%	78.44%	21.56%	76.35%	23.65%
ESM2-AVAR	62.25%	37.75%	63.73%	36.27%	62.05%	37.95%
ESM3-AVAR	57.88%	42.12%	59.32%	40.68%	57.67%	42.33%
CEM1	73.97%	26.03%				
CEM2	59.5%	40.5%				
CEM3	55.06%	44.94%				

Over the second sub-sample period 1991:1–2004:3 reported in table 9, investment shares, measured by the difference between SSI and ESM_method1_BVAR, are 14.22% of SSIM1, 25.19% of SSIM2, and 30.84% of SSIM3, while the gaps between SSI and the CE index produce investment shares of 17.26%, 26.87%, and 33.78%, respectively. These results confirm that the CE index underestimates the ESM, but not by much, with the errors in the CE index being less than 4% of the SSI index at all levels of aggregation and over all sub-sample periods. The investment shares in the second sub-period are substantially lower than those in the first sub-sample period. Over the period from 1991 to early 1994 and the period after 2001:4, there was a strong tendency for investment shares to decline over time, as shown in figure 8. We can infer that during these periods, the own rates of return on monetary assets, relative to

investment (non-monetary) shares of 29.52%, 46%, and 49.53%. These error shares are slightly higher than those computed based on ESM-BVAR, because the CE index is downward biased.

Table 8. Monetary Services Share and Investment Share, Sample Period: 1960(2)–1991(9).

	Method 1		Method 2		Method 3	
V	*VS*	*IS*	*VS*	*IS*	*VS*	*IS*
ESM1-BVAR	73.6%	26.4%	73.22%	26.78%	73.4%	26.6%
ESM2-BVAR	57.88%	42.12%	60.82%	39.18%	57.53%	42.47%
ESM3-BVAR	54.37%	45.63%	56.64%	43.36%	53.51%	46.49%
ESM1-AVAR	72.75%	27.25%	75.43%	24.57%	72.67%	27.33%
ESM2-AVAR	57.02%	42.98%	59.08%	40.92%	56.65%	43.35%
ESM3-AVAR	53.5%	46.5%	55.48%	44.52%	53.15%	46.85%
ESM1_actual	74.83%	25.17%				
ESM2_actual	58.74%	41.26%				
ESM3_actual	55.05%	44.94%				

Note: Sample period is 1960:2–1991:9. Money stock V was computed using forecasted values. VS and IS are monetary services share and investment share, respectively. Monetary services share and investment share were computed by averaging $\frac{V}{SSI} * 100$ and $(\frac{SSI-V}{SSI} * 100)$ over sample period, respectively.

Table 9. Partition of Simple-Sum Aggregates into Monetary Service and Non-Monetary Services Share (Investment Share), Sample Period: 1991(1)–2004(3).

	Method 1		Method 2		Method 3	
V	*VS*	*IS*	*VS*	*IS*	*VS*	*IS*
ESM1-BVAR	85.78%	14.22%	86.09%	13.91%	85.78%	14.22%
ESM2-BVAR	74.81%	25.19%	74.03%	25.97%	75%	25.0%
ESM3-BVAR	69.16%	30.84%	69.24%	30.76%	69.14%	30.86%
ESM1-AVAR	85.16%	14.84%	85.81%	14.19%	85.14%	14.86%
ESM2-AVAR	74.19%	25.81%	76%	24.0%	75.16%	24.84%
ESM3-AVAR	68.37%	31.63%	69.1%	30.90%	68.34%	31.66%
CEM1	82.74%	17.26%				
CEM2	73.13%	26.87%				
CEM3	66.22%	33.78%				

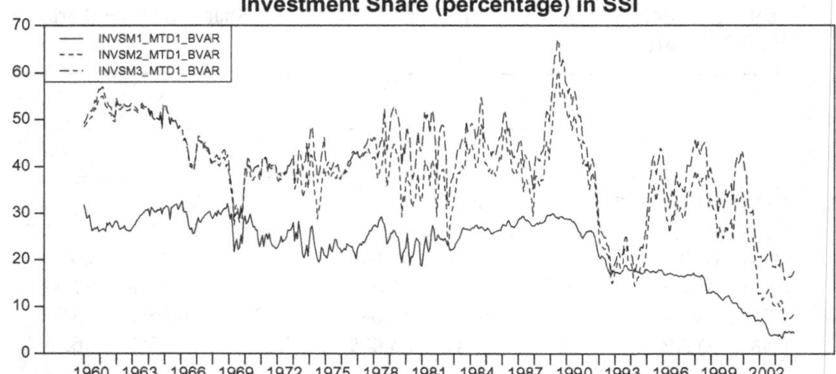

Fig. 8. Using BVAR Method 1 Forecasts.
Note: INVSM_MTD1_BVAR is investment share in percentage inherent in SSI and is computed as ((SSI-V)/(SSI))*100 where *V* is ESM_mtd1_BVAR.

the benchmark rate, have decreased, so that the investment motive for holding monetary assets declined.[18]

4.8.2.2. *Comparison across Computing Methods*[19]

When comparing the ESM across computing methods, we find that Methods 1 and 3 result in very similar values of the ESM at all levels of aggregation. As indicated in tables 7, 8, and 9, the difference between

[18]We denote ESM, computed using forecasts from the AVAR model with Method 1, Method 2, and Method 3, by ESM_mtd1_AVAR, ESM_mtd2_AVAR, and ESM_mtd3_AVAR, respectively. ESMs obtained by AVAR models displayed much higher volatilities than those displayed by their counterpart ESMs obtained by BVAR models. Nevertheless, ESMs obtained by AVAR models also produce the same patterns as ESM_mtd1_BVAR with respect to biases in the SSI and the CE index. In particular, the simple sum index is biased upward substantially, while the CE index is biased downward, but not substantially. The size of the biases in the simple sum aggregates increases with broader aggregates. In addition, the average levels of ESMs obtained by AVAR models are not much different from those of ESMs obtained by BVAR models, as shown in Tables 7, 8, and 9.

[19]We do not present the graphs for the ESMs obtained by AVAR models, nor do we present the graphs for the ESMs based on Method 2 and Method 3. Interested readers can find those results in Barnett (2006).

these two methods is less than 1%. This means that covariance terms among expected benchmark rates, and covariances between expected benchmark rates and expected monetary-service expenditures, did not seem greatly to affect measurement of the ESM. On the other hand, comparing the ESMs based on Method 1 and Method 2 over the full sample period, we found that monetary service shares estimated by Method 2 were greater than those estimated by Method 1, but the differences between the two methods were less than 3% of the SSI at all levels of aggregation. This divergence between Methods 1 and 2 results from the assumption that the benchmark rate follows a martingale process. Nevertheless, the differences in economic money stock across computing methods seem to be negligibly small, relative to the overall bias in the SSI. Furthermore, regardless of the forecast models from which forecasts are generated, and methods by which ESM is computed, certain patterns are evident. The SSI is biased upward, while the CE index is biased downward, on average, with bias less than 4% of SSI.

4.9. Discussion and Conclusion

We measure the United States capital stock of money implied by the Divisia monetary-services-flow, in a manner consistent with present-value discounting and time-varying discount rates. Based on Barnett's (1991) definition of the economic capital stock of money, we compute the economic stock of money by discounting to present value the expected monetary-services-flow expenditure, with user cost pricing of those flows. The economic stock of money nests the currency equivalent (CE) index as a special case under the assumption of martingale expectations. While the martingale expectations assumption greatly simplifies the present-value discounting, that assumption is very strong and often has motivated hesitancy to use the CE index as a stock measure. Instead of assuming martingale expectations, we use forecasts based on asymmetric vector autoregression (AVAR) and Bayesian vector autoregression

(BVAR). For comparison, we compute the ESM using actual realized future data within our sample.

We report the size of biases embedded in the SSI and the CE index. Those biases can be attributed to the two indexes' implicit assumptions. The ESM computed using BVAR forecasts implies that the simple sum index greatly exaggerates money stock through inclusion of substantial non-monetary shares. Over the period 1960:2 to 2004:3, those non-monetary shares comprised 22.76% of the stock at the M1 level, 37.11% at the M2 level, and 41.26% at the M3 level of aggregation.

The CE index almost always underestimated the economic stock of money, but the size of the bias in the CE index was less than 4% of the SSI index's bias at all levels of aggregation. Although the assumption of martingale expectations may be unappealing, the resulting bias of the CE index is very small compared with the bias of the SSI index. A particularly noteworthy conclusion of this research was the robustness of our results across forecasting models.

Prior concerns about the use of Barnett's economic capital stock of money have centered on the difficulties of discounting expected future flows and on the possible need to use sophisticated approaches of forecasting to acquire good results. We find that robustness to the forecasting method is not only high, but is so high that even the simple martingale expectations method implicit in the easily computed CE index may be adequate for most purposes. This conclusion is particularly clear, when the capital stock of money, computed with various models of expectations formation, is compared with the simple sum index. In particular, the variation in capital stock indexes with different expectations formation models is small relative to the gap between any of their paths and that of the simple sum index. Since the difference between the simple sum monetary aggregates and the discounted economic capital stock of money is large, accurate measurement of the theoretical capital stock could have important implications for understanding the wealth effects and transmission mechanism of monetary policy.

To do better than the CE index in measuring the growth rate of the monetary-asset capital stock, one can use our BVAR or AVAR model. They both outperformed the "naive" martingale forecast model implicit in the CE index. But data series that depend on forecasted variables are not likely to be preferred by governmental agencies, and we find the gains from forecasting to be small. Although based upon "naive" forecasting, the CE is not atheoretical, unlike the atheoretical simple-sum accounting index. In addition the CE index can easily be computed using data at a single point in time, with moving average smoothing of that otherwise highly volatile index.

In conclusion, the CE index can be used to measure the stock of money with reasonable accuracy, while the official simple-sum aggregate is an inappropriate measure of money stock or monetary-services flow. While the use of BVAR or AVAR forecasting can produce small gains for research purposes, we believe that the moving-average-smoothed CE index may be adequate for most policy purposes requiring a money stock variable. We believe using an appropriate measure of money stock can produce advances in understanding the wealth effects of policy. The prior hesitancy to use the theoretical economic capital-stock of money formula no longer is justified, since our finding of robustness of that formula to expectations formation removes the reason for that concern, when judged relative to the simple sum index.

Further improvements could be acquired from an adjustment to the CE index to remove the small systematic bias that we identify in that index. Introduction of risk aversion also merits research, using the approach in Barnett and Wu (2005) to risk-adjust the flow that is discounted in the ESM. Having established merits of the asset-pricing capital-stock approach to money measurement, we leave such possible refinements to future research. But it is important to recognize that the large gain in moving from the simple-sum index to the ESM, computed with any forecasting procedure, far exceeds the gains from bias correction, risk adjustment, or choice among forecasting procedures.

APPENDIX

Table A1. Out-of-Sample Forecast Performance Statistics: UVAR and AVAR.

	UVAR-M1		AVAR-M1	
	$\bar{U}_1$	$\bar{U}_2$	$\bar{U}_1$	$\bar{U}_2$
Evaluation Period	$(TE)^{m1}$	BENCH	$(TE)^{m1}$	BENCH
1991:1–2004:3	0.747	0.767	0.730	0.737
1991:1–1995:12	0.797	0.839	0.773	0.801
1996:1–2001:12	0.776	0.769	0.741	0.715
2002:1–2004:3	0.724	0.769	0.758	0.791
	UVAR-M2		AVAR-M2	
	$\bar{U}_1$	$\bar{U}_2$	$\bar{U}_1$	$\bar{U}_2$
Evaluation Period	$(TE)^{m2}$	BENCH	$(TE)^{m2}$	BENCH
1991:1–2004:3	0.721	0.763	0.716	0.738
1991:1–1995:12	0.771	0.838	0.7567	0.810
1996:1–2001:12	0.737	0.762	0.733	0.711
2002:1–2004:3	0.75	0.768	0.749	0.776
	UVAR-M3		AVAR-M3	
	$\bar{U}_1$	$\bar{U}_2$	$\bar{U}_1$	$\bar{U}_2$
Evaluation Period	$(TE)^{m3}$	BENCH	$(TE)^{m3}$	BENCH
1991:1–2004:3	0.722	0.765	0.72	0.738
1991:1–1995:12	0.777	0.837	0.766	0.81
1996:1–2001:12	0.749	0.763	0.75	0.711
2002:1–2004:3	0.76	0.78	0.753	0.777

5

Exchange Rate Determination from Monetary Fundamentals: An Aggregation Theoretic Approach[1]

William A. Barnett and Chang Ho Kwag

We incorporate aggregation and index number theory into monetary models of exchange rate determination in a manner that is internally consistent with money market equilibrium. Divisia monetary aggregates and user-cost concepts are used for money supply and opportunity-cost variables in the monetary models. We estimate a flexible price monetary model, a sticky price monetary model, and the Hooper and Morton (1982) model for the US dollar/UK pound exchange rate. We compare forecast results using mean square error, direction of change, and Diebold-Mariano statistics. We find that models with Divisia indexes are better than the random walk assumption in explaining the exchange rate fluctuations. Our results are consistent with the relevant theory and the "Barnett critique."

5.1. Introduction

Following Meese and Rogoff's (1983) (hereafter MR) finding that monetary models' exchange-rate forecasting power are no greater than that of the random walk forecast, numerous studies have sought to find better estimation and forecasting methods. We investigate an alternative approach to improvement: incorporation of index number and aggregation theory into the model in a manner assuring that the

[1]Reprinted with permission from *Frontiers in Finance and Economics* (2006), "Exchange Rate Determination from Monetary Fundamentals: an Aggregation Theoretic Approach," William A. Barnett and Chang Ho Kwag, vol. 3, no. 1, pp. 29–48. Copyright © 2006 *Frontiers in Finance and Economics.*

assumptions implicit in the data construction are internally consistent with the assumptions used in deriving the models within which the data are used.

Some of the prior attempts sought to increase the forecasting power by improving the estimation technique. Wolff (1987) used time varying coefficients, and Taylor and Peel (2000) estimated a nonlinear error correction model. Mark (1995) used a nonparametric bootstrapping method to investigate the structural models' forecasting power in the long horizon. Other prior attempts sought to expand the information sets. Groen (2000) and Mark and Sul (2001) tried to increase the structural models' forecasting power by pooling the data across countries. However, most of the results have not been clearly successful, and as a result the findings of MR still are widely accepted.[2]

These discouraging results suggest that the problem may not be solved by using better estimation or forecasting methods. Perhaps the focus needs to be directed at more fundamental problems. In this study, we switch the focus from econometrics to the fundamentals. In the monetary approach, money market equilibrium conditions, purchasing power parity (PPP), and uncovered interest parity (UIP) are basic to model structures. However, it is well known that those conditions often perform poorly empirically (e.g., Engel (1996, 2000)). Hence, several models have sought to deal with the PPP and UIP problems. The sticky price monetary model relaxes the PPP assumption. Relaxing the UIP assumption, models with risk premia appeared, such as Frankel (1984). In contrast, little attention has been given to the money market equilibrium condition or the evidence of unstable money demand.

The objective of this paper is to investigate whether the exchange-rate forecasting power of monetary models can be improved by

[2]Mark (1995) and Chinn and Meese (1995) have shown that fundamentals have forecasting power in the long horizon. But other critical studies, such as Kilian (1999) and Berkowitz and Giorwitz (2001), find that Mark's results are dependent upon assumptions on the data generating processes.

focusing on the monetary equilibrium condition. In particular, money demand may be more stable and thus the monetary equilibrium condition may perform better, if we use monetary aggregates derived from aggregation theory, instead of the commonly used atheoretical simple-sum aggregates.

Barnett (1980) derived the formula for the user cost of monetary services and the resulting theory of monetary aggregation, and produced the Divisia monetary aggregates that track the monetary quantity aggregator functions of aggregation theory. Many subsequent publications have found that using those aggregation-theoretic monetary aggregates resolves many of the "puzzles" in the literature. For a collection of much of the most important research from that literature, see Barnett and Serletis (2000), Barnett and Binner (2004), and Barnett, Fisher, and Serletis (1992). Unstable structure induced by use of simple sum monetary aggregates within models that are internally inconsistent with simple sum aggregation has been called the "Barnett critique" by Chrystal and MacDonald (1994).

We investigate performance of monetary exchange-rate determination models, when Divisia monetary aggregates are used instead of the commonly used simple sum monetary aggregates. The use of simple sum monetary aggregates within those models violates fundamental nesting conditions needed for internal consistency of the models with the data. We compare the forecasts of (5.1) monetary models with simple-sum monetary aggregates, (5.2) the same monetary models with Divisia monetary aggregates, and (5.3) the random walk model.

5.2. The Role of Money Supply and Demand in Exchange Rate Models

Since the outset of the floating exchange-rate system in the early 1970s, the monetary approach (or the asset approach in a wider concept) has emerged as the dominant exchange rate determination model. The MR (1983) research, as well as most of the succeeding empirical studies of exchange rate determination, used monetary models in estimating and forecasting exchange rates.

In monetary models, the bilateral exchange rate, defined to be the relative price of two currencies, is influenced by the supply and demand for money in the two countries. Hence, one of the main building blocks of the model is the monetary equilibrium in each country:

$$m_t - p_t = a_1 y_t - a_2 i_t, \tag{5.1}$$

$$m_t^* - p_t^* = a_1^* y_t^* - a_2^* i_t^*, \tag{5.2}$$

where m_t, p_t, y_t are the logarithms of the money supply, price level, and output respectively, and asterisk denotes foreign variable. The level of the opportunity cost (user cost) of holding money is i_t.

If the parameters are equal across countries, so that $a_1 = a_1^*, a_2 = a_2^*$, then the "flexible price monetary model" for the log exchange rate, S_t, can be shown to be the following:

$$S_t = (m_t - m_t^*) - a_1(y_t - y_t^*) + a_2(i_t - i_t^*), \tag{5.3}$$

where $S_t = p_t - p_t^*$ under purchasing power parity.

This classical flexible price monetary model provides the basic structure of the monetary approach. Although the assumptions underlying this model are generally strong, other models have relaxed the underlying assumptions and modified the structures of the flexible price model. The major assumptions that have been relaxed are price flexibility and capital mobility.

Allowing for short-run price flexibility, Dornbusch's (1976) version of the sticky price monetary model has played an important role in explaining the short-run exchange-rate overshoot. Alternatively the portfolio-balance approach relaxes the perfect capital mobility assumption and treats domestic and foreign bonds as imperfect substitutes. In that approach, the supply and demand for bonds play an important role in exchange-rate determination.

In all versions of the monetary approach, the money supply and the variables that determine money demand, such as output and monetary user costs, affect the exchange rate movements, as seen from equations (5.1), (5.2), and (5.3). As a result, we introduce the aggregation-theoretic correct monetary aggregates and their opportunity costs. Nevertheless, the simple-sum monetary aggregates and short-run interest rates are commonly used as the money supply and the opportunity cost variables in these studies, despite their known inconsistency with aggregation and index number theory. Simple sum monetary aggregates, by giving an equal and constant weight to each component monetary asset, can severely distort the information about the monetary service flows supplied in the economy, and the commonly used narrow aggregates, such as M1 and M2, cannot represent the total monetary services supplied in the economy, since those aggregates impute zero weight to the omitted components that appear only in broader aggregates.

The short-run interest rate that is used as a measure of the opportunity cost of holding money is also theoretically invalid. When a very narrow aggregate containing only currency and non-interest-bearing demand deposits is used, a suitably determined short run interest rate can measure the opportunity cost adequately; but broader aggregates include checkable NOW accounts yielding interest and other monetary assets yielding even higher rates of return. As a result, consuming the services of such assets does not require foregoing the complete short-term rate of return on nonmonetary alternative assets. Hence a short term rate of return overstates the opportunity cost, and thereby the user cost, of holding broad monetary assets that include interest-yielding monetary assets.

A large literature has shown that using the simple sum monetary aggregates and a short-run interest rate in monetary equilibrium can destabilize otherwise stable money demand. For an overview of much of that literature, see Barnett and Binner (2004). We believe that the poor performance of the monetary exchange-rate determination models may have the same source.

5.3. Aggregation and Index Number Theory

Rigorous microeconomic and aggregation-theoretic foundations were introduced into monetary economics, when Barnett (1980; 1981a,b; 1987) produced the theoretical linkage between monetary theory and aggregation theory. Recognizing that monetary assets are durable goods, he developed and applied the theory needed to construct monetary aggregates based on microeconomic aggregation theory. Since a durable good does not depreciate fully during one time period, a monetary aggregate that reflects the "monetary service flow" during a holding period is not equal to the monetary stock. In fact it more recently has been shown that the capital stock of money is the discounted present value of the aggregation-theoretic monetary service flow.

It follows that the price of the monetary service flow is the opportunity cost (user cost) of holding monetary assets per unit time. The real user-cost price has been proven by Barnett (1980) to be the present value of the interest foregone by holding the assets, when a higher rate of return is available on a pure investment asset providing no monetary services. The resulting formula for monetary asset i during current period t is:

$$\pi_{it} = \frac{R_t - \gamma_{it}}{1 + R_t}, \tag{5.4}$$

where γ_{it} is the own rate of return on asset i, and R_t is the yield available in the economy on a pure investment asset ("benchmark" asset) providing no services other than its own investment rate of return.

With the monetary service flow and its user-cost price well defined, the aggregation-theoretic monetary-service-flow aggregate can be tracked and thereby accurately measured using statistical index number theory. A class of particularly highly regarded statistical index numbers is the class of "superlative index numbers" defined by Diewert (1976) to track aggregator functions up to third order remainder terms. Two well known superlative indexes are the Fisher ideal index and the Divisia index. In this study, we use the Divisia index.[3]

Let m_{it} be nominal balances of monetary asset i in period t, let $s_{it} = \pi_{it}m_{it}/\sum \pi_{jt}m_{jt}$, and let $s_{it}^* = (1/2)(s_{it} + s_{it-1})$.[4] Then the nominal Divisia quantity index M_t is defined by:

$$\ln M_t - \ln M_{t-1} = \sum_{i=1}^{n} s_{it}^*(\ln m_{it} - \ln m_{it-1}). \tag{5.5}$$

The growth rate of the Divisia index is a weighted average of the growth rates of the component monetary assets. The weight of each component is the user-cost-evaluated value share of that component. In continuous time differential equation form, the Divisia index is exact for any aggregator function and second order in this finite change (Törnqvist) form. The corresponding real Divisia user-cost price index, Π_t, is[5]

$$\ln \Pi_t - \ln \Pi_{t-1} = \sum_{i=1}^{n} s_{it}^*(\ln \pi_{it} - \ln \pi_{it-1}). \tag{5.6}$$

[3]The choice between the Fisher ideal index and the Divisia index is of little significance, since the two indexes differ by less than the roundoff error in the component data. See Barnett (1980; 1981a,b; 1987).

[4]The extension to risk aversion under intertemporal nonseparability of preferences recently has been produced by Barnett and Wu (2005). When rates of return on monetary assets are subject to exchange-rate risk, that extension could be important. However, no empirical applications of Barnett and Wu's difficult formula have yet appeared. When the econometric problems associated with use of that risk-adjusted index number have been resolved, we anticipate that our already promising results can be further improved.

[5]Alternatively an implicit price dual to the monetary service index is defined by Fisher's weak factor reversal test. But the difference between that exact dual and the Divisia user-cost price index is negligible in most applications.

If there is a change in the interest rate on a component monetary asset, the asset holders will respond by substituting towards the assets with relatively lower user costs. A simple sum aggregate, by treating component assets as perfect substitutes, does not correctly capture any of those substitution effects among the component assets. A Divisia index treats component assets as imperfect substitutes, internalizes substitution effects, and measures the income effects, thereby capturing the exact change in the monetary service flows.

5.4. Exchange Rate Forecasting with Divisia Money and User Cost Prices

5.4.1. *Model Specification*

In accordance with the asset approach model of Hooper and Morton (1982) (hereafter HMM), the basic equation for estimation and forecasting of log exchange rates, S_t, is the following:

$$S_t = a_0 + a_1(m_t - m_t^*) + a_2(y_t - y_t^*) + a_3(i_t - i_t^*) + a_4(\dot{p}_t - \dot{p}_t^*) + a_5 ca_t + a_6 ca_t^* + u_t \tag{5.7}$$

where $\dot{p}_t$ is the expected inflation rate and ca_t is the current account deficit at time t.[6] As in the special case equation (5.3), asterisks denote foreign variables.

Two well known special cases are nested within equation (5.7). If we assume that $a_5 = a_6 = 0$, then equation (5.3) reduces to the sticky price monetary model (SPM) of Dornbush (1976). If $a_4 = a_5 = a_6 = 0$, the equation (5.7) reduces further to the flexible price monetary

[6]For the current account terms, Hooper and Morton (1982) used the cumulative current account deficit, under the assumption that long-term exchange rate changes are correlated with unanticipated shocks to the current account balances. Meese and Rogoff (1983) used cumulative deviations from trend balances as proxies for the unanticipated shocks. But cumulative deviation from trend balance is not invariant to the specification of the trend balance process. We use the current account balance itself, to avoid dependence upon a nonunique trend process specification.

model (FPM) of Frenkel (1976) and Bilson (1978), as in equation (5.3) above. We use these three models, FPM, SPM and HMM, for estimation and forecasting, but with improvement through inclusion of aggregation theoretic variables for measurement of monetary flows and opportunity costs.

5.4.2. *Data Specification and Transformation*

We use quarterly data from the United Kingdom and the United States for the period 1977:1 to 2002:3, since the Bank of England and the Federal Reserve Bank of St. Louis both provide Divisia monetary aggregate data for that time period. The exchange rate, income, interest rate, price, and current account variables are drawn from the IMF's International Financial Statistics. In particular, we use the seasonally-adjusted nominal exchange rate (US$/£), real GDP, three-month bond-equivalent Treasury bill rate (TB3MB), consumer price index (CPI), and current account deficit for each country as S_t, y_t, i_t, p_t, and ca_t respectively. The monetary aggregates, M1, M3 (for the US), and M4 (for the UK), and the component quantity and interest rate data are acquired from the databases of the Federal Reserve Bank of St. Louis and the Bank of England.

Details regarding the Federal Reserve data are available from Anderson, Jones, and Nesmith (1997a,b). For the UK monetary services indexes, the Bank of England (hereafter BOE) publishes in its Quarterly Bulletin the Divisia indices for M4, based upon Fisher, Hudson and Pradhan (1993). However, we reconstructed the UK monetary-services index in a manner consistent with the procedures and transformations used with the Federal Reserve. In particular, with the UK data we followed the BOE's classification of component monetary assets and their interest rates. However, the BOE's computation of the user cost of monetary asset is slightly different from that of the US counterpart. We used equation (5.4) in calculating the user cost of the UK monetary components for consistency with the St. Louis Federal Reserve Bank's procedure.

5.4.3. *Estimation and Forecasting*

We estimate each of the three models twice. First, we use the simple-sum monetary indexes to measure the pair (m_t, m_t^*) and the conventional short term interest rates to measure the pair of opportunity costs (i_t, i_t^*), despite the fact that some of the monetary components themselves yield interest. We repeat the estimation with the Divisia money-services index used to measure (m_t, m_t^*) and the Divisia user-cost price index used to measure the opportunity costs (i_t, i_t^*). We compare the forecasting power of the resulting six monetary models with that of a random walk forecast without drift.

We use the "rolling regression" procedure with fixed sample size in the model estimation and forecasting. In rolling regression, two-step procedures are repeated sequentially. In the first step, the model is estimated over a selected data sample and forecasted over the out-of-sample data period. In the second step, the sample period is rolled one observation forward. This two-step procedure is repeated until all the out-of-sample observations are consumed. We first estimate the model for the 41 observations from 1977:1 through 1987:1, with the out-of-sample forecast conducted over the period of 62 observations from 1987:2 through 2002:3, corresponding to the post Louvre Accord period.

There are two common problems in the exchange rate models: the explanatory variables in the model are all endogenous and are nonstationary. As result, we use vector error correction (VEC) in estimation, and we simultaneously solve the full model in forecasting. Estimating the relationships among multiple variables using vector error correction is accomplished in two steps. In the first step, cointegrating relationships are tested and estimated. An error correction term is constructed from the estimated cointegrating relations. The vector error-correction specification is a vector autoregression (VAR) in the first differences, including the error correction terms. In the second step the resulting specification is estimated over each sample period.

In some prior studies, the cointegrating vectors were estimated over the full data span. However, we estimate the cointegrating vector in each rolling period. As a result, the number of cointegrating relationships and the estimates of those relationships can vary across the sample periods.[7]

5.4.4. *Forecast Comparisons*

To evaluate the accuracy of a structural model's exchange rate forecasts, we use the ratio of the structural model's mean squared error (MSE) to that of a random walk without drift. If an MSE value is smaller than one, then the structural model has better forecasting power than the random walk forecast. For each of the six models, we compute the MSE ratios for 1 through 8 periods forward. Forecasting the direction of the change of the exchange rate is important, regardless of the magnitude of the change. As a result, we compute the direction of change (DOC) statistic, following Diebold and Mariano (1995) and Cheung, Chinn and Pascual (2002). The DOC statistic is the ratio of the number of correctly predicted directions of change to the total number of predictions. If the DOC statistic is significantly larger than 0.5, then the structural model has better direction-of-change forecasting power than a no-change assumption forecast. If the exchange rate were a random walk, the expected value of the DOC statistic would be 0.5. A test statistic value significantly smaller than 0.5 implies that the model forecasts changes in the wrong direction and thereby produces misleading information about exchange rate movements.

We also use the Diebold-Mariano (DM) statistics to compare the accuracy and direction of forecasts of the structural model with those of the random walk. The DM statistic tests the null hypothesis that

[7]Mark (1995) and Chinn and Meese (1995) impose the cointegrating vector *a priori*. MacDonald and Taylor (1993) estimated it over the entire sample.

there are no differences in the accuracies and/or directions of the two forecasts.[8]

5.5. The Empirical Results

5.5.1. *The MSE and DM Comparisons*

The MSE ratios and the DM test statistics of the models using non-aggregation-theoretic traditional data are summarized in Table 1. Each cell in the table has two entries. The first is the MSE ratio and the second, in parenthesis, is the DM test statistic. There are 24 MSE ratios produced from the three models with 8 forecasts per model. Of the 24 cases, only 7 produce MSEs that are smaller than 1.0. Among those 7 ratios, only 4 are smaller than 0.9. With the flexible monetary model and the sticky price monetary model, the ratios are less than 1.0 until the 3rd period. However after that period, the ratios become

Table 1. MSE Comparison of the Traditional Monetary Models.

	1 Period	2 Period	3 Period	4 Period	5 Period	6 Period	7 Period	8 Period
FPM	0.7206	0.8134	0.9550	1.1243	1.3911	1.6602	1.4709	1.7023
	(−1.16)	(−0.88)	(−0.26)	(0.46)	(0.86)	(1.15)	(0.88)	(1.19)
SPM	0.7532	0.8305	0.9470	1.1006	1.3401	1.5028	1.3183	1.5819
	(−0.90)	(−0.81)	(−0.30)	(0.33)	(0.65)	(0.76)	(0.47)	(0.72)
HMM	0.9214	1.0598	1.2386	1.2267	1.3003	1.3832	1.1461	1.2260
	(−0.28)	(0.23)	(1.02)	(0.91)	(0.91)	(1.16)	(0.49)	(0.69)

Note: FPM, SPM, HMM denote flexible price monetary model, sticky price monetary model, and Hooper and Morton model, respectively. The values in parenthesis are the Diebold-Mariano test statistics for forecast accuracy.

[8]There are problems in using DM statistics for evaluating out-of sample forecasts, when parameters are estimated. Nevertheless, we use the DM statistic as a source of further information, despite the limitations of the DM tests. There are two DM statistics: one for accuracy and one for direction of change. See Diebold-Mariano (1995) for detailed explanation of each. For the accuracy test, we use a rectangular lag window.

larger than 1.0. The HM model does not produce any improvement in forecasting accuracy.

The results of the three traditional structural models are generally unfavorable. These unfavorable results are reinforced by the DM test statistics. All of the DM values are between −1.64 and 1.64, thereby implying that the null hypothesis of no difference in accuracy, relative to the random walk forecast, cannot be rejected at the 10% significance level. We find that the structural models' forecasts are no better than the random walk model's forecasts of the exchange rate. These findings are consistent with previously published results that are unfavorable to the monetary models with traditional non-aggregation-theoretic monetary data.

Table 2 displays the MSE ratios and the DM test results with the Divisia monetary models. In contrast to the above results with traditional data, the Divisia monetary models produce strikingly favorable MSE ratios. Out of the 24 results, the values of 21 MSEs are smaller than 1.0. Of those 21 favorable values, 17 are smaller than 0.9. The results with the sticky price monetary model are particularly strong. All the values are within the range of 0.6035 to 0.7884, indicating that we can reduce the MSE from 20% to 40% by using Divisia monetary models, rather than the random walk forecast. The DM test statistics again produce favorable results. With the sticky

Table 2. MSE Comparison of the Divisia Monetary Models.

	1 Period	2 Period	3 Period	4 Period	5 Period	6 Period	7 Period	8 Period
FPM	0.6321	0.6075	0.5905	0.6743	0.8445	1.0346	0.9543	1.1552
	(−1.41)	(−2.36)	(−2.83)	(−1.71)	(−0.44)	(0.08)	(−0.10)	(0.27)
SPM	0.6035	0.6589	0.6641	0.6374	0.7011	0.7663	0.6806	0.7884
	(−1.64)	(−1.94)	(−2.98)	(−2.28)	(−1.19)	(−0.96)	(−1.40)	(−0.94)
HMM	0.6786	0.8679	0.9160	0.9351	0.9761	1.0184	0.8179	0.8856
	(−1.58)	(−0.61)	(−0.46)	(−0.25)	(−0.07)	(0.05)	(−0.54)	(−0.40)

Note: FPM, SPM, HMM denote flexible price monetary model, sticky price monetary model, and Hooper and Morton model, respectively. The values in parenthesis are the Diebold-Mariano test statistics for forecast accuracy.

price model, the absolute values of the DM statistics are greater than 1.64 from the 1st period through the 4th period. The flexible price model displays better forecasting results than the random walk forecasts from 2 to 4 periods forward.

These results imply that the monetary models' exchange-rate forecasting accuracy can be improved substantially by using aggregation-theoretic monetary aggregates. These results are consistent with previous research demonstrating that aggregation-theoretic monetary aggregates and use-cost prices can stabilize monetary equilibrium conditions, which are central to the monetary exchange-rate forecasting models.

5.5.2. *The DOC Results*

The traditional monetary models' DOC forecasting results are reported in Table 3. As with the MSEs, the results are not favorable to those models. For up to 2-period forecasts, the DOC values are greater than 0.5. Thus the traditional monetary models' results on direction-of-change forecasts are favorable in those cases. But beyond 2 periods, the DOC values drop below 0.5. At the 10% significance level, the DM statistics indicate that the sticky price model and the HM model-forecasts outperform the random-walk one-step-ahead forecasts. Far less favorable results are provided for

Table 3. The DOC Comparison of the Traditional Monetary Models.

	1 Period	2 Period	3 Period	4 Period	5 Period	6 Period	7 Period	8 Period
FPM	0.5645	0.5246	0.4333	0.3559	0.3621	0.3684	0.4107	0.4364
	(1.02)	(0.38)	(−1.03)	(−2.21)	(−2.10)	(−1.99)	(−1.34)	(−0.94)
SPM	0.6613	0.5738	0.4333	0.3898	0.3966	0.4386	0.5	0.4727
	(2.54)	(1.15)	(−1.03)	(−1.69)	(−1.58)	(−0.93)	(0.00)	(−0.40)
HMM	0.6935	0.5902	0.4833	0.4407	0.3793	0.4035	0.4643	0.4909
	(3.05)	(1.41)	(−0.26)	(−0.91)	(−1.84)	(−1.46)	(−0.53)	(−0.13)

Note: FPM, SPM, HMM denote flexible price monetary model, sticky price monetary model, and Hooper and Morton model, respectively. The values in parenthesis are the Diebold-Mariano test statistics for direction of change.

Table 4. The DOC Comparison of the Divisia Monetary Models.

	1 Period	2 Period	3 Period	4 Period	5 Period	6 Period	7 Period	8 Period
FPM	0.7419	0.6557	0.5833	0.5593	0.5690	0.5789	0.5714	0.5636
	(3.81)	(2.43)	(1.29)	(0.91)	(1.05)	(1.19)	(1.07)	(0.94)
SPM	0.7097	0.5574	0.5500	0.5254	0.5690	0.5789	0.6786	0.6000
	(3.30)	(0.90)	(0.77)	(0.39)	(1.05)	(1.19)	(2.67)	(1.48)
HMM	0.6613	0.6066	0.5333	0.5254	0.5517	0.5965	0.6429	0.6182
	(2.54)	(1.66)	(0.52)	(0.39)	(0.79)	(1.46)	(2.14)	(1.75)

Note: FPM, SPM, HMM denote flexible price monetary model, sticky price monetary model, and Hooper and Morton model, respectively. The values in parenthesis are the Diebold-Mariano test statistics for direction of change.

other forecast periods, such as the 4 to 6 period ahead forecasts, since the flexible price model then produces erroneous information about the direction of the change. In general, the traditional models with non-aggregation-theoretic data display very little power regarding the direction of the exchange rate movements.

Again, when Divisia monetary models are used, the results are favorable, as shown in Table 4. All the DOC values are larger than 0.5, ranging from 0.5254 to 0.7419. The DM test results also are favorable. The 1st period forecasts of all three models are significantly better than those from the random walk forecast. The 2nd period forecasts of the FPM and the HMM also are significantly improve, with 8 out of 24 being significant at the 10% level.

The Divisia monetary models, unlike the same models with non-aggregation-theoretic monetary data, produce favorable forecasting performance.

5.6. Conclusion

This paper incorporates monetary aggregation and index number theory into exchange rate determination theory. We investigate whether exchange rate forecasting power can be improved by specifying the monetary equilibrium condition more accurately. With Divisia monetary aggregates and their user costs, we find that the monetary fundamentals explain exchange rate movements more accurately than the random walk forecast.

In this study, data-availability limits us to modeling and forecasting the US dollar/UK pound exchange-rate movements. At present only the Federal Reserve of St. Louis and the Bank of England publish Divisia monetary aggregates data. Although our results with that exchange rate are strong, reversal of MR's results cannot be considered conclusive without data on more exchange rates. It is expected that Divisia data for many European countries will be available soon from the European Central Bank, in accordance with the procedures for multilateral aggregation developed by Barnett (2005). When the new European data is available, a complete analysis with several bilateral exchange rates will be possible.

6

Multilateral Aggregation-Theoretic Monetary Aggregation over Heterogeneous Countries

William A. Barnett[1]

We derive fundamental theory for measuring monetary service flows aggregated over countries within a multicountry area. We develop three increasingly restrictive approaches: (1) the heterogeneous agents approach, (2) the multilateral representative agent approach, and (3) the unilateral representative agent approach. These results are being used by the European Central Bank in construction of its Divisia monetary aggregates database, with convergence from the most general to the more restrictive approaches expected as economic convergence within the area proceeds. Our theory permits monitoring the effects of policy over a multicountry area, while also monitoring the distribution effects of policy among the countries.

6.1. Introduction

With the growth of "free trade" economic and political unions, such as NAFTA and the EU, and more profoundly the growth of economic monetary unions, such as the EMU, an increasing amount of research effort has focused on index-number-theoretic measurement problems

---

[1]Reprinted from *Journal of Econometrics* (2007), "Multilateral Aggregation-Theoretic Monetary Aggregation over Heterogeneous Countries" by William A. Barnett, vol. 136, no. 2, February, pp. 457–482. Copyright © 2007 Elsevier. This research was supported by the European Central Bank. The opinions expressed herein are those of the author and do not necessarily reflect those of the European Central Bank. The original ECB working paper, Barnett (2003), contains further results relevant to application to the European Monetary Union, and can be downloaded without charge from www.ecb.int.

associated with economic modeling and conduct of macroeconomic policy in such economic unions.[2] The need for internally consistent recursive aggregation over monetary data within and over countries is central to the objectives of that research. For those purposes, this research, unlike prior research on this subject, was conducted in a manner that produces direct, multilateral extensions of the available closed-economy results. The theory developed in this paper is currently being used by the European Central Bank in the construction of its Divisia monetary aggregates database. Further details of this research, as applied to the euro area, are available in the original ECB working paper, Barnett (2003).

Monetary aggregation and index number theory and the broader field of financial aggregation and index number theory were first rigorously connected with the literature on microeconomic aggregation and index number theory by Barnett (1980, 1987). A collection of many of his contributions to that field is available in Barnett and Serletis (2000). But Barnett's work in those publications was based upon the assumption that the data was produced by a single closed economy.

The purpose of this paper is to extend that theory to the multicountry case in a form that would be applicable to economic unions, both prior to and after the introduction of a common currency. Progress towards convergence within economic unions

[2]See, e.g., M. M. G. Fase and C. C. A. Winder (1994), Spencer (1997), Wesche (1997), Fase (2000), Beyer, Doornik, and Hendry (2001), Stracca (2001), and Reimers (2002). Two approaches have been proposed and applied by other researchers. One has been called the direct approach and the other the indirect approach. We show that the direct approach implies the existence of our most restrictive, unilateral representative agent, which requires assumptions that we consider to be very strong. The alternative indirect approach uses Divisia aggregation within countries and then *ad hoc* weighting of those within-country indexes to aggregate over countries. The indirect approach produces a result that is disconnected from theory and does not produce nesting of the multilateral or unilateral representative agent approaches.

occurs gradually. For that reason, our results are produced under a sequence of increasingly strong assumptions, beginning with (1) a heterogeneous agents approach applicable to the past under reasonable assumptions, and then progressing to (2) a new multilateral representative agent approach applicable to an economic union under reasonable convergence assumptions, and finally to (3) a unilateral representative agent approach requiring very strong assumptions, perhaps relevant to the very distant future, if at all.

At some date following the introduction of a common currency, our heterogeneous agents approach could become mathematically equivalent to the multilateral representative agent approach, since the assumptions necessary for equivalence of the two approaches are reasonably related to the long run objectives of economic monetary unions. But the far more restrictive unilateral representative agent approach requires very strong assumptions. In particular the unilateral representative agent approach would require convergence of inflation rates and interest rates across countries and would imply demographic convergence to a homogeneous population, such that the country of residence of a consumer would become irrelevant to the unilateral representative agent's decisions.

This paper's extensions of Barnett's earlier work produce a number of unexpected innovations, including the need for simultaneous use of two different consumer price indexes for internal consistency of the theory. The current paper is intended to solve the central theoretical problems associated with monetary aggregation over countries. This paper is likely to be the first in a series of papers. Later papers are planned to incorporate risk aversion, with the first step in that direction appearing in Barnett and Wu (2005). The solutions of the fundamental problems addressed in the current paper are logically prior to our planned future work on this subject.

The purposes and objectives of this research in the multicountry case are analogous to the purposes and objectives of monetary and financial aggregation and index number theory in the single country case. Data construction and measurement procedures imply the theory that can rationalize those procedures. Unless that implied theory is internally consistent with the theory used in applications of that data in modeling and policy, the data and its applications are incoherent. Such internal inconsistencies can produce the appearance of structural change, when there has been none.[3]

6.2. Definition of Variables

We define an "economic union" to be any multicountry area within which multilateral measurement and policy are relevant. Whether of not a common currency exists within the area is not part of this definition, but is relevant to the choice among assumptions we introduce. In practice, the identification of an economic union is usually by political treaty. But in economic theory, existence of such an area can be defined by a weak separability clustering condition, which need not imply the existence of a political treaty or an "optimal currency area."[4]

All results are in continuous time. Certainty equivalence is assumed within the decisions of each consumer, as would be attained under risk neutrality by replacing contemporaneously random rates of return by their expectations.

Let K be the number of countries in the economic union. We let $p_k^* = p_k^*(\mathbf{p}_k)$ be the true cost of living index in country $k \in \{1, \ldots, K\}$, where $\mathbf{p}_k = \mathbf{p}_k(t)$ is the vector of prices of consumer goods at time t and $\mathbf{x}_k = \mathbf{x}_k(t)$ is the vector of per-capita real rates of consumption of those goods in country k at time t. Let $H_k = H_k(t)$ be the population of country k at time t, and let m_{kji} be the nominal per capita holdings of asset type i located or purchased in country j but owned by economic agents in country k. The holdings are per capita relative to country k's own population, H_k. We present all results in per capita form,

[3]This phenomenon has been called the "Barnett critique" by Chrystal and MacDonald (1994).

[4]See Swofford (2000) and Drake, Mullineux, and Agung (1997).

since the per capita variables are the ones that are needed in demand functions at the aggregate level. In addition the correlation with inflation tends to be in terms of per capita flows, since increases in monetary services that produce no change in per capita monetary services just accommodate population growth.

Assume that asset holders within the economic union also sometimes hold assets in Z countries that are outside the economic union. Let N_j be the number of asset types available within country j, and let N be the total number of asset types available within all of the relevant countries $j \in \{1, \ldots, K + Z\}$, where clearly $N \geq N_j$ for all $j \in \{1, \ldots, K + Z\}$. Then the subscripts of m_{kji} have range: $k \in \{1, \ldots, K\}$, $j \in \{1, \ldots, K + Z\}$, $i \in \{1, \ldots, N\}$. We are not limiting i to be within $\{1, \ldots, N_j\}$, since we wish to associate a unique numerical value of i to each asset type, regardless of country j within which the asset is located. As a result, for each (k, j) there will necessarily be zero values of m_{kji} for $N - N_j$ values of i. If countries j and k do not share the same currency, then nominal holdings are converted to units of country k's currency using the exchange rate between country k's and country j's currencies.[5] Then $m^*_{kji} = m_{kji}/p^*_k$ is the real per capita holdings of asset i located or purchased in country j but owned by economic agents in country k.

Let $r_{kji} = r_{kji}(t)$ be the holding-period after-tax yield on asset i located or purchased in country j and owned by an economic agent in country k at instant of time t, where all asset rates of return are yield-curve adjusted to the same holding period (e.g., 30 days).[6] It

[5]Similarly we assume that prices of consumer goods are converted to units of country k's currency. Since aggregation over consumer goods is not the primary subject of this paper, our notation for consumer goods quantities, expenditures, and prices is less formal than for monetary assets.

[6]In most cases below, the adjustment for taxation will have no effect, unless the marginal tax rate is not the same on assets appearing in the numerator and denominator of the shares. See Barnett and Serletis (2000, p. 20). The yield curve adjustment of rates of return of different maturities is acquired by subtracting from the asset's yield the country's Treasury security yield of the same maturity and

is important to recognize that the subscript k identifies the country of residence of the asset holder, and not necessarily the country of location of the asset. Rates of return on foreign denominated assets owned by residents of country k are understood to be effective rates of return, net of the instantaneous expected percentage rate of change in the exchange rate between the domestic and foreign currency. At some time following the introduction of a common currency, the dependency of rates of return upon k can be expected to end, and the dependency upon j will be relevant only to holdings within the economic union of assets located in the Z countries outside the economic union. Hence at some time after the introduction of a common currency, it follows that r_{kji} will be independent of (j, k) for all $j, k \in \{1, \ldots, K\}$.

Let $R_k = R_k(t)$ be the benchmark rate of return in country k at instant of time t, where the benchmark rate of return is the rate of return received on a pure investment providing no services other than its yield.[7] Then $\pi^*_{kji}(t) = R_k(t) - r_{kji}(t)$ is the real user cost price of asset i located or purchased in country j and owned by residents of country k at time t, and $\pi_{kji} = p^*_k \pi^*_{kji}$ is the corresponding nominal user cost.[8] It does not matter whether real or nominal interest rates are used, since the inflation rate conversion between nominal and real applies to both terms in the user cost formula and hence cancels out between the two terms.

Technically speaking, whenever m_{kji} is zero, as often will happen when a particular asset type i is not available within country j, the user cost price should be the asset's reservation price in country j.

---

then adding that yield differential onto the Treasury security yield of the chosen holding period. The same holding period should be used for all assets.

[7]See the Appendix and footnotes 17 and 28 to Barnett (2003), regarding construction of a proxy for the benchmark rate.

[8]For these formulas and results, see Barnett (1978, section 3; 1980, section 3.2; or 1987, section 2.1). In discrete time, it is necessary to discount to the beginning of the period all interest paid at the end of the period. This requires dividing nominal and real user costs by $1 + R_k$.

But in practice, terms containing assets having zero quantity will drop out of all of our formulas, except when the asset's quantity becomes nonzero in the next period. In such cases, the reservation price must be imputed during the period preceding the innovation and the new goods introduction procedure must be used.[9] Since such innovations are infrequent, it usually will not be necessary to impute a reservation price or interest rate to asset holdings for which $m_{kji} = 0$.

We now define

$$\begin{aligned}
\mathbf{m}_{kj}^* &= (m_{kj1}^*, \ldots, m_{kji}^*, \ldots, m_{kjN}^*)', \\
\mathbf{m}_{kj} &= (m_{kj1}, \ldots, m_{kji}, \ldots, m_{kjN})', \\
\mathbf{r}_{kj} &= (r_{kj1}, \ldots, r_{kji}, \ldots, r_{kjN})', \\
\boldsymbol{\pi}_{kj}^* &= (\pi_{kj1}^*, \ldots, \pi_{kji}^*, \ldots, \pi_{kjN}^*)', \\
\boldsymbol{\pi}_{kj} &= (\pi_{kj1}, \ldots, \pi_{kji}, \ldots, \pi_{kjN})',
\end{aligned}$$

and let

$$\begin{aligned}
\mathbf{m}_{k}^* &= (\mathbf{m}_{k1}^*, \ldots, \mathbf{m}_{kj}^*, \ldots, \mathbf{m}_{k,K+Z}^*)', \\
\mathbf{m}_{k} &= (\mathbf{m}_{k1}, \ldots, \mathbf{m}_{kj}, \ldots, \mathbf{m}_{k,K+Z})', \\
\mathbf{r}_{k} &= (\mathbf{r}_{k1}, \ldots, \mathbf{r}_{kj}, \ldots, \mathbf{r}_{k,K+Z})', \\
\boldsymbol{\pi}_{k}^* &= (\boldsymbol{\pi}_{k1}^*, \ldots, \boldsymbol{\pi}_{kj}^*, \ldots, \boldsymbol{\pi}_{k,K+Z}^*)', \\
\boldsymbol{\pi}_{k} &= (\boldsymbol{\pi}_{k1}, \ldots, \boldsymbol{\pi}_{kj}, \ldots, \boldsymbol{\pi}_{k,K+Z})'.
\end{aligned}$$

6.3. Aggregation within Countries

Aggregation within countries uses the existing theory developed by Barnett (1980, 1987). That theory uses the economic approach to index number theory and assumes the existence of a representative agent within each country. To avoid the unnecessary imputation of

[9]For the new goods introduction procedure, see Barnett and Serletis (2000, p. 77, footnote 25) and Anderson, Jones, and Nesmith (1997b, pp. 77–78).

reservation prices to assets not being held by residents of country k, we shall restrict most of our computations to the index set $S_k = \{(j,i) : m_{kji} > 0, j \in \{1,\ldots,K+Z\}, i \in \{1,\ldots,N\}$ for all $k \in \{1,\ldots,K\}$.

Definition 1. Within each country $k \in \{1,\ldots,K\}$, define the monetary real user-cost price aggregate Π_k^*, the monetary nominal user-cost price aggregate Π_k, the real per-capita monetary services aggregate M_k^*, and the nominal per-capita monetary services aggregate M_k by the following Divisia indices:

$$d\log \Pi_k^* = \sum_{(j,i)\in S_k} w_{kji} d\log \pi_{kji}^*,$$

$$d\log \Pi_k = \sum_{(j,i)\in S_k} w_{kji} d\log \pi_{kji},$$

$$d\log M_k^* = \sum_{(j,i)\in S_k} w_{kji} d\log m_{kji}^*,$$

$$d\log M_k = \sum_{(j,i)\in S_k} w_{kji} d\log m_{kji},$$

where

$$w_{kji} = \frac{\pi_{kji} m_{kji}^*}{\boldsymbol{\pi}_k' \mathbf{m}_k} = \frac{\pi_{kji}^* m_{kji}^*}{\boldsymbol{\pi}_k^{*\prime} \mathbf{m}_k^*} = \frac{(R_k - r_{kji}) m_{kji}^*}{\sum_{(j,i)\in S_k} (R_k - r_{kji}) m_{kji}^*}$$
$$= \frac{(R_k - r_{kji}) m_{kji}}{\sum_{(j,i)\in S_k} (R_k - r_{kji}) m_{kji}}.$$

Observe that $0 \leq w_{kji} \leq 1$ for all $k \in \{1,\ldots,K\}, j \in \{1,\ldots,K+Z\}$, and $i \in \{1,\ldots,N\}$. Also observe that $\sum_{(j,i)\in S_k} w_{kji} = 1$ for all $k \in \{1,\ldots,K\}$. Hence the shares, w_{kji}, have the properties of a probability distribution for each $k \in \{1,\ldots,K\}$, and we could interpret our Divisia indexes above as Divisia growth rate means. But since it is convenient to assume the existence of a representative agent within each country, the statistical interpretation as a mean is not necessary. We instead can appeal to the Divisia index's known ability to track the aggregator function of the country's representative consumer.

The following result relating nominal to real values follows immediately.

Lemma 1. $M_k = M_k^* p_k^*$ *and* $\Pi_k = \Pi_k^* p_k^*$.

Proof. Follows from the known linear homogeneity of the Divisia index. ■

6.4. Aggregation Over Countries

Our heterogeneous agents approach to aggregation over countries is based upon the stochastic convergence approach to aggregation, championed by Theil (1967) and developed further by Barnett (1979a,b; 1981a, chap. 2). This approach not only can be used to aggregate over heterogeneous consumers, but also jointly over consumers and firms. Hence the approach is not only a heterogeneous consumers approach, but more generally is a true heterogeneous agents approach. See, e.g., Barnett and Serletis (2000, pp. 88–90 and chapter 9). By assuming the existence of a representative agent within each country, and treating those representative agents as heterogeneous agents, we produce a heterogeneous countries approach to aggregation over countries.

In aggregating within an economic union, this approach implies that the countries' characteristics, including cultures, tastes, languages, etc., were sampled from underlying theoretical populations consistent with the climates, histories, resources, geographies, neighboring population characteristics, etc. All time-varying variables then become stochastic processes. Each Divisia index aggregating over component stochastic processes becomes the sample mean of realizations of those stochastic processes, and thereby an estimate of the mean function of the underlying unknown population stochastic process. The distributions of those stochastic processes are derived distributions induced by the random sampling from country characteristics. The derived empirical distributions of the countries' solution stochastic-process growth rates impute probabilities to countries equal to their relevant expenditure shares in expenditure within the economic union.

Let e_k be the exchange rate of country k's currency relative to a market basket of currencies, such as the ecu (European currency unit), where e_k is defined in units of the market basket currency per unit of country k's currency. When extending the data backwards to before the introduction of a common currency, the exchange rates can play an important role in our results.

The stochastic convergence approach to aggregation over heterogeneous agents has traditionally been based more on statistical theory than on economic theory. But a rigorous connection with economic theory has been provided by Barnett (1979a). We shall use that interpretation in our heterogeneous agents approach, as we now explain.

Consider a possible country with representative consumer c, having utility function $U_c = U_c[u_c(\mathbf{m}_c^*), g_c(\mathbf{x}_c)]$. Assume that the differences in tastes across possible countries can be explained in terms of a vector of taste-determining variables, $\boldsymbol{\phi}_c$. The dimension of the vector of taste-determining variables must be finite, but otherwise is irrelevant to the theory.[10] Then there must exist functions U, u, and g, such that

$$U_c = U_c[u_c(\mathbf{m}_c^*), g_c(\mathbf{x}_c)] = U[u(\mathbf{m}_c^*, \boldsymbol{\phi}_c), g(\mathbf{x}_c, \boldsymbol{\phi}_c), \boldsymbol{\phi}_c]$$

for all possible countries' tastes, $\boldsymbol{\phi}_c$. Although U, u, and g are fixed functions, the random vector $\boldsymbol{\phi}_c$ of taste-determining variables causes U_c, u_c, and g_c to become random functions, reflecting the possible

[10] The assumption of finite dimensionality of $\boldsymbol{\phi}_c$ is only for notational convenience. Without that assumption, $\boldsymbol{\phi}_c$ could not be written as a vector. A sequence or continuum of taste-determining variables would not alter any of our conclusions, but would complicate the notation.

variations of tastes and their probabilities, conditionally upon their given environmental, demographic, historical, resource, and other factors in the economic union.

Assume that each possible country c's representative consumer solves the following decision problem for $(\mathbf{m}_c^*, \mathbf{x}_c)$ at each instant of time t:

$$\text{maximize } U[u(\mathbf{m}_c^*, \boldsymbol{\phi}_c), g(\mathbf{x}_c, \boldsymbol{\phi}_c), \boldsymbol{\phi}_c]$$
$$\text{subject to} \quad \mathbf{m}_c^{*\prime}\boldsymbol{\pi}_c + \mathbf{x}_c^{\prime}\mathbf{p}_c = I_c.$$

Assume that the countries and their representative agents are about to be drawn from the theoretically possible populations, but have not yet been drawn. Assume that there is an infinite number of possible countries in the economic union, so that there exists a continuous joint distribution of the random variables $(I_c, \mathbf{p}_c, e_c, \boldsymbol{\pi}_c, \boldsymbol{\phi}_c)$ at any time t. We assume that $\boldsymbol{\phi}_c$ is sampled at birth and does not change during lifetimes, so that $\boldsymbol{\phi}_c$ is not time dependent. But $\{I_c(t), \mathbf{p}_c(t), e_c(t), \boldsymbol{\pi}_c(t)\}$ are stochastic processes. Hence at any time t we can write the theoretical population distribution function of $\{I_c(t), \mathbf{p}_c(t), e_c(t), \boldsymbol{\pi}_c(t), \boldsymbol{\phi}_c\}$ at t as F_t. With distributions derived from F_t, it follows that at any t, the following are random variables: $d\log(p_c^* e_c)$, $d\log(M_c e_c)$, $d\log(M_c^*)$, $d\log(\Pi_c e_c)$, and $d\log(\Pi_c^*)$.

Using the derived distribution of those random variables, we can define their theoretical population means by $\theta_1 = E[d\log(p_c^* e_c)]$, $\theta_2 = E[d\log(M_c e_c)]$, $\theta_3 = E[d\log(M_c^*)]$, $\theta_4 = E[d\log(\Pi_c e_c)]$, and $\theta_5 = E[d\log(\Pi_c^*)]$, where $(\theta_1, \theta_2, \theta_3, \theta_4, \theta_5) = (\theta_1(t), \theta_2(t), \theta_3(t), \theta_4(t), \theta_5(t))$ is a nonstochastic function of time. Now consider sampling from the theoretical population K times to draw the $k \in \{1, \ldots, K\}$ actual countries. The countries are assumed to have representative consumers having characteristics that are produced from the continuous theoretical population distribution F_t at t.

Definition 2. Let $s_k = H_k / \sum_{\kappa=1}^{K} H_\kappa$ be country k's fraction of total economic union population.

Define the kth country's expenditure share W_k of the economic union's monetary service flow by:

$$W_k = \frac{M_k^* \Pi_k^* p_k^* e_k s_k}{\sum_{\kappa=1}^{K} M_\kappa^* \Pi_\kappa^* p_\kappa^* e_\kappa s_\kappa} = \frac{M_k \Pi_k^* e_k s_k}{\sum_{\kappa=1}^{K} M_\kappa \Pi_\kappa^* e_\kappa s_\kappa}$$
$$= \frac{M_k^* \Pi_k e_k s_k}{\sum_{\kappa=1}^{K} M_\kappa^* \Pi_\kappa e_\kappa s_\kappa}. \tag{6.1}$$

The fact that this definition is in terms of total national expenditure shares, rather than per capita shares, is evident from the fact that:

$$\frac{M_k^* \Pi_k^* p_k^* e_k s_k}{\sum_{\kappa=1}^{K} M_\kappa^* \Pi_\kappa^* p_\kappa^* e_\kappa s_\kappa} = \frac{M_k^* \Pi_k^* p_k^* e_k H_k}{\sum_{\kappa=1}^{K} M_\kappa^* \Pi_\kappa^* p_\kappa^* e_\kappa H_\kappa}.$$

Observe that $0 \leq W_k \leq 1$ for all k, and $\sum_{k=1}^{K} W_k = 1$. We thereby can treat $\{W_1, \ldots, W_K\}$ as a probability distribution in computing the following Divisia means by our stochastic heterogeneous-countries approach to aggregation over countries.

Definition 3. Aggregating over countries, define the monetary-sector-weighted Divisia consumer price index, $p^* = p^*(t)$, by:

$$d \log p^* = \sum_{k=1}^{K} W_k d \log (p_k^* e_k). \tag{6.2}$$

Definition 4. Define the economic union's nominal, M, and real, M^*, per-capita monetary service flows by:

$$d \log M = \sum_{k=1}^{K} W_k d \log (s_k M_k e_k)$$

and

$$d \log M^* = \sum_{k=1}^{K} W_k d \log (s_k M_k^*).$$

Definition 5. Define the economic union's nominal, Π, and real, Π^*, monetary user-cost prices by

$$d \log \Pi = \sum_{k=1}^{K} W_k d \log (\Pi_k e_k)$$

and

$$d \log \Pi^* = \sum_{k=1}^{K} W_k d \log \left(\Pi_k^*\right).$$

When we draw from the derived population distributions, the frequency with which we draw $d \log p_k^* e_k$, $d \log (s_k M_k e_k)$, $d\, log(s_k M_k^*)$, $d \log (\Pi_k e_k)$, and $d \log (\Pi_k^*)$ is W_k. From Khinchine's theorem, assuming independent sampling, we find that $d \log p^*$, $d \log M$, $d \log M^*$, $d \log \Pi$, and $d \log \Pi^*$ are sample means of distributions having population means equal to $\theta_1(t)$, $\theta_2(t)$, $\theta_3(t)$, $\theta_4(t)$, and $\theta_5(t)$, respectively. In addition, $d \log p^*$, $d \log M$, $d \log M^*$, $d \log \Pi$, and $d \log \Pi^*$ converge in probability as $K \to \infty$ to $\theta_1(t), \theta_2(t), \theta_3(t), \theta_4(t)$, and $\theta_5(t)$, respectively. It is this convergence to theoretical population properties that accounts for this aggregation approach's name, "the stochastic convergence approach," in Barnett (1979a).

Observe that there is no assumption that a representative agent exists over countries. We assume in this heterogeneous agents approach only that representative agents exist within countries. Aggregation over countries is defined to be estimation of the moments of the stochastic processes generated by sampling from the underlying theoretical population that produces the countries' representative agents. When in later sections we consider the existence of multilateral and unilateral representative agents over countries, we add strong assumptions about the *realized* tastes after sampling from the theoretical population.

In summary, the perspective from which our heterogeneous agents approach is produced is prior to the drawing from the theoretical distribution, so that random variables have not yet been realized and all dynamic solution paths are stochastic processes induced by the randomness of $\{I_c(t), \mathbf{p}_c(t), e_c(t), \boldsymbol{\pi}_c(t), \boldsymbol{\phi}_c\}$. No assumptions are made about the precise form in which realized tastes relate to each other across countries. The heterogeneous-agents approach tracks aggregator functions within countries. But this approach does not require assumptions sufficient for the existence of microeconomic aggregator functions over countries. After aggregating over countries, this approach tracks moments of aggregate stochastic processes and is interpreted relative to the underlying population distributions.

In contrast, our multilateral and unilateral representative agent approaches add assumptions regarding the functional relationship among realized tastes of countries already in existence, and seek to track the realized aggregator function over countries. Under those additional assumptions producing the existence of an aggregator function over the economic union, the heterogeneous agents approach reduces to the multilateral representative agent approach as a special case. Although the two approaches have different interpretations, because of the difference in perspective regarding prior versus post sampling, the multilateral economic agent approach is nevertheless mathematically a nested special case of the heterogeneous agents approach.

It is important to recognize the following proof's dependence upon the definition of p^* in equation (6.2), with the share weights determined by Definition 2. If any other weights, such as consumption-expenditure share or GDP weights, had been used in defining p^*, then Theorem 1 would not hold.

Theorem 1. $M = M^* p^*$ *and* $\Pi = \Pi^* p^*$.

Proof. The method of proof is proof by contradiction. First consider M, and suppose that $M \neq M^* p^*$. Then

$$d \log M \neq d \log (M^* p^*) = d \log M^* + d \log p^*.$$

So by Lemma 1, $\sum_{k=1}^{K} W_k d \log(s_k M_k e_k) \neq \sum_{k=1}^{K} W_k d \log(s_k M_k / p_k^*) + d \log p^*$.

$$= \sum_{k=1}^{K} W_k d \log(s_k M_k) - \sum_{k=1}^{K} W_k d \log p_k^* + d \log p^*.$$

$$\textit{Hence} \sum_{k=1}^{K} W_k d \log(s_k M_k)$$

$$\neq \sum_{k=1}^{K} W_k d \log(s_k M_k) - \sum_{k=1}^{K} W_k d \log p_k^*$$

$$+ d \log p^* - \sum_{k=1}^{K} W_k d \log e_k$$

$$= \sum_{k=1}^{K} W_k d \log(s_k M_k) - \sum_{k=1}^{K} W_k d \log(p_k^* e_k) + d \log p^*$$

$$= \sum_{k=1}^{K} W_k d \log(s_k M_k),$$

which is a contradiction. The last equality follows from equation (6.2) in Definition 3.

Now consider Π, and suppose that $\Pi \neq \Pi^* p^*$. Then

$$d \log \Pi \neq d \log \left(\Pi^* p^*\right) = d \log \Pi^* + d \log p^*.$$

By Definitions 3 and 5, it follows that

$$\sum_{k=1}^{K} W_k d \log(\Pi_k e_k) \neq \sum_{k=1}^{K} W_k d \log\left(\Pi_k^*\right) + \sum_{k=1}^{K} W_k d \log\left(p_k^* e_k\right).$$

Hence by Lemma 1, we have that

$$\sum_{k=1}^{K} W_k d\log\left(\Pi_k^* p_k^* e_k\right) \neq \sum_{k=1}^{K} W_k d\log\left(\Pi_k^*\right) + \sum_{k=1}^{K} W_k d\log\left(p_k^* e_k\right),$$

or

$$\sum_{k=1}^{K} W_k d\log\left(\Pi_k^*\right) + \sum_{k=1}^{K} W_k d\log\left(p_k^* e_k\right) \neq \sum_{k=1}^{K} W_k d\log\left(\Pi_k^*\right) + \sum_{k=1}^{K} W_k d\log\left(p_k^* e_k\right),$$

which is a contradiction. ∎

The following theorem proves Fisher's factor reversal property for the monetary quantity and user cost aggregates over countries. In particular, we prove that total expenditure on monetary services aggregated over countries is the same, whether computed from the product of the economic union's quantity and user cost aggregates or from the sum of the products within countries. The multiplications by s_k convert to per capita values relative to total economic union population, while the within-country aggregates, M_k^*, remain per capita relative to each country's own population.

Theorem 2. $M^* \Pi = \sum_{k=1}^{K} \left(M_k^* s_k\right) \Pi_k e_k.$

Proof. The method of proof is proof by contradiction. So assume that

$$d\log\left(M^*\right) + d\log\left(\Pi\right) \neq d\log\left(\sum_{k=1}^{K} M_k^* s_k \Pi_k e_k\right) = \frac{d\left(\sum_{k=1}^{K} M_k^* s_k \Pi_k e_k\right)}{\sum_{k=1}^{K} M_k^* s_k \Pi_k e_k}.$$

Hence by Definitions 4 and 5, it follows that

$$\sum_{k=1}^{K} W_k d \log (s_k M_k^*) + \sum_{k=1}^{K} W_k d \log (\Pi_k e_k) \neq \frac{d\left(\sum_{k=1}^{K} M_k^* s_k \Pi_k e_k\right)}{\sum_{k=1}^{K} M_k^* s_k \Pi_k e_k}.$$

Multiplying through by $\sum_{k=1}^{K} M_k^* s_k \Pi_k e_k$ and using Definition 2, we get

$$\sum_{k=1}^{K} (M_k^* s_k \Pi_k e_k) d \log (s_k M_k^*) + \sum_{k=1}^{K} (M_k^* s_k \Pi_k e_k) d \log (\Pi_k e_k) \neq d\left(\sum_{k=1}^{K} M_k^* s_k \Pi_k e_k\right).$$

So

$$\sum_{k=1}^{K} (M_k^* s_k \Pi_k e_k) \frac{d\left(s_k M_k^*\right)}{s_k M_k^*} + \sum_{k=1}^{K} (M_k^* s_k \Pi_k e_k) \frac{d\left(\Pi_k e_k\right)}{\Pi_k e_k} \neq \sum_{k=1}^{K} d\left(M_k^* s_k \Pi_k e_k\right).$$

Hence

$$\sum_{k=1}^{K} (\Pi_k e_k) d\left(s_k M_k^*\right) + \sum_{k=1}^{K} \left(M_k^* s_k\right) d\left(\Pi_k e_k\right) \neq \sum_{k=1}^{K} d\left(M_k^* s_k \Pi_k e_k\right).$$

But taking the total differential of $M_k^* s_k \Pi_k e_k$, we have

$$d(M_k^* s_k \Pi_k e_k) = (\Pi_k e_k)\, d(M_k^* s_k) + (M_k^* s_k) d\left(\Pi_k e_k\right),$$

so that

$$\sum_{k=1}^{K}(\Pi_k e_k)d\left(s_k M_k^*\right)+\sum_{k=1}^{K}\left(M_k^* s_k\right)d\left(\Pi_k e_k\right)$$
$$\neq \sum_{k=1}^{K}(\Pi_k e_k)d(M_k^* s_k)+\sum_{k=1}^{K}\left(M_k^* s_k\right)d(\Pi_k e_k),$$

which is a contradiction. ■

6.5. Special Cases

We now consider some special cases of our results. First we consider the case of purchasing power parity. While the purchasing power parity assumption is not applicable to many economic unions, this special case is useful in understanding the forms of the more general formulas we have derived without purchasing power parity and could be useful in applying this theory to other economic unions in which purchasing power parity may apply.

6.5.1. *Purchasing Power Parity*

Definition 6. We define $E = \{e_k\colon k = 1, \ldots, K\}$ to satisfy purchasing power parity, if $p_j^*/p_i^* = e_i/e_j$ for all countries $i, j \in \{1, \ldots, K\}$. Under this definition, it equivalently follows that there exists a price p^0 such that $p^0 = p_i^* e_i = p_j^* e_j$ for all $i, j \in \{1, \ldots, K\}$.

Theorem 3. *If E satisfies purchasing power parity, then*

$$W_k = \frac{M_k^* \Pi_k^* s_k}{\sum_{\kappa=1}^{K} M_\kappa^* \Pi_\kappa^* s_\kappa} \tag{6.3}$$

Proof. See Barnett (2003). ■

Theorem 4. *If E satisfies purchasing power parity, then*

$$d\log p^* = d\log\left(p_k^* e_k\right) \tag{6.4}$$

for all countries $k \in \{1, \ldots, K\}$.

Proof. See Barnett (2003). ■

Comparing (6.3) with (6.1), and (6.4) with (6.2) displays the sources of the complications in (6.1) and (6.2) caused by violations of purchasing power parity.

6.5.2. *Multilateral Representative Agent over the Economic Union*

In this section, we define the concept of a multilateral representative agent. In the next section, we define a unilateral representative agent over countries to be a representative agent who considers the same goods in different countries to be perfect substitutes, regardless of the country of residence of the purchaser or the country within which the good or asset is acquired. The existence of a unilateral representative agent has been implicit in the existing studies using the "direct method" of aggregation over monetary assets in the euro area. As we shall show, the existence of a unilateral representative agent requires extremely strong assumptions. Without a homogeneous culture and the vast population migrations that could produce that uniformity, this assumption will not apply. The existence of a multilateral representative agent requires far more reasonable assumptions.

If tastes across countries do converge in the distant future, the convergence is more likely to be towards a homogeneous multilateral representative agent, which we shall define, rather than towards a unilateral representative agent. A homogeneous multilateral representative agent recognizes the existence of country specific tastes, but equates those tastes across countries. A unilateral representative agent does not recognize the relevancy of countries at all and thereby does not recognize the existence of country specific tastes. Country specific utility functions cannot be factored out of the economic union's tastes (i.e., weak separability of country tastes fails); and the country subscripts, j and k, disappear from the decision of the unilateral representative agent. The allocation of goods across countries is indeterminate in that case.

6.5.2.1. *Multilateral Representative Agent with Heterogeneous Tastes*

We begin by defining relevant assumptions and produce the theory of a multilateral representative agent. We show that the existence of a multilateral representative agent is a special case of our heterogeneous countries theory. We further show that a homogeneous multilateral representative agent exists under stronger assumptions.

As described in the previous section, our representative agent approach for aggregating over countries treats countries as already realized, so that variables and functions no longer are random. Hence we can consider realized functional structure aggregated over realized countries. The following assumption is needed, and begins to become weak only after the introduction of a common currency.

Assumption 1. Suppose there is convergence over the economic union in the following sense. Let there exist $R = R(t)$ such that $R_k = R(t)$ for all $k \in \{1, \ldots, K\}$ and all t.

The existence of a representative agent is necessary and sufficient for the nonexistence of distribution effects.[11] Distribution effects introduce second moments and possibly higher order moments into demand functions aggregated over consumers. The existence of such second and higher order moments in the macroeconomy can cause policy to influence distributions of income and wealth across consumers. Assumption 1 rules out certain possible distribution effects. Additional assumptions ruling out other sources of distribution effects will be needed as we consider further special cases.

By its definition, the benchmark asset, unlike "monetary" assets, provides no services other than its investment rate of return, and hence cannot enter the utility function of an infinitely lived representative agent.[12] Therefore, differences in tastes across countries

---

[11] See Gorman (1953).

[12] See, e.g., Barnett and Serletis (2000, p. 53). In the finite planning horizon case, the benchmark asset enters utility only in the terminal period to produce a savings motive to endow the next planning horizon.

play no role in decisions regarding benchmark asset holdings by a representative agent within the economic union. For that reason, the existence of a common benchmark rate for all countries is necessary for a representative agent over countries. A representative agent within the economic union would hold only the highest yielding of multiple possible benchmark assets. This conclusion is not necessary in our thereby-more-general heterogeneous countries approach.

With Assumption 1, we also can consider the following stronger assumption. We assume that all K countries have already been drawn from their theoretical population of potential countries. Then the tastes of the representative consumers in each country are realized and are no longer random. The following assumption produces the existence of aggregator functions, (U, V, G), over the individual realized countries' tastes, (u_k, g_k), for $k \in \{1, \ldots, K\}$.

Assumption 2a: Assume that there exists a representative consumer over the economic union. Within that representative agent's intertemporal utility function, assume that $(\mathbf{m}_1^*(t), \ldots, \mathbf{m}_K^*(t), \mathbf{x}_1(t), \ldots, \mathbf{x}_K(t))$ is intertemporally weakly separable from $(\mathbf{m}_1^*(\tau), \ldots, \mathbf{m}_K^*(\tau), \mathbf{x}_1(\tau), \ldots, \mathbf{x}_K(\tau))$ for all $t \neq \tau$, and also assume that monetary assets are weakly separable from consumer goods.

As defined in Section 1, $\mathbf{x}_k$ is the vector of instantaneous per-capita goods consumption rates in country k relative to the population of country k. Then $s_k\mathbf{x}_k$ is the per-capita real consumption vector relative to total economic union population, $H = \sum_{k=1}^{K} H_k$. Since contemporaneous consumption of goods and services is weakly separable from future consumption, a contemporaneous category utility function exists of the form

$$U = U[\breve{V}(s_1\mathbf{m}_1^*, \ldots, s_K\mathbf{m}_K^*), \breve{G}(s_1\mathbf{x}_1, \ldots, s_K\mathbf{x}_K)], \qquad (6.5a)$$

where $\breve{V}$ and $\breve{G}$ are linearly homogeneous.

Assumption 2b: Assume further that consumption of monetary assets and goods are weakly separable among countries, so that the contemporaneous utility function has the blockwise weakly separable form

$$U = U\{V[s_1 u_1(\mathbf{m}_1^*), \ldots, s_K u_K(\mathbf{m}_K^*)], G[s_1 g_1(\mathbf{x}_1), \ldots, s_K g_K(\mathbf{x}_K)]\}. \tag{6.5b}$$

Assume that the functions V, G, u_k, and g_k do not change over time and are linearly homogeneous for all $k \in \{1, \ldots, K\}$.[13]

The dependency of u_k and g_k on k permits heterogeneity of tastes across countries. In the next subsection, we shall explore the special case of homogeneity of tastes across countries. As in our heterogeneous agents approach, the subscript k identifies the country of residence of the owner of the asset and not necessarily the country within which the asset is purchased or located. Hence, equation (6.5b) requires that the tastes that determine the utility functions, u_k and g_k, are those of the residents of country k, regardless of the country within which the residents have deposited their assets. Note that equation (6.5a) does not require that tastes of consumer's residing in country k exist independently of the tastes of consumers residing in other countries. The existence of stable country-specific tastes, u_k and g_k, exist only under the stronger assumption (6.5b).

Equation (6.5b) could equivalently be written as

$$U = U\{V[u_1(s_1\mathbf{m}_1^*), \ldots, u_K(s_K\mathbf{m}_K^*)], G[g_1(s_1\mathbf{x}_1), \ldots, g_K(s_K\mathbf{x}_K)]\},$$

because of the linear homogeneity of the utility functions, u_k and g_k. But we prefer the form of equation (6.5b), since it makes clear our ability to aggregate first within countries to acquire the within-country monetary aggregates, $M_k^* = u_k(\mathbf{m}_k^*)$, and the within-country consumer goods aggregates, $X_k = g_k(\mathbf{x}_k)$. Note that M_k^* and X_k are in per capita terms relative to country k's population. We then can

[13]The assumption that the functions do not move over time does not preclude subjective discounting of future utility within the integrand of the intertemporal utility integral.

aggregate over countries to acquire the economic union's monetary aggregate over countries, $M^* = V[s_1 u_1(\mathbf{m}_1^*), \ldots, s_K u_K(\mathbf{m}_K^*)] = V[s_1 M_1^*, \ldots, s_K M_K^*]$, and the economic union's consumer goods aggregate over countries, $X = G[s_1 g_1(\mathbf{x}_1), \ldots, s_K g_K(\mathbf{x}_K)] = G[s_1 X_1, \ldots, s_K X_K]$. Note that M* and X are in per capita terms relative to total economic union population. Our proofs below demonstrate the capability to aggregate recursively in that manner.

Under Assumptions 1, 2a, and 2b, let $I = I(t)$ be the instantaneous rate of expenditure. It is budgeted to t by the representative consumer in a prior stage intertemporal allocation. Then we can define the following contemporaneous, conditional decision at instant of time t.

Decision 1: Choose $(\mathbf{m}_1^*, \ldots, \mathbf{m}_K^*, \mathbf{x}_1, \ldots, \mathbf{x}_K)$ to

$$\text{maximize } \mathrm{U}\{V[s_1 u_1(\mathbf{m}_1^*), \ldots, s_K u_K(\mathbf{m}_K^*)], G[s_1 g_1(\mathbf{x}_1), \ldots, s_K g_K(\mathbf{x}_K)]\}$$

$$\text{subject to} \sum_{k=1}^{K} s_k \mathbf{m}_k^{*\prime} \boldsymbol{\pi}_k e_k + \sum_{k=1}^{K} s_k \mathbf{x}_k' \mathbf{p}_k e_k = I.$$

Definition 7. We define a multilateral representative consumer to be an economic agent who solves Decision 1 under Assumptions 1, 2a, and 2b.

Note that our definitions of real and nominal money balances have not changed from those in Section 1. Nominal balances owned by residents of country k are deflated by p_k^* to acquire real balances, where p_k^* is the unit cost function dual to the consumer goods quantity aggregator function, $g_k(\mathbf{x}_k)$, within country k. We are not yet accepting assumptions that would be sufficient for existence of a single consumer-price index that could be used to deflate nominal balances within all countries in the economic union to real balances in those countries. Hence p_k^* is not independent of k. Our economic union consumer-goods price aggregate, p^*, is relevant to deflation of monetary balances only after monetary balances have been aggregated over countries.

Observe that Assumption 1 does not require convergence of rates of return on all monetary assets across countries. To produce the multilateral representative consumer, Assumption 1 requires only that consumers in all countries of the economic union have access to the same benchmark rate of return on pure investment. We now consider the implications of a multilateral representative agent. In the next section, we then focus on the case of a unilateral representative agent, requiring the adoption of very strong assumptions.

The following lemmas now are immediate.

Lemma 2. *Under Assumptions 1, 2a, and 2b, the representative consumer's allocation of $I(t)$ over goods and monetary services will solve Decision 1.*

Proof. Follows from known results on two stage budgeting, where the first stage is intertemporal. One need only redefine the variables in the continuous time analog to Barnett (1978, section 3; 1980, section 3.1; or 1987, sections 2.1–2.2). ∎

Lemma 3. *Under Assumptions 1, 2a, and 2b, let $X_k = g_k(\mathbf{x}_k)$ be the exact consumer goods per-capita quantity aggregate over $\mathbf{x}_k$ for country k, relative to the population of country k, and let $X = G(s_1X_1, \ldots, s_KX_K)$ be the exact consumer goods per capita quantity aggregate over countries, relative to total economic union population. Then p_k^* is the exact price dual to X_k, and P^* is the exact price dual to X, where P^* is defined such that*

$$d\log P^* = \sum_{k=1}^{K}\left(\frac{X_k p_k^* e_k}{\sum_{\kappa=1}^{K} X_\kappa p_\kappa^* e_\kappa}\right) d\log p_k^* e_k. \tag{6.6}$$

Proof. The result regarding p_k^* follows, since it was defined in Section 1 to be the true cost of living index of X_k. The result on P^* follows by a proof analogous to that of Theorem 2, since duality of P^* and X implies, from factor reversal, that

$$XP^* = \sum_{k=1}^{K} X_k p_k^* e_k. \tag{6.7}$$

This equation accounts for the form of the share weights in equation (6.6). ■

Note that P^*, defined by equation (6.6), and p^*, defined by equation (6.2), are not the same. Both consumer price indexes are needed for different purposes, as we shall discuss further below. Now consider the following decision, within which aggregation over consumer goods has already occurred.

Decision 2: Choose $(\mathbf{m}_1^*, \ldots, \mathbf{m}_K^*, X)$ to

$$\text{maximize } U\{V[s_1 u_1(\mathbf{m}_1^*), \ldots, s_K u_K(\mathbf{m}_K^*)], X\}$$
$$\text{subject to} \sum_{k=1}^{K} s_k \mathbf{m}_k^{*\prime} \boldsymbol{\pi}_k e_k + XP^* = I.$$

The following theorem establishes the connection between Decisions 1 and 2.

Theorem 5. *Under Assumptions* 1, 2a, *and* 2b, *let* $(\mathbf{m}_1^*, \ldots, \mathbf{m}_K^*, \mathbf{x}_1, \ldots, \mathbf{x}_K)$ *solve Decision 1, and let X and P^* be defined as in Lemma* 3. *Then* $(\mathbf{m}_1^*, \ldots, \mathbf{m}_K^*, X)$ *will solve Decision* 2.

Proof. Follows from Lemma 3 and well known results on two stage budgeting. ■

Theorem 5 permits us to concentrate on aggregation over monetary assets within countries and then over countries, while using a quantity and price aggregate for consumer goods. Theorem 5 also demonstrates our need for the P^* price index in the prior aggregation over consumer goods.

In Decision 3, we now define a "second stage" decision, in which funds preallocated to monetary-services expenditure within the economic union are allocated over countries. In Decision 4, we then define a "third stage" decision, in which funds preallocated to monetary-services expenditure within the each country are allocated over assets in the country.

Let Π_k for each $k \in \{1, \ldots, K\}$ be as in Definition 1. We then can define the following decision.

Decision 3: For given value of X, choose $(M_1^*, \ldots, M_K^*)$ to

$$\text{maximize } V(s_1 M_1^*, \ldots, s_K M_K^*)$$

$$\text{subject to} \sum_{k=1}^{K} s_k M_k^* \Pi_k e_k = I - XP^*. \tag{6.8}$$

Decision 4: For each $k \in \{1, \ldots, K\}$ choose $\mathbf{m}_k^*$ to

$$\text{maximize } \mathrm{u}_k(\mathbf{m}_k^*)$$

$$\text{subject to } \mathbf{m}_k^{*\prime} \boldsymbol{\pi}_k = M_k^* \Pi_k.$$

The following two corollaries to Theorem 5 relate to Decisions 3 and 4.

Corollary 1 to Theorem 5. *Under Assumptions* 1, 2a, *and* 2b, *let* $(\mathbf{m}_1^*, \ldots, \mathbf{m}_K^*, X)$ *solve Decision* 2. *Define* P^* *as in equation* (6.6) *and the vector of user costs* $\Pi = (\Pi_1, \ldots, \Pi_K)$ *as in Definition* 1. *Then* $(M_1^*, \ldots, M_K^*)$ *will solve Decision* 3, *where* $M_k^* = u_k(\mathbf{m}_k^*)$ *for all* $k \in \{1, \ldots, K\}$.

Proof. Follows from well known results on two stage budgeting. ■

Corollary 2 to Theorem 5. *Under Assumptions* 1, 2a, *and* 2b, *let* $(\mathbf{m}_1^*, \ldots, \mathbf{m}_K^*, X)$ *solve Decision* 2, *and let* $M_k^* = u_k(\mathbf{m}_k^*)$ *for all* $k \in \{1, \ldots, K\}$. *Define* Π_k *as in Definition* 1. *Then* $\mathbf{m}_k^*$ *also will solve Decision* 4 *for all* $k \in \{1, \ldots, K\}$.

Proof. Follows from well known results on two stage budgeting and a simple proof by contradiction. Suppose $M_k^* = u_k(\mathbf{m}_k^*)$, but $\mathbf{m}_k^*$ does not solve Decision 4 for all $k \in \{1, \ldots, K\}$. Then $(\mathbf{m}_1^*, \ldots, \mathbf{m}_K^*, X)$ cannot solve Decision 2. ■

Decision 4 defines the representative consumers assumed to exist within countries in Section 2. Under the assumptions in Definition 7 for the existence of a multilateral representative consumer, Corollary 2 to Theorem 5 proves that the decisions of the representative consumers in Section 2 are nested as conditional decisions within the decision of the multilateral representative consumer. Hence our results in Section 2 can be used to aggregate within countries, regardless of whether aggregation over countries is by our heterogeneous countries approach or by our multilateral representative consumer approach.

After the aggregation within countries is complete, Corollary 1 to Theorem 5 demonstrates that Decision 3 can be used to aggregate over countries, if we accept the assumptions necessary for the existence of a multilateral representative agent. The monetary quantity aggregator function for aggregation over countries then is V, and a Divisia index can be used to track V in the usual manner.

Observe that Decision 4 would be unaffected, if the vector of within-country user costs $\boldsymbol{\pi}_k$ and the aggregate within-country user cost Π_k were changed to real user costs, since all that would be involved is the division of each constraint by p_k^*. Hence that constraint would continue to hold, if all values in the constraint were in real terms.

But observe that in Decisions 2 and 3, the consumer price index P^* on the right hand side of equation (6.8) is not the same as the consumer price index p_k^* needed to deflate the user costs on the left hand side to real value. In addition, the consumer price index p_k^* used to deflate each term on the left hand side is different for each $k \in \{1, \ldots, K\}$. Hence the constraint would be broken, if all variables on both sides of the constraint were replaced by real values. This would amount to dividing each term by a different price index. Also recall that conversion of $\mathbf{m}_k^*$ to nominal balances requires multiplication by p_k^*, which is different for each country k.

The following illustration can further clarify the need for two price indexes in modeling. Consider the following decision using the exact aggregates both over monetary assets and goods within the economic union.

Decision 5: Choose (M^*, X) to

$$\text{maximize } U(M^*, X)$$
$$\text{subject to} \quad M^*\Pi + XP^* = I.$$

The solution will be of the form

$$\begin{pmatrix} M^* \\ X \end{pmatrix} = D(I, \Pi, P^*) = D(I, \Pi^* p^*, P^*). \tag{6.9a}$$

But by Lemma 1 and the homogeneity of degree zero of demand, we equivalently can write:

$$\begin{pmatrix} M^* \\ X \end{pmatrix} = D\left(\frac{I}{p^*}, \Pi^*, \frac{P^*}{p^*}\right), \tag{6.9b}$$

or

$$\begin{pmatrix} M^* \\ X \end{pmatrix} = \widehat{D}\left(\frac{I}{P^*}, \frac{\Pi^* p^*}{P^*}\right), \tag{6.9c}$$

where

$$\widehat{D}\left(\frac{I}{P^*}, \frac{\Pi^* p^*}{P^*}\right) = D\left(\frac{I}{P^*}, \frac{\Pi^* p^*}{P^*}, 1\right).$$

As can be seen from equations (9b) and (9c), there is no way to remove the simultaneous dependence of the solution demand function systems upon the two price indexes, P^* and p^*. The form of the demand system in (9a) is in terms of nominal total expenditure ("income"), I. The form of the demand system in (9b) is in terms of real income relative to p^* aggregate prices. The form in (9c) is in terms of real income relative to P^* aggregate prices. None of the three possible forms results in either p^* or P^* canceling out. In addition, Lemma 1 requires that conversion of M* to nominal balances must be relative to p^* prices.

The following theorem establishes the relationship between our heterogeneous countries approach and our multilateral representative agent approach.

Theorem 6. *Under Assumptions 1, 2a, and 2b, let* $(M_1^*, \ldots, M_K^*)$ *solve Decision 3, and let* M^* *be as defined in Definition 4. Then*

$$d \log M^* = d \log V(s_1 M_1^*, \ldots, s_K M_K^*).$$

Proof. Follows from the exact tracking of the Divisia index in continuous time. ■

Our multilateral representative agent theory produces conditions under which an economic (rather than statistical) monetary aggregate exists over countries. When an economic monetary aggregator function, V, exists over countries, Theorem 6 shows that our index number M^*, introduced in Definition 4, will exactly track the theoretical aggregate. In particular, we have demonstrated that our heterogeneous agents approach for aggregating over countries reduces to the multilateral approach under assumptions 1, 2a, and 2b, since both approaches then produce the same monetary aggregate, M^*, over countries. In addition, Π_k and Π_k^* defined in Definition 5 will remain dual to M^*, since the proofs of Theorems 1 and 2 remain valid under Assumptions 1, 2a, and 2b.

We have demonstrated at all stages of aggregation that our multilateral representative agent approach is nested within our heterogeneous countries approach as a special case under Assumptions 1, 2a, and 2b. Theorem 6 is the result at the level of aggregation over countries, while Corollary 2 to Theorem 5 is the result for aggregation within countries.

Also observe that since the proofs of Theorems 1 and 2 remain valid under our additional assumptions in this section, it follows that we must continue to deflate nominal M aggregated over countries to real M^* using p^*, not P^*. The correct dual to aggregate real consumption X is P^*, which should be used to deflate nominal to real consumption expenditure. Regarding the computation of P^*

and its possible use as an inflation target, see Diewert (2002). It is important to recognize that p^* and P^* both play important roles in this theory, and neither is an acceptable substitute for the other.[14] These conclusions hold in both our heterogeneous countries approach and in the multilateral representative agents special case acquired when the benchmark rate is the same for all countries in the economic union.

6.5.2.2. *Multilateral Representative Agent with Homogeneous Tastes*

We now proceed to the far more restrictive case of a homogeneous multilateral representative agent who imputes identical tastes to the residents of all countries in the economic union. An initial necessary assumption is Assumption 1. As shown by Theorem 7 below, the seeming paradox of the existence of two consumer price indices — p^* to deflate nominal money balances to real balances and P^* to deflate nominal consumption expenditure to real aggregate consumption — disappears under the following additional important assumption.

Assumption 3: Suppose there is convergence over the economic union in the following strong sense. Let there exist $\hat{P} = \hat{P}(t)$such that

$$\frac{d}{dt}[\log(p_k^*(t)e_k(t))] = \frac{d}{dt}[\log \hat{P}(t)] \tag{6.10}$$

for all $k \in \{1, \ldots, K\}$ and all t.

[14]Although perhaps somewhat surprising, the need for two different consumer price indexes is not entirely without precedent. The theory that produces the relative price version of Theil's (1971, p. 578, eq. 6.19) Rotterdam consumer demand system model also requires two consumer price indexes: the Divisia price index with average share weights to deflate nominal income to real income and the Frisch consumer price index with marginal budget share weights to deflate nominal to real relative prices. But that Rotterdam model phenomenon has a different source.

The following theorem is immediate.

Theorem 7. *Under Assumption 3, the following equation holds for all nonnegative* $(e_1, \ldots, e_K)$ *and all nonnegative* $(p_1^*, \ldots, p_K^*)$*:*

$$d \log p^*(p_1^* e_1, \ldots, p_K^* e_K)$$
$$= d \log P^*(p_1^* e_1, \ldots, p_K^* e_K).$$

Proof. By equation (6.10), $d \log (p_k^* e_k) = d \log \hat{P}$ for all $k \in \{1, \ldots, K\}$ and all t. Hence $d \log p^* = d \log \hat{P}$ by equation (6.2), and $d \log P^* = d \log \hat{P}$ by equation (6.10). So $d \log p^* = d \log P^*$. ■

We now consider further the case of a homogeneous multilateral representative agent, but first we shall need the following lemma.

Lemma 4. *Under Assumptions 1, 2a, 2b, and 3, there exists g such that* $g_k = g$ *for all* $k \in \{1, \ldots, K\}$ *so that tastes for consumer goods are identical across countries.*

Proof. By equation (6.10), it follows that $d \log[p_k^*(t) e_k(t)] = d \log \hat{P}[\mathbf{p}_k(t) e_k(t)]$ for all $k \in \{1, \ldots, K\}$. Hence the same consumer goods price aggregator function $\hat{P}$ applies for all $k \in \{1, \ldots, K\}$. But the consumer goods quantity aggregator function, g_k, is dual to the consumer goods price aggregator function. Hence the consumer goods quantity aggregator functions g_k must also be independent of k. ■

To move further towards the existence of a homogeneous multilateral representative consumer, we also need the following assumption, which is analogous to Assumption 3.

Assumption 4: Suppose that convergence over the economic union results in the existence of $\hat{\Pi}$ such that

$$\frac{d}{dt}\left[\log\left(\Pi_k(t) e_k(t)\right)\right] = \frac{d}{dt}[\log \hat{\Pi}(t)]$$

for all $k \in \{1, \ldots, K\}$ and all t.

Clearly under this assumption, it follows from Definition 5 that $\hat{\Pi}(t) = \Pi(t)$ for all t. The following lemma depends heavily upon Assumption 4.

Lemma 5. *Under Assumptions 1, 2a, 2b, and 4, there exists u such that $u_k = u$ for all $k \in \{1, \ldots, K\}$, so that tastes for monetary services are identical across countries.*

Proof. Analogous to the proof of Lemma 4. ■

The form of Decision 1 now is as follows.

Decision 1a: Choose $(\mathbf{m}_1^*, \ldots, \mathbf{m}_K^*, \mathbf{x}_1, \ldots, \mathbf{x}_K)$ to

$$\text{maximize } U\{V[s_1 u(\mathbf{m}_1^*), \ldots, s_K u(\mathbf{m}_K^*)], G[s_1 g(\mathbf{x}_1), \ldots, s_K g(\mathbf{x}_K)]\}$$
$$\text{subject to } \textstyle\sum_{k=1}^{K} s_k \mathbf{m}_k^{*\prime} \boldsymbol{\pi}_k e_k + \sum_{k=1}^{K} s_k \mathbf{x}_k^{\prime} \mathbf{p}_k e_k = I.$$

Observation 1: Under Assumptions 1, 2a, 2b, 3, and 4, the solutions to Decisions 1 and 1a will be the same, as is evident from Lemmas 4 and 5. Because of the homogeneity of tastes across countries in Decision 1a, we have the following definition.

Definition 8. We define a homogeneous multilateral representative agent to be an economic agent who solves Decision 1a under Assumptions 1, 2a, 2b, 3, and 4.

Observe that despite the homogeneity of tastes across countries, the decision remains multilateral, as a result of the assumption of blockwise weak separability of tastes across countries. That separability assumption produces existence of within-country tastes, u, independent of consumption in other countries. The fact that the tastes are identical for all countries in the economic union does not negate the existence of those tastes, u.

In econometric studies, there could be reason to investigate convergence of the general multilateral representative consumer towards the homogeneous multilateral representative agent. But for data construction purposes, we see no advantage to adopting the homogeneous multilateral representative agent model. We have shown that the general multilateral representative agent model can be used to construct aggregates recursively, first within countries and then across countries. When producing the aggregates within countries, there is not benefit to imposing uniformity of tastes across countries.

In the next section, we explore the unilateral representative agent model that would produce a large gain in data construction simplification, but only under a very strong assumption that is not likely to be reasonable within the near future, if ever.

6.5.3. *Existence of a Unilateral Representative Agent over the Economic Union*

A unilateral representative agent considers the same goods and assets to be perfect substitutes, regardless of the country within which the goods and assets are purchased and regardless of the country within which the purchaser resides. Under this assumption, our subscripts j and k will be irrelevant to the tastes of the unilateral representative agent. Only the subscript i will matter, since countries, and thereby country subscripts, will be irrelevant to the decision.

We no longer can accept Assumption 2b, but instead will have to make a much stronger, but nonnested, assumption. Assumption 2b assumed weak separability among countries of residence of consumers. But a unilateral representative agent neither recognizes the country of residence of a consumer nor the country within which a good or asset was acquired. Hence tastes specific to a country no longer exist. It is important to recognize the fundamental difference between the homogeneous multilateral representative consumer and the unilateral representative consumer. The former imputes identical tastes to each country's residents, but does recognize the existence of different countries and the existence of the identical tastes, u, within each country. But the unilateral representative consumer does not impute existence of weakly separable tastes to the residents of any country in the economic union.

Since we no longer can assume weak separability among countries, we shall have to rewrite Decision 1 as:

Decision 1b: Choose $(\mathbf{m}_1^*, \ldots, \mathbf{m}_K^*, \mathbf{x}_1, \ldots, \mathbf{x}_K)$ to

$$\text{maximize } U[\breve{V}(s_1\mathbf{m}_1^*, \ldots, s_K\mathbf{m}_K^*), \breve{G}(s_1\mathbf{x}_1, \ldots, s_K\mathbf{x}_K)]$$

$$\text{subject to } \textstyle\sum_{k=1}^{K} s_k \mathbf{m}_k^{*\prime} \boldsymbol{\pi}_k e_k + \sum_{k=1}^{K} s_k \mathbf{x}_k' \mathbf{p}_k e_k = I.$$

Hence we now replace Assumption 2b with the following much stronger assumption, which is neither necessary nor sufficient for Assumption 2b.

Assumption 5: Let $\mathbf{m}^* = \sum_{k=1}^{K} \sum_{j=1}^{K+Z} s_k \mathbf{m}_{kj}^*$, and $\mathbf{x} = \sum_{k=1}^{K} s_k \mathbf{x}_k$. Suppose there exists linearly homogeneous $\hat{V}$ such that $\hat{V}(\mathbf{m}^*) = \breve{V}(s_1\mathbf{m}_1^*, \ldots, s_K\mathbf{m}_K^*)$, where $\breve{V}$ is as defined in equation (6.5a) . Then for any i, all monetary assets of that type are perfect substitutes, regardless of the country within which they are located or the country in which the owner resides. Analogously for consumer goods, assume there exists $\hat{G}$ such that $\hat{G}(\mathbf{x}) = \breve{G}(s_1\mathbf{x}_1, \ldots, s_K\mathbf{x}_K)$, where $\breve{G}$ is as defined in equation (6.5a). Hence for any i, all consumer goods of that type are perfect substitutes, regardless of the country within which they are located or the country in which the owner resides. Further assume that there exist $\boldsymbol{\pi}(t)$ and $\mathbf{p}(t)$ such that $\boldsymbol{\pi}_{kj}(t)e_k(t) = \boldsymbol{\pi}(t)$ and $\mathbf{p}_k(t)\, e_k(t) = \mathbf{p}(t)$ for all $k \in \{1, \ldots, K\}, j \in \{1, \ldots, K+Z\}$, and all t.

The assumptions $\boldsymbol{\pi}_{kj}(t)e_k(t) = \boldsymbol{\pi}(t)$ and $\mathbf{p}_k(t)e_k(t) = \mathbf{p}(t)$ are needed to avoid corner solutions allocating no consumption to residents of some countries. Otherwise, with perfect substitutability across countries of residence, all consumption of each good by the unilateral representative agent would be allocated to residents of the country having the lowest price of that good. Under Assumption 5, Decision 1b now becomes Decision 1c, defined as follows.

Decision 1c: Choose $(\mathbf{m}^*, \mathbf{x})$ to

$$\text{maximize } U[\hat{V}(\mathbf{m}^*), \hat{G}(\mathbf{x})]$$

$$\text{subject to } \mathbf{m}^{*\prime}\boldsymbol{\pi} + \mathbf{x}'\mathbf{p} = I.$$

The following theorem demonstrates that Decision 1c is the decision of a unilateral representative consumer for the economic union.

Theorem 8. *Let* $(\mathbf{m}_1^*, \ldots, \mathbf{m}_K^*, \mathbf{x}_1, \ldots, \mathbf{x}_K)$ *solve Decision 1b, and let* $\mathbf{m}^*$ *and* $\mathbf{x}$ *be as defined in Assumption 5. Under Assumptions 1, 2a, and 5, it follows that* $\mathbf{m}^*$ *and* $\mathbf{x}$ *will solve Decision 1c.*

Proof. Observe that there is no need to include Assumptions 3 or 4 in this theorem, since Assumption 5 implies Assumptions 3 and 4. The result follows directly from the theorem's assumptions and the definitions of $\mathbf{m}^*$ and $\mathbf{x}$. ■

We thereby are led to the following definition.

Definition 9. Under Assumptions 1, 2a, and 5, we define a unilateral representative consumer to be an economic agent who solves Decision 1c.

Note that a unilateral economic agent recognizes no differences in tastes among countries, either for the owner's country of residence or for the country within which the asset or good is located or purchased. But in a more fundamental sense, observe that in general it is impossible to factor out of $\hat{V}(\mathbf{m}^*)$ or $\hat{G}(\mathbf{x})$ the consumption or asset holdings of residents of any country. Hence country specific separable subfunction u_k or g_k, do not exist, and hence separable tastes of residents of a country do not exist. In fact for any solution for $(\mathbf{m}^*,\mathbf{x})$ to Decision 1c, the allocation of asset holdings and consumption expenditure to countries is indeterminate. Assumptions 3 and 4 have been omitted from Theorem 8, because of redundancy with Assumption 5. But Assumption 2b, which also has been omitted, is not redundant, but rather is omitted since it contradicts Assumption 5. The unilateral representative agent exists under much stronger assumptions than the multilateral representative agent. But the unilateral representative agent is not a nested special case of the multilateral representative agent, whether in its general or homogeneous form.[15]

The multilateral representative agent model of Decision 1 is far more reasonable, requiring only Assumptions 1, 2a, and 2b. But we see from Theorem 6 that our heterogeneous agents approach would produce the same results as the multilateral representative agent theory, if the necessary conditions for existence of a multilateral representative agent were satisfied.

6.6. Interest Rate Aggregation

Since interest rates play important roles in policy, it could be useful to compute the interest rate aggregate that is dual to the Divisia monetary quantity index. We show that the correct interest rate aggregate is not the one in common use by central banks, and we view the commonly used interest rate aggregates to be unacceptable. In particular we provide the correct formula for aggregating interest rates jointly over monetary assets and over countries.

Let $\bar{r}_k$ be the dual aggregate interest rate for country k. It follows from Definition 1 and the definition of the vector of component user costs prices, $\boldsymbol{\pi}_k^*$ that $R_k - \bar{r}_k = \Pi_k^*$, where $\Pi_k^* = \Pi_k^*(\boldsymbol{\pi}_k^*)$. Hence $\bar{r}_k$ easily can be computed from $\bar{r}_k = R_k - \Pi_k^*$. In discrete time when $\pi_{ki}^* = (R_k - r_{ki})/(1 + R_k)$, it follows that $(R_k - \bar{r}_k)/(1 + R_k) = \Pi_k^*$, with $\bar{r}_k$ being computed by solving that equation.

---

[15]Decision 1c is the representative agent model previously used in some studies to aggregate within the euro area. But the required convergence conditions, Assumptions 1, 2a, and 5 and the implied Assumptions 3 and 4, are clearly very strong, since they imply decision independence of the country of residence of purchasers and of the country of location of the purchase. Rather than requiring identical tastes of consumers among all countries in the economic union, as in the homogeneous multilateral representative agent case, the unilateral representative agent case implies nonexistence of separable tastes or cultures for any country, through irrelevancy of the location of the purchaser or of the purchased good or asset.

After aggregating over countries, the interest rate that is dual to M* is similarly easy to compute, if the same benchmark rate applies to all countries. In that case, which we believe not likely to be applicable prior to the introduction of a common currency, our heterogeneous agents approach to aggregating over countries becomes mathematically equivalent to our multilateral representative agent approach.

Let $R = R(t)$ be the common benchmark rate applying to all countries in the economic union, and let $\bar{r} = \bar{r}(t)$ be the interest rate aggregate dual to M^*. In continuous time, it follows that $R - \bar{r} = \Pi^*$, where $\Pi^* = \Pi^*(t) = \Pi^*(\Pi_1^*, \ldots, \Pi_K^*)$ Hence $\bar{r}$ easily can be computed from $\bar{r} = R - \Pi^*$. Analogously in discrete time, it follows that $(R - \bar{r})/(1 + R) = \Pi^*$, with $\bar{r}$ being computed by solving that equation.[16]

Note that our aggregation-theoretic interest-rate aggregates are not the interest-rate weighted averages often used in this literature.

6.7. Divisia Second Moments

Our use of the stochastic approach to aggregation lends itself naturally to the computation of Divisia second moments, although in the above sections we have provided only the Divisia first moments. In this tradition, the "Divisia index" is synonymous with the Divisia growth rate mean. We believe that the Divisia growth rate variance could be especially useful for exploring distribution effects of policy within an economic union and progress towards convergence. We propose below some potentially useful Divisia growth rate variances. Conversion of our continuous time formulas to their discrete time version is analogous to that available for the within-country Divisia

---

[16]In the heterogeneous agents approach, there does not exist a common benchmark rate that can be imputed to all countries. Under those circumstances, the aggregation theoretic method of producing the interest rate aggregate can be found in Barnett (2000, p. 278, equation 5).

quantity and user cost growth rate variances in Barnett and Serletis (2000, p. 172, eqs. 4 and 7).

We believe that the Divisia growth rate variances could be especially useful when computed about the Divisia means of the following growth rates: (i) the monetary quantity growth rates, d log M and d log M^*, in Definition 4, (ii) the Divisia means of the user cost price growth rates, $d \log \Pi$ and $d \log \Pi^*$, in Definition 5, and (iii) the inflation growth rate, $d \log p^*$, in equation (6.2) or the inflation growth rate, $d \log P^*$, in equation (6.6). Repeating those Divisia mean formulas and producing the analogous Divisia variances, we have the following formulas.

The Divisia growth rate means are in Definitions 3, 4, and 5 and equation (6.6).

The analogous Divisia growth rate variances are $K = \sum_{k=1}^{K} W_k [d \log (s_k M_k e_k) - d \log M]^2$, $K^* = \sum_{k=1}^{K} W_k [d \log (s_k M_k^*) - d \log M^*]^2$, $J = \sum_{k=1}^{K} W_k [d \log (\Pi_k e_k) - d \log \Pi]^2$, $J^* = \sum_{k=1}^{K} W_k [d \log (\Pi_k^*) - d \log \Pi^*]^2$, $G_M = \sum_{k=1}^{K} W_k [d \log p_k^* e_k - d \log p^*]^2$, and $G = \sum_{k=1}^{K} B_k [d \log p_k^* e_k - d \log P^*]^2$. An additional potentially useful Divisia growth rate variance is that of the monetary expenditure share growth rates $\Psi = \sum_{k=1}^{K} W_k [d \log W_k - d \log W]^2$, where $d \log W = \sum_{k=1}^{K} W_k d \log W_k$.

The Divisia monetary services growth rate variances, K and K^*, and the Divisia monetary-services expenditure-share growth-rate variance, Ψ, are measures of the dispersion of monetary service growth rates across countries in nominal and real terms, respectively, while the Divisia inflation rate variances, G and G_M, are measures of the dispersion of inflation rates across countries. Increasing values of K, K^*, Ψ, and G over time are indications of growth in the distribution effects of monetary policy over the countries of the economic union. Decreases in K, K^*, Ψ, and G over time are indications of convergence towards more uniform effects of policy over the economic union. If variations in K, K^*, and Ψ tend to precede those of G, then there is an implication of causality. The converse could indicate that policy is accommodating other causal factors.

The Divisia growth rate variances, J and J^*, are measures of the progress of harmonization of financial markets over countries and hence are less directly connected with monetary policy and more directly connected with structural progress in the unification of money markets over the economic union.

6.8. Conclusions

We advocate use of Barnett's (1980) representative agent approach to Divisia aggregation within countries and then our heterogeneous countries approach to aggregation over countries. Our stochastic approach to aggregation over countries lends itself naturally to computation of Divisia second moments. We advocate computation of Divisia variance growth rates about the Divisia means across countries. Those Divisia second moments could provide useful information about the distribution effects of policy and about progress towards convergence over an economic union, such as the EMU.

We define and produce the theory relevant to a third very restrictive case, which we call the unilateral representative agent approach. This approach, which we show to be implied by some early studies of euro-area monetary aggregation, may be relevant to aggregation over states or provinces of a single country, but not likely for aggregation over different countries within an economic union.

With the heterogeneous countries or multilateral representative agent approach, we find the need for two different consumer price indexes: one for use in deflating nominal to real monetary balances after aggregation over countries, and one for deflating nominal to real consumer goods expenditure. The imputation of either index to both uses would produce a serious specification error. Only under our very restrictive homogeneous multilateral representative agent assumptions or the even-more-restrictive unilateral representative agent assumptions do the growth rates of the two consumer price indexes become equal.

The choice among our nested assumption structures for aggregation must be consistent with the assumptions made in producing the models within which the data is to be used. In fact it is attainment of that internal consistency that is the primary objective of index number and aggregation theory. Without that coherence between aggregator function structure and the econometric models within which aggregates are embedded, stable structure can appear to become unstable.

7

Measurement Error in Monetary Aggregates: A Markov Switching Factor Approach[1]

William A. Barnett, Marcelle Chauvet
and Heather L. R. Tierney

This paper compares the different dynamics of the simple sum monetary aggregates and the Divisia monetary aggregate indexes over time, over the business cycle, and across high and low inflation and interest rate phases. Although traditional comparisons of the series sometimes suggest that simple sum and Divisia monetary aggregates share similar dynamics, there are important differences during certain periods, such as around turning points. These differences cannot be evaluated by their average behavior. We use a factor model with regime switching. The model separates out the common movements underlying the monetary aggregate indexes, summarized in the dynamic factor, from individual variations in each individual series, captured by the idiosyncratic terms. The idiosyncratic terms and the measurement errors reveal where the monetary indexes differ. We find several new results. In general, the idiosyncratic terms for both the simple sum aggregates and the Divisia indexes display a business cycle pattern, especially since 1980. They generally rise around the end of high interest rate phases — a couple of quarters before the beginning of recessions — and fall during recessions to subsequently converge to their average in the beginning of expansions. We find that the major differences between the simple sum aggregates and Divisia indexes occur around the beginnings and ends of economic recessions, and during some high interest rate phases. We note the inferences' policy relevance, which is particularly dramatic at the broadest (M3) level of aggregation. Indeed, as Belongia (1996) has observed in this regard, "measurement matters."

[1]Reprinted with permission from *Macroeconomic Dynamics* (2009), "Measurement Error in Monetary Aggregates: A Markov Switching Factor Approach" by William A. Barnett, Marcelle Chauvet, and Heather L. R. Tierney, vol. 13, supplement S2, September, pp. 381–412.

7.1. Introduction

There is a vast literature on the appropriateness of aggregating over monetary asset components using simple summation. Linear aggregation can be based on Hickisian aggregation (Hicks 1946), but that theory only holds under the unreasonable assumption that the user-cost prices of the services of individual money assets do not change over time. This condition implies that each asset is a perfect substitute for the others within the set of components. Simple sum aggregation is an even more severe special case of that highly restrictive, linear aggregation, since simple summation requires that the coefficients of the linear aggregator function all be the same. This, in turn, implies that the constant user-cost prices among monetary assets be exactly equal to each other. Not only must the assets be perfect substitutes, but must be perfect one-for-one substitutes — i.e., must be indistinguishable assets, with one unit of each asset being a perfect substitute for exactly one unit of each of the other assets.

In reality, financial assets provide different services, and each such asset yields its own particular rate of return. As a result, the user costs, which measure foregone interest and thereby opportunity cost, are not constant and are not equal across financial assets. The relative prices of U.S. monetary assets fluctuate considerably, and the interest rates paid on many monetary assets are not equal to the zero interest rate paid on currency. These observations have motivated serious concerns about the reliability of the simple sum aggregation method, which has been disreputable in the literature on index number theory and aggregation theory for over a century. In addition, an increasing number of imperfect substitute short-term financial assets have emerged in recent decades. Since monetary aggregates produced from simple summation do not accurately measure the quantities of monetary services chosen by optimizing agents, shifts in the series can be spurious, as those shifts do not necessarily reflect a change in the utility derived from money holdings.

Microeconomic aggregation theory offers an appealing alternative approach to the definition of money, compared to the atheoretical simple-sum method. The quantity index under the aggregation theoretic approach extracts and measures the income effects of changes in relative prices and is invariant to substitution effects, which do not alter utility and thereby do not alter perceived services received. The simple sum index, on the other hand, does not distinguish between income and substitution effects, if the aggregate's components are not perfect substitutes in identical ratios, and thereby the simple sum index confounds together substitution effects with actual services received. The aggregation-theoretic monetary aggregator function, which correctly internalizes substitution effects, can be tracked accurately by the Divisia quantity index, constructed by using expenditure shares as the component growth-rate weights. Barnett (1978,1980) derived the formula for the theoretical user-cost price of a monetary asset, needed in computation of the Divisia index's share weights, and thereby originated the Divisia monetary aggregates. The growth rate weights resulting from this approach are different across assets, depending on all of the quantities and interest rates in each share, and those weights can be time-varying at each point in time. For a detailed description of the theory underlying this construction, see Barnett (1982,1987).

It is important to understand that the direction in which an asset's growth-rate weight will change with an interest rate change is not predictable in advance. Consider Cobb-Douglas utility. Its shares are independent of relative prices, and hence of the interest rates within the component user cost prices. For other utility functions, the direction of the change in shares with a price change, or equivalently with an interest rate change, depends upon whether the own price elasticity of demand exceeds or is less than -1. In elementary microeconomic theory, this often overlooked phenomenon produces the famous "diamonds versus water paradox" and is the source of most of the misunderstandings of the Divisia monetary aggregates' weighting, as explained by Barnett (1983).

Several authors have studied the empirical properties of the Divisia index compared with the simple sum index. The earliest comparisons are in Barnett (1982) and Barnett, Offenbacher, and Spindt (1984). More recent examples include Belongia (1996), Belongia and Ireland (2006), and Schunk (2001), and the comprehensive survey found in Barnett and Serletis (2000). In particular, Belongia (1996) replicates some studies on the impact of money on economic activity and compares results acquired using a Divisia index instead of the originally used simple sum index, Schunk (2001) investigates the forecasting performance of the Divisia index compared with the simple sum aggregates, and Belongia and Ireland (2006) explore the policy implications in the dual space of aggregated user costs and interest rates. Barnett and Serletis (2000) collect together and reprint seminal journal articles from this literature.[2]

In this paper we compare the different dynamics of simple sum monetary aggregates and the Divisia indexes, not only over time, but also over the business cycle and across high and low inflation and interest rate phases. The potential differences between the series can be economically very important. If one of the indexes corresponds to a better measure of money, its dynamical differences from the official simple sum aggregates increase the already considerable uncertainty regarding the effectiveness and appropriateness of current monetary policy. We aim to study the differences and whether they occur during particular periods. Information about the state of monetary growth becomes particularly relevant for policymakers, when inflation enters a high growth phase or the economy begins to weaken. In fact Barnett (1997) has argued and documented the connection between the decline in the policy credibility of monetary aggregates and defects that are peculiar to simple sum aggregation.

Although traditional comparisons of the series sometimes suggest that they share similar long run dynamics, there are differences during certain important periods, such as around turning points. These differences cannot be evaluated by long run average behavior. Our

[2]Other overviews of published theoretical and empirical results in this literature are available in Barnett, Fisher, and Serletis (1992) and Serletis (2006).

proposed approach offers several ways in which these differences can be analyzed. A nonlinear dynamic factor model is used to separate out the common movements underlying the monetary aggregate indexes, summarized in the latent dynamic factor, from individual variations specific to each of the indexes, captured by the idiosyncratic terms. The idiosyncratic terms and the measurement errors reveal where the monetary indexes differ.[3] The idiosyncratic terms show the movements that are peculiar to each series, whereas the measurement error captures the remaining noise inherent in the data. That is, the dynamic factor represents simultaneous downturn and upturn movements in money growth rate indexes. If only one of the indexes declines, this would be captured by its idiosyncratic term.

We model both the common factor as well as the idiosyncratic terms for each index as following different Markov processes. Given that the idiosyncratic movements are peculiar to each index, the idiosyncratic terms' Markov processes are assumed to be independent of each other. In addition, we allow the idiosyncratic terms to follow autoregressive processes. These assumptions entail a very flexible framework that can capture the dynamics of the differences across the indexes without imposing dependence between them.

[3]In aggregation theory measurement error refers to the tracking error in a nonparametric index number's approximation to the aggregator function of microeconomic theory, where the aggregator function is the subutility or subproduction function that is weakly separable within tastes or technology of an economic agent's complete utility or production function. Consequently, aggregator functions are increasing and concave and need to be estimated econometrically. On the other hand, state space models use the term measurement error to mean un-modeled noise, which is not captured by the state variable or idiosyncratic terms. In this paper, measurement error refers to this latter definition, which can be expected to be correlated with the former, when the behavior of the data process is consistent with microeconomic theory. But it should be acknowledged that neither concept of measurement error can be directly derived from the other. In fact the state space model concept of measurement error is more directly connected with the statistical ("atomistic") approach to index number theory than to the more recent "economic approach," which is at its best when data is not aggregated over economic agents.

Factor models with regime switching have been widely used to represent business cycles (see e.g., Chauvet 1998, 2001, Kim and Nelson 1998, among several others), but without relationship to aggregation theory. Our proposed model differs from the literature in its complexity, as it includes estimation of the parameters of three independent Markov processes. In addition, the focus is not only on the estimated common factor, but on the idiosyncratic terms that reflect the divergences between the monetary aggregate indexes in a manner relevant to aggregation theory.

To our knowledge, there is no parallel work in the literature that formally compares simple sum aggregate with the Divisia index directly, using a multivariate time-series framework to *estimate* the dynamical differences between these series. Our contribution goes beyond the simple comparison over time, as we also focus on major measurement errors that might have occurred during some periods, such as around the beginnings or ends of recessions or in transition times, as from low (high) to high (low) inflation or interest rate phases.

We estimate three models, one for each pair of the monetary indexes: simple sum M_1 and Divisia MSI_1 (Model 1), simple sum M_2 and Divisia MSI_2 (Model 2), and simple sum M_3 and Divisia MSI_3 (Model 3), where MSI is the monetary services index computed from the Divisia index by the St. Louis Federal Reserve Bank. Our findings confirm some of the findings of the previous literature in addition to producing several new results.

In general, the idiosyncratic terms for both the simple sum aggregates and the Divisia indexes display a business cycle pattern, especially since 1980. They generally rise around the end of high interest rate phases — a couple of quarters before the beginning of recessions — and fall during recessions to converge subsequently to their average behavior during the beginnings of expansions. We find that the major differences between the simple sum aggregates and Divisia indexes occur around the beginnings and ends of economic recessions, and during some high interest rate phases. This is particularly the case for the period between 1977 and 1983, which includes a slowdown, two recessions, two recoveries, and the change in the Federal Reserve's operating procedure during the "monetarist experiment" period. Notice that this period also corresponds to a high interest rate phase. Another time during which we find that the indexes diverge substantially is around the 1990 recession. A more detailed summary of findings is found in section 4.

7.2. Monetary Aggregation Theory

7.2.1. *Monetary Aggregation*

Aggregation theory and index-number theory have been used to generate official governmental data since the 1920s. One exception still exists. The monetary quantity aggregates and interest rate aggregates supplied by many central banks are not based on index-number or aggregation theory, but rather are the simple unweighted sums of the component quantities and the quantity-weighted or arithmetic averages of interest rates. The predictable consequence has been induced instability of money demand and supply functions, and a series of 'puzzles' in the resulting applied literature. In contrast, the Divisia monetary aggregates, originated by Barnett (1980), are derived directly from economic index-number theory. Financial aggregation and index number theory was first rigorously connected with the literature on microeconomic aggregation and index number theory by Barnett (1980; 1987).

Data construction and measurement procedures imply the theory that can rationalize the aggregation procedure. The assumptions implicit in the data construction procedures must be consistent with the assumptions made in producing the models within which the data are to be used. Unless the theory is internally consistent, the data and its applications are incoherent. Without that coherence between aggregator function structure and the econometric models within which the aggregates are embedded, stable structure can appear to be unstable. This phenomenon has been called the 'Barnett critique' by Chrystal and MacDonald (1994).

7.2.2. *Aggregation Theory versus Index Number Theory*

The exact aggregates of microeconomic aggregation theory depend on unknown aggregator functions, which typically are utility, production, cost, or distance functions. Such functions must first be econometrically estimated. Hence the resulting exact quantity and price indexes become estimator- and specification-dependent. This dependency is troublesome to governmental agencies, which therefore view aggregation theory as a research tool rather than a data construction procedure.

Statistical index-number theory, on the other hand, provides indexes which are computable directly from quantity and price data, without estimation of unknown parameters. Within the literature on aggregation theory, such index numbers depend jointly on prices and quantities, but not on unknown parameters. In a sense, index number theory trades joint dependency on prices and quantities for dependence on unknown parameters. Examples of such statistical index numbers are the Laspeyres, Paasche, Divisia, Fisher ideal, and Törnqvist indexes.

The loose link between index number theory and aggregation theory was tightened, when Diewert (1976) defined the class of second-order 'superlative' index numbers, which track any unknown aggregator function up to the second order. Statistical index number theory became part of microeconomic theory, as economic aggregation theory had been for decades, with statistical index numbers judged by their non-parametric tracking ability to the aggregator functions of aggregation theory.

For decades, the link between statistical index number theory and microeconomic aggregation theory was weaker for aggregating over monetary quantities than for aggregating over other goods and asset quantities. Once monetary assets began yielding interest long ago, monetary assets became imperfect substitutes for each other, and the 'price' of monetary-asset services was no longer clearly defined. That problem was solved by Barnett (1978; 1980), who derived the formula for the user cost of demanded monetary services.[4]

Barnett's results on the user cost of the services of monetary assets set the stage for introducing index number theory into monetary economics.

7.2.3. *The Economic Decision*

Consider a decision problem over monetary assets. The decision problem will be defined in the simplest manner that renders the relevant literature on economic aggregation over goods immediately applicable.[5] Initially we shall assume perfect certainty.

Let $\mathbf{m}_t' = (m_{1t}, m_{2t}, \ldots, m_{nt})$ be the vector of real balances of monetary assets during period t, let $\boldsymbol{r}_t$ be the vector of nominal holding-period yields for monetary assets during period t, and let

---

[4]Subsequently Barnett (1987) derived the formula for the user cost of supplied monetary services. A regulatory wedge can exist between the demand and supply-side user costs, if non-payment of interest on required reserves imposes an implicit tax on banks.

[5]Our research in this paper is not dependent upon this simple decision problem, as shown by Barnett (1987), who proved that the same aggregator function and index number theory applies, regardless of whether the initial model has money in the utility function, or money in a production function, or neither, so long as there is intertemporal separability of structure and certain assumptions are satisfied for aggregation over economic agents. The aggregator function is the derived function that has been shown in general equilibrium always to exist, if money has positive value in equilibrium, regardless of the motive for holding money. See, e.g., Arrow and Hahn (1971), Stanley Fischer (1974), Phlips and Spinnewyn (1982), and Poterba and Rotemberg (1987). Analogously, Feenstra (1986, p. 271) demonstrated "a functional equivalence between using real balances as an argument of the utility function and entering money into liquidity costs which appear in the budget constraints." The converse mapping from the money in the aggregator (utility or production) function approach to the explicit motive is not unique, but in this paper we are not seeking to identify the motives for holding money.

R_t be the one period holding yield on the benchmark asset during period t. The benchmark asset is defined to be a pure investment that provides no services other than its yield, R_t, so that the asset is held solely to accumulate wealth. Thus, R_t is the maximum holding period yield in the economy in period t.

Let y_t be the real value of total budgeted expenditure on monetary services during period t. Under simplifying assumptions for data within one country, the conversion between nominal and real expenditure on the monetary services of one or more assets is accomplished using the true cost of living index on consumer goods.[6] The optimal portfolio allocation decision is:

$$\begin{aligned} &\text{maximize} \quad u(\mathbf{m}_t) \\ &\text{subject to} \quad \boldsymbol{\pi}_t'\mathbf{m}_t = y_t, \end{aligned} \tag{7.1}$$

where $\boldsymbol{\pi}_t' = (\pi_{1t}, \ldots, \pi_{nt})$ is the vector of monetary-asset real user costs, with

$$\pi_{it} = \frac{R_t - r_{it}}{1 + R_t} \tag{7.2}$$

The function u is the decision maker's utility function, assumed to be monotonically increasing and strictly concave.[7] The user cost formula (7.2), derived by Barnett (1978; 1980), measures the forgone interest or opportunity cost of holding monetary asset i, when the higher yielding benchmark asset could have been held.

Let $\mathbf{m}_t^*$ be derived by solving decision (7.1). Under the assumption of linearly homogeneous utility, the exact monetary aggregate of economic theory is the utility level associated with holding the portfolio, and hence is the optimized value of the decision's

[6]The multilateral open economy extension is available in Barnett (2007).

[7]To be an admissible quantity aggregator function, the function u must be weakly separable within the consumer's complete utility function over all goods and services. Producing a reliable test for weak separability is the subject of much intensive research, most recently by Barnett and Peretti (2009).

objective function:

$$M_t = u(\mathbf{m}_t^*). \tag{7.3}$$

7.2.4. *The Divisia Index*

Although equation (7.3) is exactly correct, it depends upon the unknown function, u. Nevertheless, statistical index-number theory enables us to track M_t exactly without estimating the unknown function, u. In continuous time, the monetary aggregate, $M_t = u(\mathbf{m}_t^*)$, can be tracked exactly by the Divisia index, which solves the differential equation

$$\frac{d \log M_t}{dt} = \sum_i s_{it} \frac{d \log m_{it}^*}{dt} \tag{7.4}$$

for M_t, where

$$s_{it} = \frac{\pi_{it} m_{it}^*}{y_t}$$

is the i'th asset's share in expenditure on the total portfolio's service flow.[8] The dual user cost price aggregate $\Pi_t = \Pi(\boldsymbol{\pi}_t)$, can be tracked exactly by the Divisia price index, which solves the differential equation

$$\frac{d \log \Pi_t}{dt} = \sum_i s_{it} \frac{d \log \pi_{it}}{dt}. \tag{7.5}$$

The user cost dual satisfies Fisher's factor reversal in continuous time:

$$\Pi_t M_t = \boldsymbol{\pi}_t' \mathbf{m}_t. \tag{7.6}$$

As a formula for aggregating over quantities of perishable consumer goods, that index was first proposed by François Divisia (1925), with market prices of those goods inserted in place of the user

[8] In equation (7.4), it is understood that the result is in continuous time, so the time subscripts are a short hand for functions of time. We use t to be the time period in discrete time, but the instant of time in continuous time.

costs in equation (7.4). In continuous time, the Divisia index, under conventional neoclassical assumptions, is exact. In discrete time, the Törnqvist approximation is:

$$\log M_t - \log M_{t-1} = \sum_i \bar{s}_{it}(\log m^*_{it} - \log m^*_{i,t-1}), \qquad (7.7)$$

where

$$\bar{s}_{it} = \frac{1}{2}(s_{it} + s_{i,t-1}).$$

In discrete time, we often call equation (7.7) simply the Divisia quantity index.[9] After the quantity index is computed from (7.7), the user cost aggregate most commonly is computed directly from equation (7.6).

7.2.5. *Risk Adjustment*

Extension of index number theory to the case of risk was introduced by Barnett, Liu and Jensen (2000), who derived the extended theory from Euler equations rather than from the perfect-certainty first-order conditions used in the earlier index number-theory literature. Since that extension is based upon the consumption capital-asset-pricing model (CCAPM), the extension is subject to the 'equity premium puzzle' of smaller-than-necessary adjustment for risk. We believe that the under-correction produced by CCAPM results from its assumption of intertemporal blockwise strong separability of goods and services within preferences. Barnett and Wu (2005) have extended Barnett, Liu, and Jensen's result to the case of risk aversion with intertemporally non-separable tastes.[10]

[9]Diewert (1976) defines a 'superlative index number' to be one that is exactly correct for a quadratic approximation to the aggregator function. The discretization (7.7) to the Divisia index is in the superlative class, since it is exact for the quadratic translog specification to an aggregator function.

[10]The Federal Reserve Bank of St. Louis Divisia database, which we use in this paper, is not risk corrected. In addition, it is not adjusted for differences in marginal taxation rates on different asset returns or for sweeps, and its clustering

7.2.6. *Dual Space*

User cost aggregates are duals to monetary quantity aggregates. Either implies the other uniquely. In addition, user-cost aggregates imply the corresponding interest-rate aggregates uniquely. The interest-rate aggregate r_t implied by the user-cost aggregate Π_t is the solution for r_t to the equation:

$$\frac{R_t - r_t}{1 + R_t} = \Pi_t.$$

Accordingly, any monetary policy that operates through the opportunity cost of money (that is, interest rates) has a dual policy operating through the monetary quantity aggregate, and vice versa. Aggregation theory implies no preference for either of the two dual policy procedures or for any other approach to policy, so long as the policy does not violate principles of aggregation theory. In our current state-space comparisons, we model in quantity space rather than the user-cost-price or interest-rate dual spaces. Regarding policy in the dual space, see Barnett (1987) and Belongia and Ireland (2006).

7.3. The State Space Model

Let $\mathbf{Y}_t$ be the n x 1 vector of monetary indexes, where n is the number of monetary indexes in the model.

$$\Delta \mathbf{Y}_t = \boldsymbol{\lambda} \Delta F_t + \mathbf{G} \boldsymbol{\tau}_t + \mathbf{v}_t, \tag{7.8}$$

where $\Delta = 1 - L$ and L is the lag operator. Changes in the monetary aggregates, $\Delta \mathbf{Y}_t$, are modeled as a function of a scalar unobservable factor that summarizes their commonalities, ΔF_t, an

of components into groups was not based upon tests of weak separability, but rather on the Federal Reserve's official clustering. The St. Louis Federal Reserve Bank is in the process of revising its MSI database, perhaps to incorporate some of those adjustments. Regarding sweep adjustment, see Jones, Dutkowsky, and Elger (2005). At the present stage of this research, we felt it was best to use data publicly available from the Federal Reserve, so we did not modify the St. Louis Federal Reserve's MSI database in any ways.

idiosyncratic component n x 1 vector, which captures the movements peculiar to each index, $\mathbf{v}_t$, and a potential time trend $\boldsymbol{\tau}_t$. The factor loadings, $\boldsymbol{\lambda}$, measure the sensitivity of the series to the dynamic factor, ΔF_t.[11] The matrix $\mathbf{G}$ is a diagonal matrix, containing the vector of time trend coefficients, $\boldsymbol{\gamma}$, on its diagonal, while $\boldsymbol{\tau}_t$ is the vector of time trends. Both the dynamic factor and the idiosyncratic terms follow autoregressive processes:

$$\Delta F_t = \alpha_{S_t} + \phi(L)\Delta F_{t-1} + \eta_t \quad \eta_1 \sim N(0, \sigma^2), \tag{7.9}$$

$$\mathbf{v}_t = \boldsymbol{\Gamma}_{S_t^h} + \mathbf{d}(L)\mathbf{v}_{t-1} + \boldsymbol{\varepsilon}_t, \quad \boldsymbol{\varepsilon}_t \sim \text{i.i.d. } N(\mathbf{0}, \boldsymbol{\Sigma}), \tag{7.10}$$

where η_t is the common shock to the latent dynamic factor, and $\boldsymbol{\varepsilon}_t$ are the measurement errors. In order to capture potential nonlinearities across different monetary regimes, the intercept of the monetary factor switches regimes according to a Markov variable, S_t, where $\alpha_{S_t} = \alpha_0 + \alpha_1 S_t^\alpha$, and $S_t^\alpha = 0, 1$. That is, monetary indexes can either be in an expansionary regime, where the mean growth rate of money is positive ($S_t^\alpha = 1$), or in a contractionary phase with a lower or negative mean growth rate ($S_t^\alpha = 0$).

We also assume that the idiosyncratic terms for each index follow *distinct* two-state Markov processes, by allowing their drift terms, $\boldsymbol{\Gamma}_{S_t^h}$, to switch between regimes. For example, in the case of two monetary indexes, $n = 2$, there will be two idiosyncratic terms, each one following an independent Markov process S_t^β and S_t^δ, where $S_t^\beta = 0, 1$ and $S_t^\delta = 0, 1$. Notice that we do not constraint the Markov variables S_t^α, S_t^β and S_t^δ to be dependent of each other, but allow them instead to move according to their own dynamics. In fact, there is no reason to expect that the idiosyncratic terms would move in a similar manner to each other or to the dynamic factor, since by construction

[11]The factor loading for the Divisia monetary index series is set equal to one to provide a scale for the latent dynamic factor. This normalization is a necessary condition for identification of the factor, and the choice of parameter scale does not affect any of the time series properties of the dynamic factor or the correlation with its components.

they represent movements peculiar to each index not captured by the common factor.

The switches from one state to another is determined by the transition probabilities of the first-order two-state Markov processes, $p_{ij}^k = P(S_t^k = j|S_{t-1}^k = i)$, where $\sum_{j=0}^{1} p_{ij}^k = 1,\ i,j = 0,1$, with $k = \alpha, \beta, \delta$ identifying the Markov processes for the dynamic factor and the two idiosyncratic terms, respectively.

The model separates out the common signal underlying the monetary aggregates from individual variations in each of the indexes. The dynamic factor captures simultaneous downturns and upturns in money growth indexes. On the other hand, if only one of the variables declines, e.g., M1, this would not characterize a general monetary contraction in the model and would be captured by the M1 idiosyncratic term. A general monetary contraction (expansion) will occur when all n variables decrease (increase) at about the same time. That is, η_t and $\mathbf{v}_t$ are assumed to be mutually independent at all leads and lags for all n variables, and $\mathbf{d}(\mathrm{L})$ is diagonal. The dynamic factor is the outcome of averaging out the discrete states. Although the n monetary indexes represent different measurements of money, the estimated dynamic factor is a nonlinear combination of them, representing broader movements in monetary aggregates in the U.S. On the other hand, once a contraction or expansion is clearly under way, the idiosyncratic term for a particular aggregate can be highly informative near a turning point.

Dynamic factor models with regime switching have been widely used to represent business cycles. The proposed model differs from the literature in its complexity, as it includes estimation of the parameters of three independent Markov processes.

The model is cast in state space form, where (7.11) and (7.12) are the measurement and transition equations, respectively:

$$\Delta \mathbf{Y}_t = \mathbf{Z}\boldsymbol{\xi}_t + \mathbf{G}\boldsymbol{\tau}_t \tag{7.11}$$

$$\boldsymbol{\xi}_t = \boldsymbol{\mu}_{\xi_{st}} + \mathbf{T}\boldsymbol{\xi}_{t-1} + \mathbf{u}_t. \tag{7.12}$$

A particular state space representation for the estimated indicator using two variables is:

$$\Delta \mathbf{Y}_t = \begin{bmatrix} \Delta Y_{1t} \\ \Delta Y_{2t} \end{bmatrix}, \ \mathbf{Z} = \begin{bmatrix} \lambda_1 \ 1 \ 0 \ 0 \\ 1 \ 0 \ 1 \ 0 \end{bmatrix}, \ \boldsymbol{\xi}_t = \begin{bmatrix} \Delta F_t \\ v_{1t} \\ v_{2t} \\ F_{t-1} \end{bmatrix}, \ \boldsymbol{\mu}_{\xi_{st}} = \begin{bmatrix} \alpha_{st} \\ \beta_{st} \\ \delta_{st} \\ 0 \end{bmatrix},$$

$$\mathbf{T} = \begin{bmatrix} \phi_1 & 0 & 0 & 0 \\ 0 & d_1 & 0 & 0 \\ 0 & 0 & d_2 & 0 \\ 1 & 0 & 0 & 1 \end{bmatrix}, \ \mathbf{G} = \begin{bmatrix} \gamma_1 & 0 \\ 0 & \gamma_2 \end{bmatrix} \quad \text{and} \quad \mathbf{u}_t = \begin{bmatrix} \eta_t \\ \varepsilon_{1t} \\ \varepsilon_{2t} \\ 0 \end{bmatrix}.$$

The term F_{t-1} is included in the state vector to allow estimation of the dynamic factor in levels from the identity $\Delta F_{t-1} = F_{t-1} - F_{t-2}$.

The model is estimated using an extended version of the nonlinear Kalman filter to compute the latent dynamic factor and each one of three Markov processes. The nonlinear filter forms forecasts of the unobserved state vector, $\boldsymbol{\xi}_{t|t-1}^{(i,j)}$, and the associated mean squared error matrices, $\boldsymbol{\theta}_{t|t-1}^{(i,j)}$, based on information, $\mathbf{I}_{t-1} \equiv [\Delta \mathbf{Y}'_{t-1}, \Delta \mathbf{Y}'_{t-2}, \ldots, \Delta \mathbf{Y}'_1]'$, available up to time $t-1$ on the Markov state S_t, with each $S_t = S_t^{\alpha}, S_t^{\beta}, S_t^{\delta}$ taking on the value j, and S_{t-1} taking on the value i, for $i, j = 0, 1$:

$$\boldsymbol{\xi}_{t|t-1}^{(i,j)} = E(\boldsymbol{\xi}_t | \mathbf{I}_{t-1}, S_t = j, S_{t-1} = i) \tag{7.13}$$

$$\boldsymbol{\theta}_{t|t-1}^{(i,j)} = E[(\boldsymbol{\xi}_t - \boldsymbol{\xi}_{t|t-1})(\boldsymbol{\xi}_t - \boldsymbol{\xi}_{t|t-1})' | \mathbf{I}_{t-1}, S_t = j, S_{t-1} = i)]. \tag{7.14}$$

The filter uses as inputs the joint probability of the Markov-switching states at time $t-1$ and t, conditional on information up to $t-1$, $P(S_{t-1} = i, S_t = j | \mathbf{I}_{t-1})$; an inference $\boldsymbol{\xi}_{t-1|t-1}^{(i,j)}$ about the state vector using information up to $t-1$, given $S_{t-1} = i$ and $S_t = j$; and the mean squared error matrices, $\{\boldsymbol{\theta}_{t-1|t-1}^{(i,j)}\}$. The outputs are their one-step updated values. The nonlinear Kalman filter is:

$$\boldsymbol{\xi}_{t|t-1}^{(i,j)} = \boldsymbol{\mu}_{\xi_{st}} + \mathbf{T}\boldsymbol{\xi}_{t-1|t-1}^{i} \tag{7.15}$$

(prediction equations)

$$\boldsymbol{\theta}_{t|t-1}^{(i,j)} = \mathbf{T}\boldsymbol{\theta}_{t-1|t-1}^{i}\mathbf{T}' + \mathbf{H} \tag{7.16}$$

$$\boldsymbol{\xi}_{t|t}^{(i,j)} = \boldsymbol{\xi}_{t|t-1}^{(i,j)} + \mathbf{K}_t^{(i,j)}\mathbf{N}_{t|t-1}^{(i,j)} \tag{7.17}$$

(updating equations)

$$\boldsymbol{\theta}_{t|t}^{(i,j)} = (\mathbf{I}_n - \mathbf{K}_t^{(i,j)}\mathbf{Z})\boldsymbol{\theta}_{t|t-1}^{(i,j)}, \tag{7.18}$$

where $\mathbf{H}$ is the variance-covariance matrix of the vector of disturbances $\mathbf{u}_t$, $\mathbf{I}_n$ is the identity matrix, $\mathbf{K}_t^{(i,j)} = \boldsymbol{\theta}_{t|t-1}^{(i,j)}\mathbf{Z}'[\mathbf{Q}_t^{(i,j)}]^{-1}$, $\mathbf{N}_{t|t-1}^{(i,j)} = \Delta\mathbf{Y}_t - \mathbf{Z}\boldsymbol{\xi}_{t|t-1}^{(i,j)}$ is the conditional forecast error of $\Delta\mathbf{Y}_t$, and $\mathbf{Q}_t^{(i,j)} = \mathbf{Z}\boldsymbol{\theta}_{t|t-1}^{(i,j)}\mathbf{Z}'$ is its conditional variance.

The probability terms are computed using Hamilton's filter, for each $S_t = S_t^{\alpha}, S_t^{\beta}, S_t^{\delta}$, as:

$$P(S_{t-1} = i, S_t = j|\mathbf{I}_{t-1}) = p^{ij}\sum_{h=0}^{1} P(S_{t-2} = h, S_{t-1} = i|\mathbf{I}_{t-1}). \tag{7.19}$$

From these joint conditional probabilities, the density of $\Delta\mathbf{Y}_t$ conditional on S_{t-1}, S_t, and $\mathbf{I}_{t-1}$ is:

$$f(\Delta\mathbf{Y}_t|S_{t-1} = i, S_t = j, \mathbf{I}_{t-1}) = [(2\pi)^{-n/2}|\mathbf{Q}_t^{(i,j)}|^{-1/2}\exp\left(-\frac{1}{2}\mathbf{N}_{t|t-1}^{(i,j)'}\mathbf{Q}_t^{(i,j)^{-1}}\mathbf{N}_{t|t-1}^{(i,j)}\right). \tag{7.20}$$

The joint probability density of states and observations is then calculated by multiplying each element of (7.19) by the corresponding element of (7.20):

$$f(\Delta\mathbf{Y}_t, S_{t-1} = i, S_t = j|\mathbf{I}_{t-1}) = f(\Delta\mathbf{Y}_t|S_{t-1} = i, S_t = j, \mathbf{I}_{t-1})P(S_{t-1} = i, S_t = j|\mathbf{I}_{t-1}). \tag{7.21}$$

The probability density of $\Delta \mathbf{Y}_t$ given $\mathbf{I}_{t-1}$ is:

$$f(\Delta \mathbf{Y}_t|\mathbf{I}_{t-1}) = \sum_{j=0}^{1}\sum_{i=0}^{1} f(\Delta \mathbf{Y}_t, S_{t-1} = i, S_t = j|\mathbf{I}_{t-1}). \tag{7.22}$$

The joint probability density of states is calculated by dividing each element of (7.14) by the corresponding element of (7.22):

$$P(S_{t-1} = i, S_t = j|\mathbf{I}_t) = f(\Delta \mathbf{Y}_t, S_{t-1} = i, S_t = j|\mathbf{I}_{t-1})/f(\Delta \mathbf{Y}_t|\mathbf{I}_{t-1}) \tag{7.23}$$

Finally, summing over the states in (7.23), we obtain the filtered probabilities of expansions or recessions:

$$P(S_t = j|\mathbf{I}_t) = \sum_{i=0}^{1} P(S_{t-1} = i, S_t = j|\mathbf{I}_t). \tag{7.24}$$

As with the linear Kalman filter, the algorithm calculates recursively one-step-ahead predictions and updates equations of the dynamic factor and the mean squared error matrices, given the parameters of the model and starting values for $\boldsymbol{\xi}^j_{t|t}, \boldsymbol{\theta}^j_{t|t}$, and the probabilities of the Markov states. However, for each date t the nonlinear filter computes 2^k forecasts, where k is the number of states, and at each iteration the number of cases is multiplied by k. This implies that the algorithm would be computationally unfeasible, even for the simplest cases. Kim (1994), based on Harrison and Stevens (1976), proposes an approximation introduced through $\boldsymbol{\xi}^j_{t|t}$ and $\boldsymbol{\theta}^j_{t|t}$ for $t > 1$. This approximation consists of truncating the updating equations into averages weighted by the probabilities of the Markov states.

At each t, the conditional likelihood of the observable variables is obtained as a by-product of the algorithm from equation (7.20), which is used to estimate the unknown model parameters. The filter evaluates this likelihood function, which is then maximized with respect to the model parameters using a nonlinear optimization algorithm. The maximum likelihood estimators and the sample data are then used in a final application of the filter to draw inferences about the dynamic factor and probabilities, based on information available at time t. The final estimated state vector is calculated as:

$$\boldsymbol{\xi}_{t|t} = \sum_{i=0}^{1} P(S_t = j|\mathbf{I}_t)\boldsymbol{\xi}^{j}_{t|t}.$$

The estimation is implemented through a numerical procedure. The nonlinear discrete filter produces two outputs: the state vector, $\boldsymbol{\xi}_{t|t}$, containing the dynamic factor and the idiosyncratic terms, along with the associated probabilities of the Markov states. The filtered probabilities give at time t the probability of the Markov state, using only information available at t, $P(S_t = 0, 1|\mathbf{I}_t)$. On the other hand, the smoothing probabilities are obtained through backward recursion using the information in the full sample, $P(S_t = 0, 1|\mathbf{I}_T)$.

7.4. Empirical Results

7.4.1. *Data*

We use the federal funds rate as the interest rate in defining high and low interest rate phases and the log first difference of consumer price index as the inflation rate in defining high and low inflation phases. Those two series and the simple sum monetary aggregates, M1, M2, and M3, as well as their corresponding "monetary service indexes" (Divisia), MSI1, MSI2, MSI3, were all obtained from the Federal Reserve Bank of Saint Louis. The Research Division of the Saint Louis Federal Bank produces the MSI indexes on a regular basis using equation (7.7). The MSI Divisia indexes measure the flow of monetary services obtained by households and firms from holding monetary assets. For the theory and methodology utilized in the construction of these indexes, and for details of the construction of these indexes, see Anderson, Jones, and Nesmith (1997a and b). For a survey of the theory of monetary aggregation, empirical comparisons of monetary aggregates, and reprints of seminal papers on the subject, see Barnett and Serletis (2000). We use quarterly data from 1960:2 to

2005:4, which is the sample period during which the Divisia indexes data were available at the time that this research was conducted.

7.4.2. *Specification Tests*

The dynamic factor structure captures cyclical comovements underlying the observable variables. We find that the resulting dynamic factor is highly correlated with all of the monetary aggregates used in its construction. As a result, it is clear that the structure was not imposed on the data by assuming large idiosyncratic errors.

In addition, tests for the number of states strongly support the single factor specification. This conclusion is tested in different ways. First, the eigenvalues of the correlation matrix of the common factor indicate adequacy of the single factor specification.[12] Second, the model assumes that the factor summarizes the common dynamic correlation underlying the observable variables. Consequently, the idiosyncratic terms in $\mathbf{v}_t$ are uncorrelated with the observed variables in $\Delta\mathbf{Y}_t$.[13] To test this assumption, the idiosyncratic terms $\mathbf{v}_t$ are regressed on six lags of the observable variables $\Delta\mathbf{Y}_t$, and the parameters of the equations are found to be insignificantly different from zero. In addition, the one-step-ahead conditional forecast errors, $\mathbf{N}_{t|t-1}$, obtained from the filter described in section 2, are not predictable by lags of the observable variables. These results support the single factor specification, since these error terms are not capturing common information underlying the observable variables.

With respect to the measurement errors, $\boldsymbol{\varepsilon}_t$, the i.i.d. assumption is tested using Ljung-Box statistics on their sample autocorrelation and

[12]The magnitude of the n eigenvalues for each factor reflects how much of the correlation among the observable variables is explained by $k \leq n$ potential factors. For each of the three composite indicators, there is only one eigenvalue greater than one, while the others are close to zero.

[13]The model was estimated allowing either AR(1) or AR(0) processes for the disturbances $\Delta\mathbf{v}_t$. The likelihood ratio test favors the AR(1) specification at the 1% level.

the BDS test proposed by Brock, Dechert, Scheinkman, and LeBaron (1996).[14] Both tests fail to reject the i.i.d. assumption at any level.

7.4.3. *High and Low Inflation and Interest Rate Phases*

We study changes in monetary growth across business cycle phases and across high and low inflation and interest rate periods. We use economic recessions and expansions as dated by the NBER to analyze changes across business cycle states. Regarding inflation, we are mostly interested in identifying periods during which there is a persistent change in this series. We classify a high inflation phase as one in which inflation increases persistently for several quarters until it reaches a peak. Analogously, low inflation phases start when inflation falls for several quarters until it reaches a trough. A high (low) inflation phase may include periods during which the level of inflation is still relatively low (high) but is increasing (decreasing) persistently. That is, the level of inflation is not as relevant as its rate of change. For example, inflation was historically low in the early 2000s, but since its derivative turned positive in 2002:1 and remained so for a couple of quarters, this date indicates the beginning of a high inflation phase.

The metric proposed to determine inflation phases is as follows: a high inflation phase starts in quarter t, if inflation π_{t-1} was in a low phase in quarter $t-1$ and $\pi_{t+2} \geq \pi_{t+1} \geq \pi_t \geq \pi_{t-1}$. That is, inflation grows for three consecutive quarters. A low inflation phase starts in quarter t, if inflation π_{t-1} was in a high phase in quarter $t-1$ and $\pi_{t+1} < \pi_t < \pi_{t-1}$. That is, inflation falls for two consecutive quarters. This is similar to the rule of thumb of two quarters decrease (increase) in GDP to determine the beginning

[14]The BDS test requires prior settings of two calibration parameters: embedding dimensions, m, and norm bound, ε. We set $m = 2, 3, 4, 5, 6$ months and $\varepsilon =$ standard deviation of the univariate disturbance time series, assumed to have constant mean function and constant conditional variance.

of recessions (expansions), although we use an asymmetric number of quarters for high and low phases based on inflation persistence. However, the results do not change, if we use instead two quarters decrease or increase.

We also use the Bry and Boschan (1971) routine to determine inflation phases. Bry and Boschan (B-B) formalize turning point dating rules into a computer routine, which has been refined by Haywood (1973) to include an amplitude criterion.[15] The turning points obtained coincide with our proposed criterion described above. In fact, both methods select turning points that would be easily picked simply by visual inspection of the smoothed series.

The resulting inflation phases are plotted in Figure 1a together with inflation, smoothed inflation, and NBER recessions. When inflation starts increasing, it does so slowly and steadily. However,

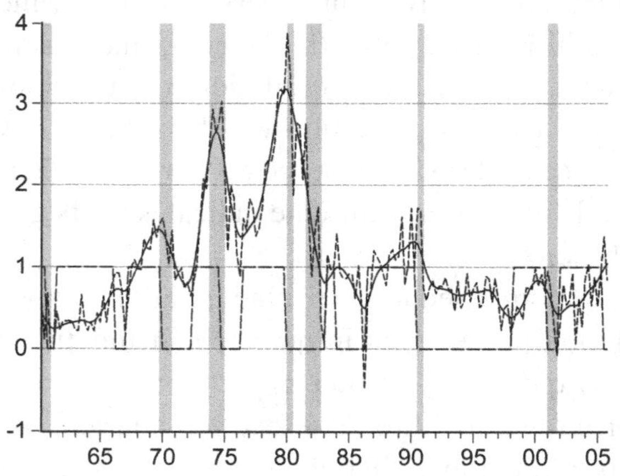

Fig. 1a. Smoothed Inflation (—), Inflation (- - -), High Inflation Phases (– – –), and NBER Recessions (Shaded Area).

[15]The main steps of the B-B routine are: (1) the data are smoothed after outliers are discarded; (2) preliminary turning points are selected and compared with the ones in the original series; (3) duration of the phases is checked, and if duration is below 6 months, the turning points are disregarded; (4) amplitude criterion is applied, based on a moving standard deviation of the series. In the end, the program selects turning points that would be easily picked simply by visual inspection.

when inflation falls, it drops abruptly, making it easier to identify the beginning of a low inflation phase than the start of a high inflation phase. Notice that inflation phases are associated with NBER recessions. In particular, all recessions begin around the end of high inflation phases. In addition, there were only two high inflation phases, in 1983–1984 and in 2002, during which a recession did not follow. However, the economy entered a slowdown in 1984–1986.

With respect to interest rate, the determination of peaks and troughs is simplified by the fact that this series is smoother than inflation. We use a similar metric to the one used for inflation. However, using two or three quarters of change as the cut off for dating the phases results in exactly the same dating. Thus, we use the following metric: a high interest rate phase starts in quarter t, if interest rate i_{t-1} was in a low phase in quarter $t-1$ and if $i_{t+1} \geq i_t \geq i_{t-1}$; and a low interest rate phase starts in quarter t, if interest rate i_{t-1} was in a high phase in quarter $t-1$ and if $i_{t+1} < i_t < i_{t-1}$. That is, the turning point of interest rate phases takes place, when the interest rate falls or rises for two consecutive quarters. Once again, we use the Bry and Boschan (1971) routine to determine interest rate phases and find the same turning points as the two-consecutive-quarter rule of thumb.

The interest rate phases are shown in Figure 1b as well as interest rate, smoothed interest rate, and NBER recessions. Interest rate phases are also associated with the NBER recessions and expansions — the peak generally is at, or right before, economic recessions, whereas the trough is roughly in the middle of expansions. One exception is for the most recent expansion, in which the high interest phase started a lot earlier, at the trough of the 2001 recession.

7.4.4. *Estimates*

Table 1 displays the maximum likelihood estimates of the Markov switching dynamic factor model applied to the monetary aggregates.

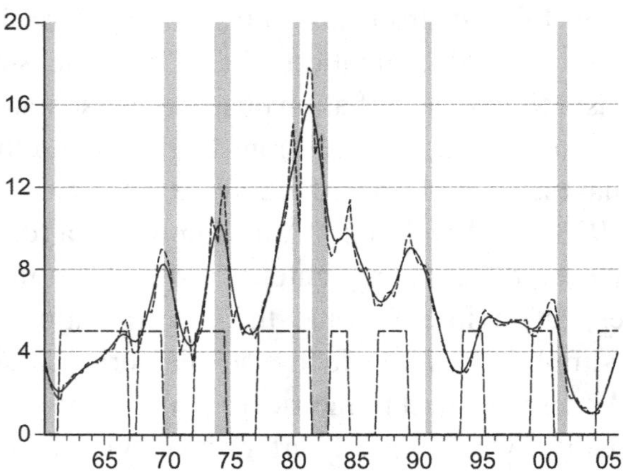

Fig. 1b. Smoothed Interest Rates (—), Interest Rates (- - -), High Interest Rates Phases (– – –), and NBER Recessions (Shaded Area).

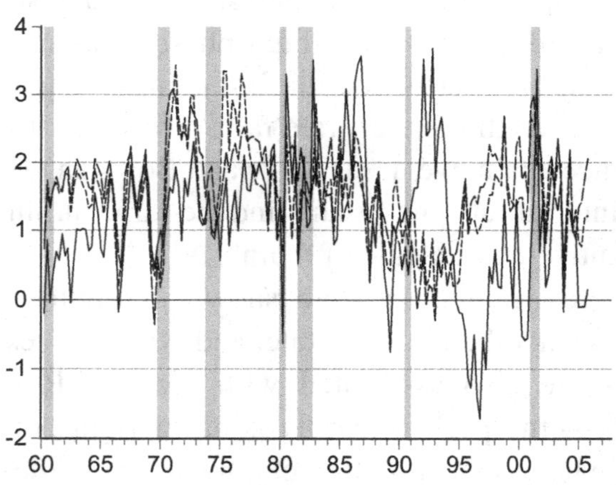

Fig. 1c. Dynamic Factors from the Pairs M1-MSI1 Growth (—), M2-MSI2 Growth (- - -), M3-MSI3 Growth (– – –), and NBER Recessions (Shaded Area).

Three models were estimated, one for each pair of the monetary indexes: M_1 and MSI_1 (Model 1), M_2 and MSI_2 (Model 2), and M_3 and MSI_3 (Model 3).

The Markov states for the factors are statistically significant across the specifications. For models 1 and 3, state 1 has a positive

Table 1. Maximum Likelihood Estimates.

Parameters	M1 and MSI1	M2 and MSI2	M3 and MSI3
α_0	−0.226	0.621	−0.767
	(0.022)	(0.115)	(0.137)
α_1	0.636	0.731	0.949
	(0.226)	(0.195)	(0.141)
Φ	0.556	0.518	0.497
	(0.070)	(0.082)	(0.071)
d_M	0.431	0.976	0.962
	(0.084)	(0.020)	(0.039)
d_{MSI}	0.979	0.589	0.603
	(0.010)	(0.095)	(0.075)
σ^2	0.511	0.254	0.157
	(0.056)	(0.038)	(0.026)
σ_M^2	0.030	0.006	0.005
	(0.003)	(0.003)	(0.002)
σ_{MSI}^2	1.099	0.047	0.093
	(0.018)	(0.007)	(0.011)
λ_M	1.099	0.977	1.172
	(0.018)	(0.034)	(0.054)
p_{00}^{α}	0.987	0.970	0.857
	(0.016)	(0.031)	(0.076)
p_{11}^{α}	0.941	0.795	0.967
	(0.059)	(0.150)	(0.022)
p_{00}^{β}	0.560	0.633	0.992
	(0.209)	(0.144)	(0.009)
p_{11}^{β}	0.967	0.977	0.976
	(0.019)	(0.011)	(0.021)
p_{00}^{δ}	0.954	0.681	0.679
	(0.019)	(0.138)	(0.136)
p_{11}^{δ}	0.701	0.971	0.972
	(0.137)	(0.014)	(0.014)
β_0	−0.322	−0.549	−0.040
	(0.063)	(0.059)	(0.010)
β_1	0.024	0.009	0.262
	(0.012)	(0.002)	(0.015)
δ_0	−0.018	−0.703	−0.857
	(0.010)	(0.433)	(0.086)
δ_1	0.096	0.008	0.051
	(0.020)	(0.003)	(0.020)
τ	0.002	0.002	0.004
	(0.001)	(0.001)	(0.0007)
Log L(θ)	−88.404	−68.893	−77.295

Asymptotic standard errors in parentheses.

mean growth rate, α_1, while state 0 has a negative mean growth rate, α_0. For model 2, the mean growth rates in both states are positive, although the mean growth rate in state 0 is smaller than in state 1, and they both are statistically significant at the 1% level.

The autoregressive coefficient for the factor, ϕ, is positive and near 0.5 across all specifications. The factor loadings measure how changes in the dynamic factor affect changes in the observable variables. The loadings for the Divisia monetary indexes are set equal to one to provide a scale for the latent dynamic factors. This normalization is a necessary condition for identification of the factors. The choice of parameter scale does not affect any of the time series properties of the dynamic factor or the correlation with its components. We find that the estimated factor loading for the simple sum monetary aggregate is positive and close to one across all models, indicating that the Divisia index and the simple sum aggregate have a similar and proportional impact on the factor for each model.

All other parameters of the model are statistically significant as well. We discuss their dynamics for each model below.

7.4.5. *Simple M1 Aggregate and Divisia M1*

The factor extracted from the growth rates of the simple sum aggregate M1 and from the growth rate of the Divisia M1 (MSI1) index is plotted in Figure 2a together with the probabilities of low monetary growth and NBER recessions (DF1). During the 1960s and 1970s, the factor is mostly positive with an average quarterly growth of 1.2%. In the second half of the sample, there are times during which money growth decreases substantially, reaching negative values. The smoothed probabilities identify four phases of negative monetary growth during this second half: 1989:1–1989:4, 1994:4–1997:2, 2000:2–2000:4, and 2005:1–20005:3; and a pulse change in 1980:2.

With correlation values of 0.988 for M1 and 0.998 for MSI1, respectively (Table 2), the dynamic factor is highly correlated with its components. Notice that M1 and MSI1 are more correlated with

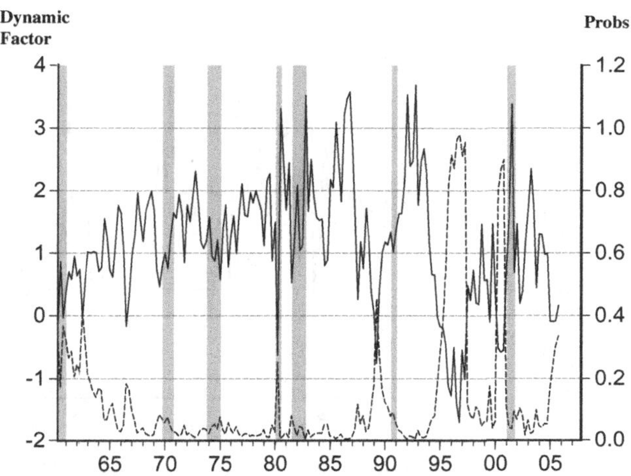

Fig. 2a. Dynamic Factor (—) and Probabilities of High Monetary Growth Based on M1 and MSI1 (- - -), and NBER Recessions (Shaded Area).

Table 2. Correlation Coefficients between Monetary Indexes and Dynamic Factors.

Parameters	$\mathbf{M_1}$	$\mathbf{MSI_1}$	$\mathbf{M_2}$	$\mathbf{MSI_2}$	$\mathbf{M_3}$	$\mathbf{MSI_3}$
$\mathbf{DFM_1}$	0.988	0.998	0.337	0.423	0.150	0.265
$\mathbf{DFM_2}$	0.354	0.339	0.947	0.963	0.767	0.883
$\mathbf{DFM_3}$	0.120	0.128	0.793	0.732	0.987	0.902
$\mathbf{M_1}$	1	0.984	0.354	0.429	0.139	0.260
$\mathbf{MSI_1}$	0.984	1	0.332	0.418	0.151	0.261
$\mathbf{M_2}$	0.354	0.332	1	0.894	0.802	0.806
$\mathbf{MSI_2}$	0.429	0.418	0.894	1	0.693	0.904
$\mathbf{M_3}$	0.139	0.151	0.802	0.693	1	0.858
$\mathbf{MSI_3}$	0.260	0.261	0.806	0.904	0.858	1

the factor than with each other. Figure 2b plots these series and NBER recessions. Although the comparison of the series suggests that they share very similar dynamics, there are important differences during certain times and around turning points that cannot be evaluated by their average behavior. The idiosyncratic terms and the measurement errors reveal where the monetary indexes differ.

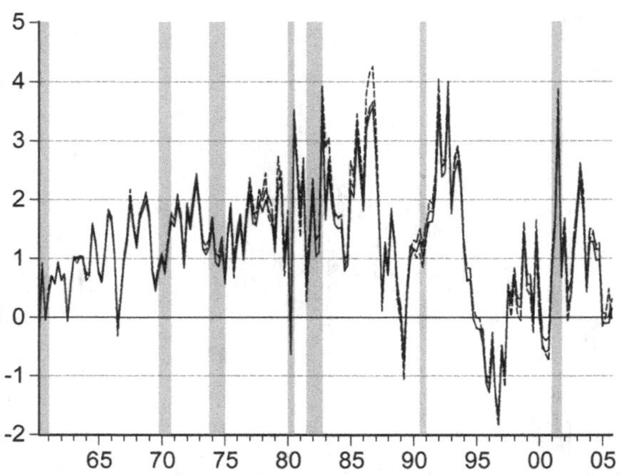

Fig. 2b. Dynamic Factor (—), Rate of Growth of M1 (---) and MSI1 (–––), and NBER Recessions (Shaded Area).

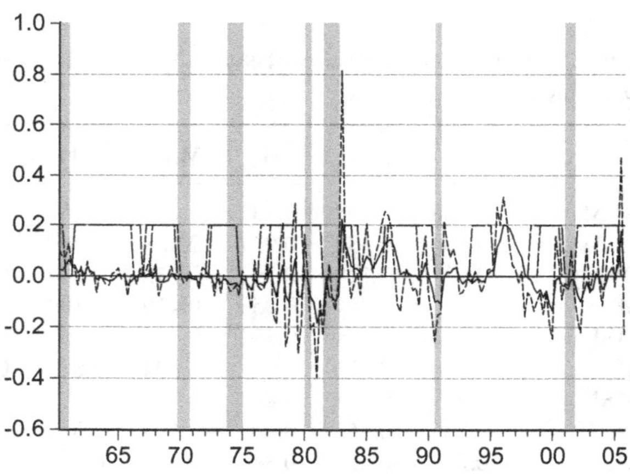

Fig. 2c. Idiosyncratic Terms for M1 (---) and MSI1 Growth (—), High Interest Rate Phases (–––), High Inflation Phases (–--), and NBER Recessions (Shaded Area).

The idiosyncratic term for MSI1 is highly autocorrelated (0.98) and smooth, whereas the one for M1 is a lot less persistent (0.48) and more jagged (Table 1 and Figure 2c). Both idiosyncratic terms display a business cycle pattern from 1980 on. In particular, they rise before the beginnings of recessions and fall during recessions,

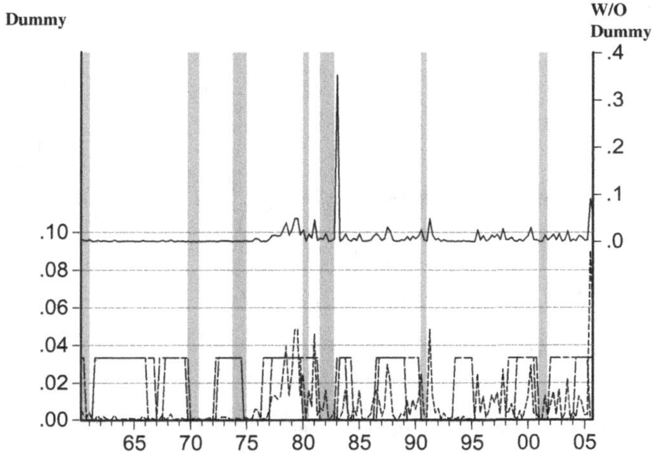

Fig. 2d. Difference between Idiosyncratic Terms for M1 and MSI1 Growth without (—), and with Dummy (---), High Interest Rate Phases (–––), High Inflation Phases (---), and NBER Recessions (Shaded Area).

but subsequently converge to their average in the beginnings of expansions. During the 1980s' and 1990s' expansions, the idiosyncratic terms increased steadily until reaching a peak in the middle of these expansions.

Figure 2d plots the squared difference between the idiosyncratic terms for M1 and MSI1, NBER recessions, and phases of high inflation and interest rates. From 1960 until 1976 the difference between them was almost zero. However, analysis of the second part of the sample uncovers some interesting divergent patterns. The major differences took place right around the beginning or end of recessions. Notice that the beginning of recessions is also the end of high interest rate and inflation phases. The largest differences occurred at the end of the 1981–82 recession and in 2005:3, followed by divergences before the 1980–81 and 1981–82 recessions and at the trough of the 1990–91 recession. In addition, persistent differences took place during high phases of inflation and interest rates. It can be observed that differences also occur, when there are some major changes in the magnitude of monetary growth. This is especially the case between

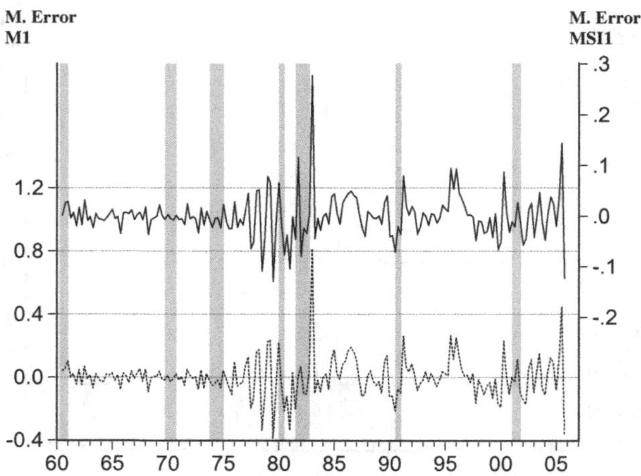

Fig. 2e. Measurement Errors for M1 (lower) and MSI1 Growth (upper), High Interest Rate Phases and High Inflation Phases (—), and NBER Recessions (Shaded Area).

1994:4–1997:2, when both the rate of growth of M1 and of the Divisia index, MSI1, decreased substantially to negative values.

Figure 2e shows the measurement error from simple sum aggregate M1 growth, from Divisia M1 growth (MSI1), and NBER recessions. The measurement error from Divisia growth is a lot smaller than from simple sum M1 growth throughout the sample. As discussed in the previous section, linear and nonlinear tests fail to reject the hypothesis of i.i.d. for the measurement errors. However, some interesting patterns can be observed in their squared differences. Since 1984, the measurement error of M1 growth is greater than of Divisia growth in the middle of expansions and smaller from the second half of expansions until around the beginning of recessions. The difference becomes positive during recessions but reverts to negative at their end. The major difference between the two took place in the first quarter of 1983, when the measurement error for M1 growth reached its maximum value.

Figure 2f shows the squared difference between the measurement errors. As for the idiosyncratic terms, the difference between the measurement errors is almost zero before 1976. However, its highest

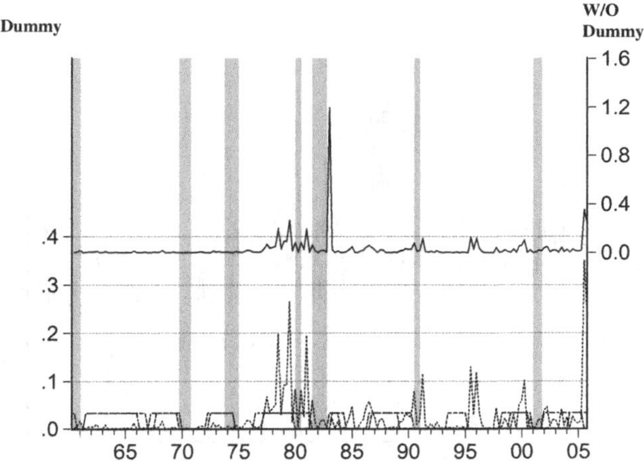

Fig. 2f. Difference between Measurement Errors for M1 and MSI1 Growth without (upper) and with Dummy (lower), High Interest Rate Phases and High Inflation Phases (—), and NBER Recessions (Shaded Area).

levels occurred during the high inflation phase between 1977 and 1983. It also increased at the peak and trough of the 1990–1991 recession and between 1999 and 2000, during the high inflation and interest rate phase that preceded the 2001 recession. As for the idiosyncratic terms, the only time that the difference between the two measurement errors was large, but not associated with a high inflation or interest rate phase or a recession, was between 1995–1996. This period corresponds to a shift of monetary growth from historically positive to very negative.

This analysis confirms previous results (see e.g., Belongia 1996), which find large differences between M1 and Divisia MSI1 between 1984 and 1987 and between 1995 and 1997, with the former being greater than the latter.

7.4.6. *Simple M2 Aggregate and Divisia M2*

The dynamic factor obtained from the growth rates of the simple sum aggregate M2 and from the Divisia M2 (MSI2) is highly correlated with these series, with correlations of 0.95 and 0.96, respectively

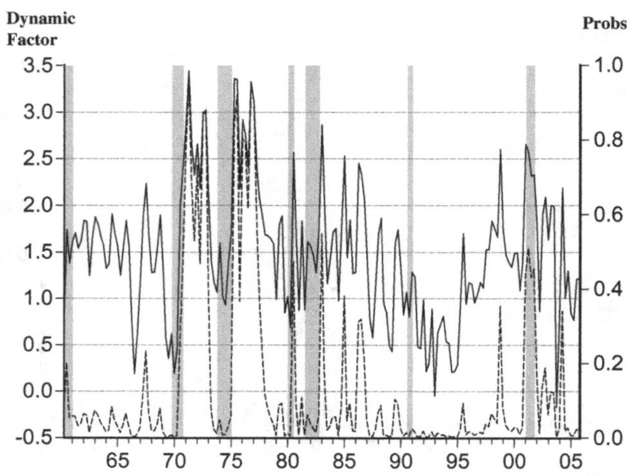

Fig. 3a. Dynamic Factor (—) and Probabilities of High Monetary Growth Based on M2 and MSI2 (- - -), and NBER Recessions (Shaded Area).

(Table 2). Figure 3a shows this factor (DF2) and the probabilities of high monetary growth. The most noticeable feature of the factor (and of its components) is its rise during 1970–73 and during 1975–78. These periods are captured by the smoothed probabilities, as well as the fast monetary growth phases following the 1980–81 and 1981–82 recessions, and during the 2001 recession. Other periods during which money growth was well above its average included 1985–86 and 1998, as depicted by the probabilities.

The dynamics of the factor DM1 differ substantially from the factor DM2, especially after 1990 (Figures 1c and 3b), and the overall correlation between them is only 0.34. First, the DM1 factor does not increase as substantially as the DM2 factor in the 1970s. Second, the DM2 factor moves in the opposite direction from the DM1 factor during 1991–1994, with DM2 reaching its highest level of growth during this period. A divergent movement also takes place in 1995–1996, when DM1 grows and DM2 falls. This same pattern is found by comparing the growth rate of M1 and MSI1 with M2 and MSI2.

The idiosyncratic terms for M2 and MSI2 are shown in Figure 3c. There are marked differences between them. Although they generally

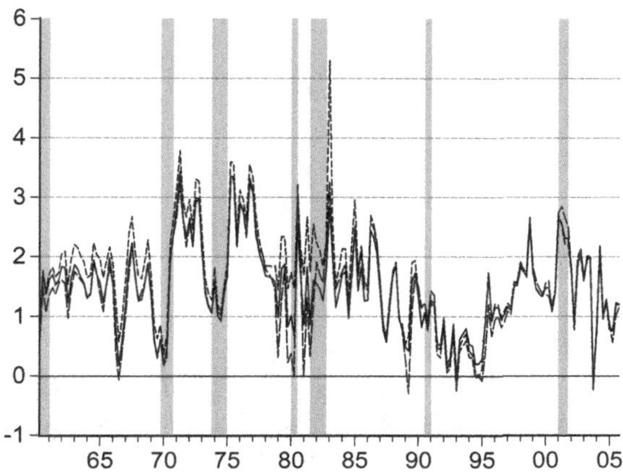

Fig. 3b. Dynamic Factor (—), Rate of Growth of M2 (- - -) and MSI2 (– – –), and NBER Recessions (Shaded Area).

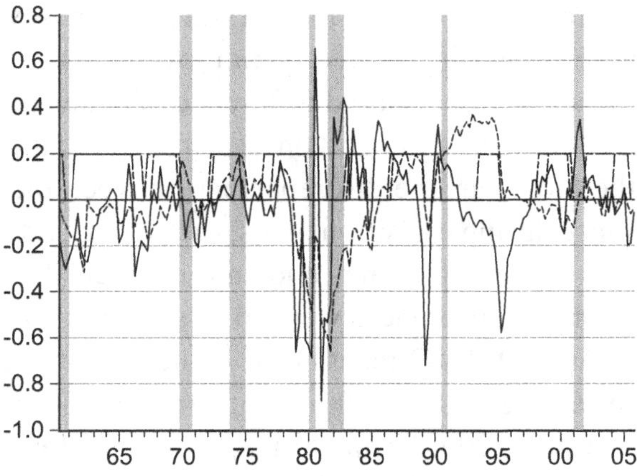

Fig. 3c. Idiosyncratic Terms for M2 (- - -) and MSI2 Growth (—), High Interest Rate Phases (– – –), High Inflation Phases (– – –), and NBER Recessions (Shaded Area).

move in the same direction in the first part of the sample, they differ substantially around turning points and in the second period. For example, the idiosyncratic term for M2 increased during the 1970 and 1974–75 recessions, even when interest rate was already in a low phase. The idiosyncratic term for the MSI2, on the other hand,

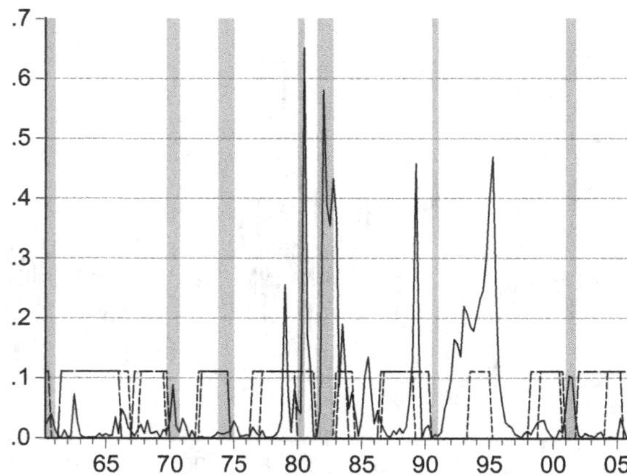

Fig. 3d. Difference between Idiosyncratic Terms for M2 and MSI2 Growth (—), High Interest Rate Phases (– – –), High Inflation Phases (- - -), and NBER Recessions (Shaded Area).

decreased during these periods. From 1982 there are several instances in which these series display divergent movements.

Figure 3d shows the squared difference between these two series along with NBER recessions and phases of high inflation and interest rates. For the most part the discrepancies between the idiosyncratic terms take place during transition times, such as around business cycle turning points or the beginnings and ends of interest rate or inflation phases. The largest differences were from the middle to the trough of the 1980–81 and 1981–82 recessions, at the end of the high interest rate phase in 1989 (and the beginning of an economic slowdown), and between 1991 and 1996. In this last period the differences were not only large, but they were also the longest in the sample, corresponding to cyclical movements of DM1 and DM2 in opposite directions as explained above. There were other important divergences, such as the ones during the 1970 and 1990 recessions, and during the transitions from tight to loose monetary policies.

Figure 3e plots the difference between the measurement errors for M2 and MSI2 growth. The main discrepancies between these two series occur between 1979 and 1982. This period includes a slowdown, two recessions and a small recovery, and coincides with

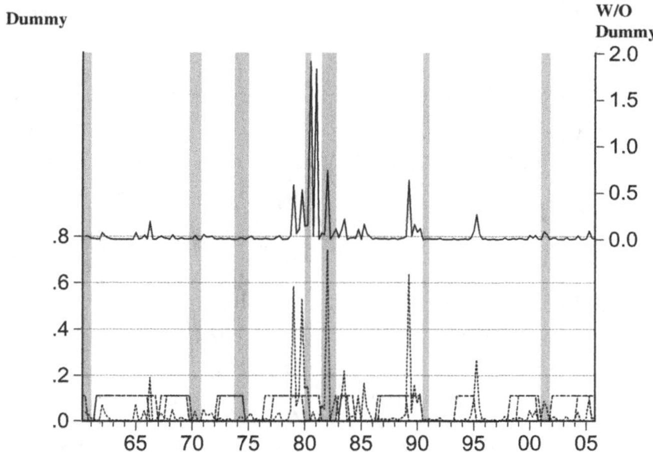

Fig. 3e. Difference between Measurement Errors for M2 and MSI2 Growth without (upper) and with Dummy (lower), High Interest Rate Phases and High Inflation Phases (—), and NBER Recessions (Shaded Area).

the time during which the Federal Reserve changed its operating procedures.

Another time during which these series differ is in the transition between two phases in 1989. In particular, a large difference takes place at the peak of the interest rates cycle. While interest rate started decreasing in 1989:2, inflation remained in a high phase until 1990:2.

7.4.7. *Simple M3 Aggregate and Divisia M3*

Figure 4a shows the dynamic factor (DF3) resulting from the growth rates of the simple sum aggregate M3 and from Divisia M3 (MSI3), while Figure 1c compares the three dynamic factors, DF1, DF2, and DF3. The factor DF1 moves in the opposite direction from the factors DF2 and DF3 during some periods, whereas in general DF2 and DF3 display very similar dynamics (Figure 1c). However, DF3 growth (as well as M3 and MSI3 growth) was not as high in the 1970s as DF2 growth. In fact, the Markov probabilities for DF3 capture instead a large drop in the underlying M3 and MSI3 growth between 1989:2 and 1995:1 as being the most salient variation in the series. Other

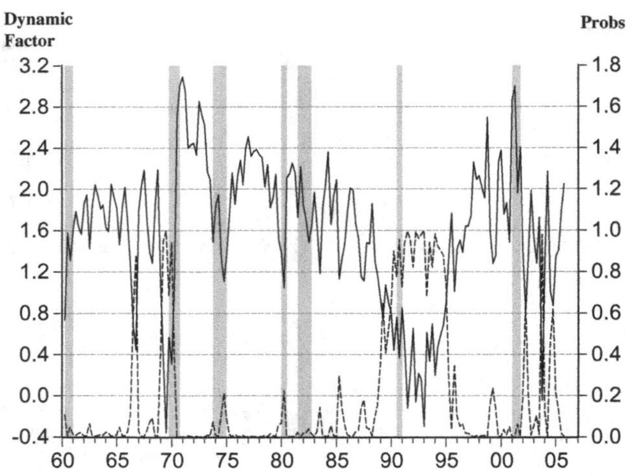

Fig. 4a. Dynamic Factor (—) and Probabilities of Low Monetary Growth Based on M3 and MSI3 (- - -), and NBER Recessions (Shaded Area).

important low growth phases captured by the probabilities are in 1966, between 1969–70, in 2002, and in 2004–05.

The dynamic factor DF3 is highly correlated with M3 and MSI3 growth, but more so with the former (0.98) than with the latter (0.90) (Table 2). However, the correlation between the dynamic factor and the growth of MSI3 is a lot higher, if the period between 1978 and 1982 is excluded. During this time, MSI3 growth oscillated substantially (Figure 4b).

The idiosyncratic terms for M3 and MSI3 growth are shown in Figure 4c. The term corresponding to M3 is smoother and has smaller fluctuations. Although they have generally similar dynamics, the two idiosyncratic terms differ substantially during some important periods. Figure 4d plots their squared difference. The major divergences between M3 and MSI3 growth coincide in time and amplitude with the differences between M2 and MSI2 growth. The largest discrepancies took place during the high inflation phase between 1978 and 1981, and during the 1981–82 recession. Times of high uncertainty are associated with larger asynchronous movements between M3 and MSI3 growth, such as during recessions or at interest

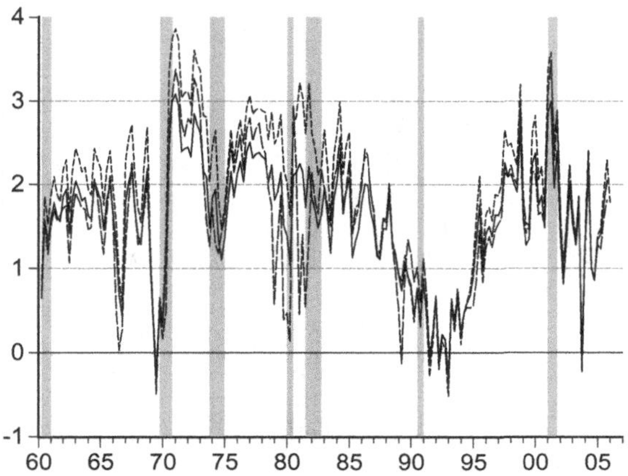

Fig. 4b. Dynamic Factor (—), Rate of Growth of M3 (---) and MSI3 (–––), and NBER Recessions (Shaded Area).

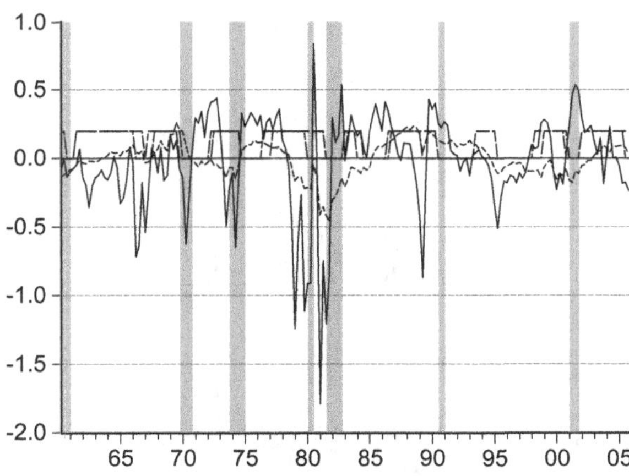

Fig. 4c. Idiosyncratic Terms for M3 (---) and MSI3 Growth (—), High Interest Rate Phases (–––), High Inflation Phases (–––), and NBER Recessions (Shaded Area).

rate turning points. This is the case, for example, between 1989 and 1990, when the high interest rate phase ended, but inflation remained in a high phase until right before the beginning of the 1990 recession. This is also the case in 1965–67, during the 1969–70 and 1990–91

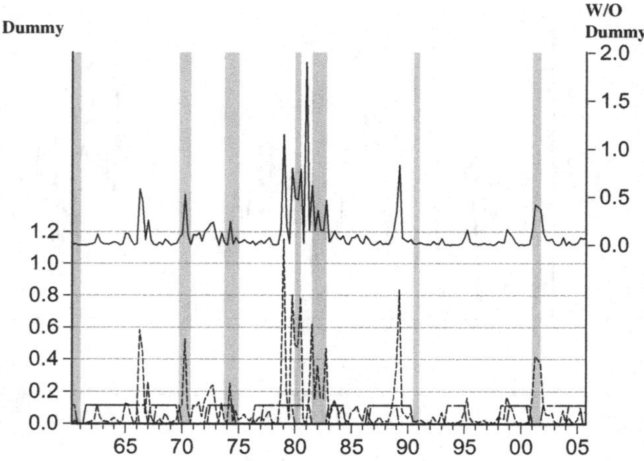

Fig. 4d. Difference between Idiosyncratic Terms for M3 and MSI3 Growth Without (—), and With Dummy (- - -), High Interest Rate Phases (– – –), High Inflation Phases (- - -), and NBER Recessions (Shaded Area).

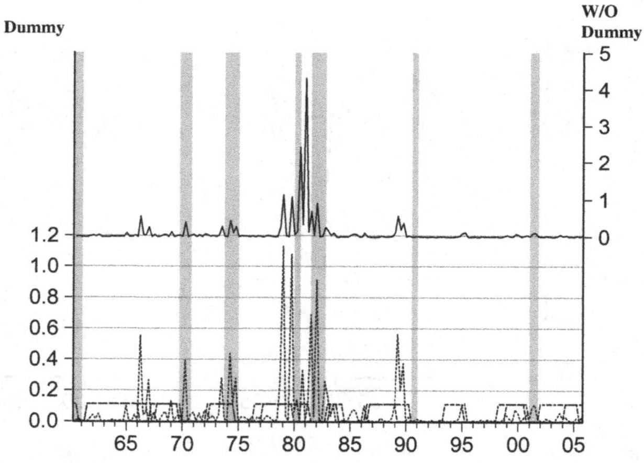

Fig. 4e. Difference between Measurement Errors for M3 and MSI3 Growth without (upper) and with Dummy (lower), High Interest Rate Phases and High Inflation Phases (—), and NBER Recessions (Shaded Area).

recessions, and during the 1972–74 period, which corresponds to a high inflation phase and recession.

Another way of gauging the differences between M3 and MSI3 growth is through the measurement errors. Figure 4e shows the squared difference between their measurement errors. Analysis of these series indicates that the major differences took place in 1979:4, 1982:1, and in the middle of the 1969–73 recession, in addition to the dissimilarities captured by the idiosyncratic terms.

7.5. Summary of Findings

These differences are economically very important. If one of the aggregates corresponds to a better measure of economic monetary services in the economy than the other, their differences add to the uncertainty about the economy and about the effectiveness and appropriateness of monetary policy — exactly at times during which information about the state of monetary growth is premium, such as around business cycle turning points and changes in inflation phases.

In general, the idiosyncratic terms for both the simple sum aggregates and the Divisia indexes display a business cycle pattern, especially since 1980. Those terms generally rise around the end of high interest rate phases (i.e., a couple of quarters before the beginning of recessions), fall during recessions, and subsequently converge to their average in the beginning of expansions.

We find that the major differences between the simple sum aggregates and Divisia indexes occur around the beginnings and ends of economic recessions, and during some high interest rate phases. This is particularly the case for the period between 1977 and 1983, which includes a slowdown, two recessions, two recoveries and the change in the Federal Reserve's operating procedure. Notice that this period also corresponds to a high interest rate phase, which took place from 1977:2 to 1981:2. Another period during which the indexes diverge substantially is around the 1990 recession.

In the case of M1 and MSI1, the main divergence between the two indexes is in 1983:1. The idiosyncratic term for M1 counter-intuitively increased to its highest level during a quarter that marked the beginning of a high interest rate phase. The MSI1, on the other hand, had only a minor rise. At that time, Milton Friedman, based on the movements of the official simple sum monetary aggregates, warned in newspapers and magazines that this ‘monetary explosion’ was bounded to be followed by a contractionary policy by the Federal Reserve, and thereby would lead to another period of stagflation. William Barnett, on the other hand, correctly predicted that there was no reason for concern, since monetary growth was at its average rate, based on the Divisia index data. In fact, Barnett correctly determined *in real time* that the large increase in simple sum money was a ‘statistical blip’ produced by the defects in simple sum monetary aggregation. In fact the two conflicting predictions appeared most dramatically on exactly the same day: September 26, 1983, *Newsweek*, (Friedman) and September 26, 1983, *Forbes* (Barnett), both full page articles.[16]

The differences and similarities between the pairs M2-MSI2 (model 2) and M3-MSI3 (model 3) are closer than the ones for M1 and MSI1 (model 1). First, the Divisia indexes MSI2 and MSI3 decrease a lot more before recessions (at the peak of inflation phases) and increase substantially more during recessions and recoveries (low interest rate phases) than the simple sum aggregates M2 and M3, respectively. That is, the dynamics of these Divisia indexes correspond more closely to the expected movements related to interest rates and inflation.

A noticeable difference between the Divisia MSI2 and the simple sum aggregate M2 is their movement in opposite directions between

[16]This is hardly the only such example of monetary policy puzzles associated with monetary aggregation problems. For more examples, see Barnett (1997) and Barnett and Chauvet (2009). It is perhaps paradoxical that Friedman was mislead by confidence in Federal Reserve monetary aggregates data, since he was highly critical of the Federal Reserve, and since Friedman and Schwartz (1970, pp. 151–152) were among the first to make clear the nature of the Federal Reserve's data aggregation error, when they wrote: “The [simple summation] procedure is a very special case of the more general approach. In brief, the general approach consists of regarding each asset as a joint product having different degrees of ‘moneyness,’ and defining the quantity of money as the weighted sum of the aggregated value of all assets .... We conjecture that this approach deserves and will get much more attention than it has so far received.”

1991 and 1995. During the recovery after the 1990 recession, M2 increased more than MSI2, while interest rates were falling. However, M2 continued to increase even during the high interest rate phase that started in 1993:3 and ended in 1995:1. On the other hand, MSI2 showed a movement more consistent with changes in interest rates, which decreased during this period.

Another difference that is observable in both pairs M2-MSI2 and M2-MSI3 is their behavior at the end of the 1981 recession, when there was a large increase in the idiosyncratic terms from the Divisia indexes, and only a minor rise for the simple sum aggregates. Accordingly, the Divisia indexes display a business cycle pattern more consistent with monetary policy.

With respect to MSI3 and the simple sum aggregate M3, the idiosyncratic terms for these series move in opposite directions on several occasions. In particular, this term for the Divisia index increases during the expansion in the early 1970s, while the idiosyncratic term for M3 counter-intuitively decreases. In addition, the idiosyncratic term for M3 shows a steady increase, since the end of the 1981–82 recession until 1989, thereby showing no link with the high interest rate phase that took place during 1986:4–1989:1. On the other hand, the term for MSI3 increased during the low inflation phase following the 1981–82 recession, but fell during this high interest rate phase. More recently, the idiosyncratic term from the M3 has been counter intuitively high during the latest high interest rate phase that started in 2004, whereas the Divisia MSI3 shows the expected decrease.

7.6. Conclusions

Microeconomic aggregation theory offers an appealing alternative to the disreputable simple-sum method of aggregation. The quantity index under the aggregation-theoretic approach passes through and measures income effects while internalizing and removing substitution effects, which are at constant utility and hence cannot reflect a change in perceived services. The simple sum index, on the other hand, confounds together income and substitution effects, unless components are one-to-one perfect substitutes, i.e., indistinguishable goods. In this paper we compare the dynamic empirical differences between the theory-based definition of money, tracked nonparametrically by the Divisia index, and the simple sum monetary aggregates, traditionally used by central banks and currently in low repute within the economics profession.

Our focus is not only on differences in their average behavior, but also their behavior during some important periods of time, such as around business cycle turning points and across high and low inflation and interest rate phases. We propose a factor model with regime switching to evaluate the common dynamics of the indexes, as well as their idiosyncratic movements.

The state-space time-series approach provides a highly promising direction for research into aggregation theory, index number theory, and economic policy. In this paper we have introduced the connection between the state-space time-series approach to assessing measurement error and the aggregation theoretic concept, with emphasis upon the relevancy to monetary aggregation and monetary policy.

We find some interesting new results. The idiosyncratic terms for both indexes display a business cycle pattern, especially since 1980. The period between 1977 and 1983 is the one during which the most notable differences take place. This period not only includes a slowdown, two recessions, two recoveries, and the change in the Federal Reserve's operating procedure, but also corresponds to a high interest rate phase, which occurred from 1977:2 to 1981:2.

In general, we find that the major differences between the simple sum aggregates and Divisia indexes occur around the beginnings and ends of economic recessions, and during some high interest rate phases. These are times in which information on monetary aggregates is premium for policymakers.

We would once again wish to draw attention to one especially clear figure: Figure 4c. Properly weighted broad aggregates are the best measures of monetary service flows, as observed by Lucas (2000, p. 270), who wrote: "I share the widely held opinion that M1 is too narrow an aggregate for this period [the 1990s], and I think that the Divisia approach offers much the best prospects for resolving this difficulty." As a result, those measures that are specific to (i.e., idiosyncratic to) simple sum M3 and Divisia M3 are of particular interest. Compare Divisia M3's idiosyncratic downward spikes in Figure 4c with simple sum M3's idiosyncratic behavior and then compare the relative predictive ability of the two extracted idiosyncratic terms with respect to NBER recessions. Figure 4c speaks for itself.

References

Anderson, RG, BE Jones, and TD Nesmith (1997a). Introduction to the St. Louis Monetary Services Index Project, *Federal Reserve Bank of St. Louis Review*, **79**(1): 25–30.

Anderson, RG, BE Jones, and TD Nesmith (1997b). Building new monetary services indexes: concepts, data, and methods, *Federal Reserve Bank of St. Louis Review*, **79**(1): 53–82.

Arrow, KJ and F Hahn (1971). *General Competitive Analysis*, Holden-Day, San Francisco.

Ashley, R, D Patterson, and M Hinich (1986). A diagnostic test for non-linear serial dependence in time series fitting errors, *Journal of Time Series Analysis*, **7**: 165–178.

Barnett, WA (1978). The user cost of money, *Economic Letters*, **1**: 145–149. Reprinted in WA Barnett and A Serletis (eds.), (2000). *The Theory of Monetary Aggregation*, North-Holland, Amsterdam, Chapter 1, pp. 6–10.

Barnett, WA (1979a). Theoretical foundations for the Rotterdam model, *Review of Economic Studies*, **46**: 109–130.

Barnett, WA (1979b). The joint allocation of leisure and goods expenditure, *Econometrica*, **47**: 539–563.

Barnett, WA (1980). Economic monetary aggregates: an application of aggregation and index number theory, *Journal of Econometrics*, **14**: 11–48. Reprinted in WA Barnett and A Serletis, (eds.), (2000). *The Theory of Monetary Aggregation*, North-Holland, Amsterdam.

Barnett, WA (1981a). *Consumer Goods and Labor Supply: Goods, Monetary Assets, and Time*, Elsevier, Amsterdam.

Barnett, WA (1981b). The new monetary aggregates: a comment, *Journal of Money, Credit, and Banking*, **13**: 485–489.

Barnett, WA (1982). The optimal level of monetary aggregation, *Journal of Money, Credit, and Banking*, **14**, 687–710. Reprinted in WA Barnett and A Serletis (eds.), (2000). *The Theory of Monetary Aggregation*, North-Holland, Amsterdam, Chapter 7, pp. 125–149.

Barnett, WA (1983). Understanding the new Divisia monetary aggregate, *Review of Public Data Use*, **11**: 349–355. Reprinted in WA Barnett and A Serletis (eds.), (2000). *The Theory of Monetary Aggregation*, North-Holland, Amsterdam, Chapter 4, pp. 100–108.

Barnett, WA (1987). The microeconomic theory of monetary aggregation, in WA Barnett and KJ Singleton (eds.), *New Approaches to Monetary Economics*, Cambridge University Press, pp. 115–168. Reprinted in WA Barnett and A Serletis (eds.), (2000). *The Theory of Monetary Aggregation*, North-Holland, Amsterdam, Chapter 3, pp. 49–99.

Barnett, WA (1991). A reply to Julio J. Rotemberg, in MT Belongia (ed.), *Monetary Policy on the 75th Anniversary of the Federal Reserve System*. Kluwer Academic, Boston: pp. 232–244. Reprinted in WA Barnett and A. Serletis, (eds.), (2000). *The Theory of Monetary Aggregation*, North Holland, Amsterdam.

Barnett, WA (1995). Exact aggregation under risk, in WA Barnett, M Salles, H Moulin, and N Schofield (eds.), (2000). Social Choice, Welfare and Ethics, Cambridge University Press, Cambridge. Reprinted in: WA Barnett and A Serletis (eds.), The Theory of Monetary Aggregation, North-Holland, Amsterdam.

Barnett, WA (1997). Which road leads to stable money demand? *The Economic Journal*, **107**: 1171–1185. Reprinted in WA Barnett and A Serletis (eds.), (2000). *The Theory of Monetary Aggregation*, North-Holland, Amsterdam, Chapter 24, pp. 577–592.

Barnett, WA (2003). Aggregation-theoretic monetary aggregation over the Euro area when countries are heterogeneous, *ECB Working Paper No. 260*, European Central Bank, Frankfurt.

Barnett, WA (2007). Multilateral aggregation-theoretic monetary aggregation over heterogeneous countries, *Journal of Econometrics*, **136**(2): 457–482.

Barnett, WA and J Binner (eds.) (2004). *Functional Structure and Approximation in Econometrics*, North-Holland, Amsterdam.

Barnett, WA and M Chauvet (2009). International financial aggregation and index number theory: a chronological half-century empirical overview, *Open Economics Review*, **20**(1): 1–37.

Barnett, WA and M Chauvet (2010). How better monetary statistics could have signaled the financial crisis, *Journal of Econometrics*, forthcoming.

Barnett, WA and JH Hahm (1994). Financial firm production of monetary services: a generalized symmetric barnett variable profit function approach, *Journal of Business and Economic Statistics*, **12**: 33–46. Reprinted in WA Barnett and J Binner (eds.), (2004). *Functional Structure and Approximation in Econometrics*, North-Holland, Amsterdam, Chapter 15, pp. 351–380.

Barnett, WA and C-H Kwag (2006). Exchange rate determination from monetary fundamentals: an aggregation theoretic approach, *Frontiers in Finance and Economics*, **3**(1): 29–48.

Barnett, WA and Y Liu (2000). Beyond the risk neutral utility function, in MT Belongia and JE Binner (eds.), *Divisia Monetary Aggregates: Theory and Practice*, Palgrave, London, 11–27.

Barnett, WA and P de Peretti (2009). A necessary and sufficient stochastic semi-nonparametric test for weak separability, *Macroeconomic Dynamics*, **13**: 317–334.

Barnett, WA and A Serletis (eds.) (2000). *The Theory of Monetary Aggregation*, North-Holland, Amsterdam.

Barnett, WA and S Wu (2005). On the user costs of risky monetary assets, *Annals of Finance*, **1**: 35–50.

Barnett, WA and H Xu (1998). Stochastic volatility in interest rates and nonlinearity in velocity, *International Journal of Systems Science*, **29**: 1189–1201.

Barnett, WA and G Zhou (1994a). Financial firm's production and supply-side monetary aggregation under dynamic uncertainty, *Federal Reserve Bank of St. Louis Review*, **76**: 133–165. Reprinted in WA Barnett and A Serletis (eds.), (2000). *The Theory of Monetary Aggregation*, North Holland, Amsterdam, Chapter 21.

Barnett, WA and G Zhou (1994b). Partition of M2+ as a joint product: commentary, *Federal Reserve Bank of St. Louis Review*, **76**: 53–62.

Barnett, WA, U Chae, and J Keating (2006). The discounted economic stock of money with VAR forecasting, *Annals of Finance*, **2**(2): 229–258.

Barnett, WA, M Chauvet, and HLR Tierney (2009). Measurement error in monetary aggregates: a markov switching factor approach, *Macroeconomic Dynamics*, **13**: 381–412.

Barnett, WA, D Fisher, and A Serletis (1992). Consumer theory and the demand for money, *Journal of Economic Literature*, **30**: 2086–2119. Reprinted in WA Barnett and A Serletis (eds.), (2000). Chapter 18.

Barnett, WA, J Geweke, and M Wolfe (1991a). Seminonparametric Bayesian estimation of the asymptotically ideal production model, *Journal of Econometrics*, **49**: 5–50.

Barnett, WA, J Geweke, and M Wolfe (1991b). Seminonparametric bayesian estimation of consumer and factor demand models, in WA Barnett, B Cornet, C D'Aspremont, J Gabszewicz, and A Mas-Colell (eds.), *Equilibrium Theory and Applications*, Cambridge University Press, Cambridge, 425–480.

Barnett, WA, J Geweke, and P Yue (1991). Seminonparametric Bayesian estimation of the asymptotically ideal model: the AIM demand system, in WA Barnett, G Tauchen, and J Powell (eds.), *Nonparametric and Semiparametric Methods in Econometrics and Statistics*, Cambridge University Press, Cambridge, 127–174.

Barnett, WA, MJ Hinich, and WE Weber (1986). The regulatory wedge between the demand-side and supply-side aggregation-theoretic monetary aggregates, *Journal of Econometrics*, **33**: 165–185. Reprinted in WA Barnett and A Serletis (eds.) (2000). *The Theory of Monetary Aggregation*, North-Holland, Amsterdam, Chapter 19, pp. 433–453.

Barnett, WA, M Hinich, and P Yue (1991). Monitoring monetary aggregates under risk aversion, in MT Belongia (ed.), *Monetary Policy on the 75th Anniverary of the Federal Reserve System*, Kluwer, Amsterdam, 189–222. Reprinted in WA Barnett and A Serletis (eds.) (2000). *The Theory of Monetary Aggregation*, North-Holland, Amsterdam, Chapter 11.

Barnett, WA, M Hinich, and P Yue (2000). The exact theoretical rational expectations monetary aggregate, *Macroeconomic Dynamics*, **4**: 197–221.

Barnett, WA, M Kirova, and M Pasupathy (1995). Estimating policy-invariant deep parameters in the financial sector when risk and growth matter, *Journal of Money, Credit, and Banking*, **27**: 1402–1430. Reprinted in WA Barnett and A Serletis (eds.), (2000). *The Theory of Monetary Aggregation*, North-Holland, Amsterdam, Chapter 22.

Barnett, WA, Y Liu, and M Jensen (1997). The CAPM risk adjustment for exact aggregation over financial assets, *Macroeconomic Dynamics*, **1**: 485–512. Reprinted in WA Barnett and A Serletis (eds.), (2000). *The Theory of Monetary Aggregation*, North-Holland, Amsterdam.

Barnett, WA, EK Offenbacher, and PA Spindt (1984). The new Divisia monetary aggregates, *Journal of Political Economy*, **92**: 1049–1085. Reprinted in WA Barnett and A Serletis (eds.), (2000). *The Theory of Monetary Aggregation*, North-Holland, Amsterdam, Chapter 17, pp. 360–388.

Barnett, WA, AR Gallant, MJ Hinich, JA Jungeilges, DT Kaplan, and MJ Jensen (1995). Robustness of nonlinearity and chaos tests to measurement error, inference method, and sample size, *Journal of Economic Behavior and Organization*, **27**: 301–320.

Barnett, WA, AR Gallant, MJ Hinich, JA Jungeilges, DT Kaplan, and MJ Jensen (1997). A single blind controlled competition among tests for non-linearity and chaos, *Journal of Econometrics*, **77**: 297–302.

Batchelor, R (1989). A monetary services index for the UK, Mimeo, Department of Economics, City University, London.

Belongia, MT (1996). Measurement matters: recent results from monetary economics re-examined, *Journal of Political Economy*, **104**: 1065–1083.

Belongia, MT and J Binner (eds.) (2000). *Divisia Monetary Aggregates: Theory and Practice*, Palgrave, Basingstoke.

Belongia, MT and J Chalfant (1989). The changing empirical definition of money: some estimates from a model of the demand for money substitutes, *Journal of Political Economy*, **97**: 387–398.

Belongia, MT and A Chrystal (1991). An admissible monetary aggregate for the United Kingdom, *Review of Economics and Statistics*, **73**: 497–503.

Belongia, MT and P Ireland (2006). The own-price of money and the channels of monetary transmission, *Journal of Money Credit and Banking*, **38**(2), 429–445.

Berkowitz, J and L Giorgianni (2001). Long-horizon exchange rate predictability? *Review of Economics and Statistics*, **83**: 81–91.

Beyer, A, JA Doornik, and DF Hendry (2001). Constructing historical euro-zone data, *Economic Journal*, **111**: 308–327.

Bilson, JFO (1978). The monetary approach to the exchange rate: some empirical evidence, *IMF Staff Papers*, **25**: 48–75.

Blanchard, OJ and S Fischer (1989). *Lectures on Macroeconomics*, MIT Press, Cambridge.

Breeden, D, M Gibbons, and R Litzenberger (1989). Empirical tests of the consumption CAPM, *Journal of Finance*, **44**: 231–262.

Brock, WA, WD Dechert, JA Schenkman, and B LeBaron (1996). A test for independence based on the correlation dimension, *Econometric Reviews*, **15**(3): 197–235.

Bry, G and C Boschan (1971). *Cyclical Analysis of Times Series: Selected Procedures and Computer Programs*, National Bureau of Economic Research, New York.

Campbell, JY (1996). Understanding risk and return, *Journal of Political Economy*, **104**: 298–345.

Campbell, JY and JH Cochrane (1999). By force of habit: a consumption-based explanation of aggregate stock market behavior, *Journal of Political Economy*, **107**: 205–251.

Chauvet, M (1998). An econometric characterization of business cycle dynamics with factor structure and regime switches, *International Economic Review*, **39**(4): 969–996.

Chauvet, M (2001). A monthly indicator of brazilian GDP, in *Brazilian Review of Econometrics*, **21**(1).

Chen, NF, R Roll, and S Ross (1986). Economic forces and the stock market, *Journal of Business*, **29**: 383–403.

Cheung, Y-W, MD Chinn, and AG Pascual (2002). Empirical exchange rate models of the nineties: are any fit to survive? NBER Working Paper 9393.

Chinn, MD and RA Meese (1995). Banking on currency forecasts: how predictable is change in money? *Journal of International Economics*, **38**: 161–178.

Chrystal, KA and R MacDonald (1994). Empirical evidence on the recent behavior and usefulness of simple-sum and weighted measures of the money stock. *Federal Reserve Bank of St. Louis Review*, **76**: 73–109.

Cochrane, JH (2000). *Asset Pricing*, Princeton Press, Princeton, NJ.

Cockerline, J and J Murray (1981). A comparison of alternative methods of monetary aggregation: some preliminary evidence, Technical Report #28, Bank of Canada.

Diebold, FX and RS Mariano (1995). Comparing predictive accuracy, *Journal of Business and Economic Statistics*, **13**: 253–263.

Diewert, WE (1976). Exact and superlative index numbers, *Journal of Econometrics*, **4**: 115–145.

Diewert, WE (2002). Harmonized indexes of consumer prices: their conceptual foundations, *Swiss Journal of Economics and Statistics*, **138**: 547–637.

Divisia, F (1925). L'Indice monétaire et la théorie de la monnaie, *Revue d'Economie Politique*, **39**: 980–1008.

Doan, T, RB Litterman, and CA Sims (1984). Forecasting and conditional projection using realistic prior distributions, *Econometric Reviews*, **3**: 1–144.

Dornbusch, R (1976). Expectations and exchange rate dynamics, *Journal of Political Economy*, **84**: 1161–1176.

Drake, L (1992). The substitutability of financial assets in the U.K. and the implication for monetary aggregation, *Manchester School of Economics and Social Studies*, **60**: 221–248.

Drake, L, A Mullineux, and J Agung (1997). One Divisia money for Europe? *Applied Economics*, **29**: 775–786.

Engel, C (1996). The forward discount anomaly and the risk premium: a survey of recent evidence, *Journal of Empirical Finance*, **3**: 123–192.

Engel, C (2000). Long-run PPP may not hold after all, *Journal of International Economics*, **51**: 243–273.

Fama, EF and K French (1992). The cross-section of expected stock returns, *Journal of Finance*, **47**: 427–465.

Fase, MMG (1985). Monetary control: the Dutch experience: some reflections on the liquidity ratio. in C van Ewijk and JJ Klant (eds.), *Monetary Conditions for Economic Recovery*, Martinus Nijhoff, Dordrecht: 95–125.

Fase, MMG (2000). Divisia aggregates and the demand for money in core EMU, in MT Belongia and JE Binner (eds.), *Divisia Monetary Aggregates: Theory and Practice*, Macmillan, London, pp. 138–169.

Fase, MMG and CCA Winder (1994). Money demand within EMU: an analysis with the Divisia measure, De Nederlandsche Bank NV, Amsterdam, pp. 25–55.

Fayyad, SK (1986). Monetary asset component grouping and aggregation: an inquiry into the definition of money. Ph.D. Dissertation, University of Texas, Austin, Texas.

Feenstra, RC (1986). Functional equivalence between liquidity costs and the utility of money, *Journal of Monetary Economics*, **17**: 271–291.

Fischer, S (1974). Money and the production function, *Economic Inquiry*, **12**: 517–533.

Fisher, I (1922). *The Making of Index Numbers: A Study of Their Varieties, Tests, and Reliability*, Houghton Mifflin, Boston.

Fisher, P, S Hudson, and M Pradhan (1993). Divisia measures of money, *Bank of England Quarterly Bulletin*, May, 240–255.

Frenkel, JA (1976). A monetary approach to the exchange rate: doctrinal aspects and empirical evidence, *Scandinavian Journal of Economics*, **2**: 200–224.

Frankel, JA (1984). Tests of monetary and portfolio balance models of exchange rate determination, in JFO Bilson and RC Marston (eds.), *Exchange Rate Theory and Practice*, pp. 239–259.

Friedman, M and A Schwartz (1970). *Monetary Statistics of the United States: Estimation, Sources, Methods, and Data*, Columbia University Press, New York.

Goldfeld, SM (1973). The demand for money revisited, *Brookings Papers on Economic Activity*, **3**: 577–638.

Gorman, WM (1953). Community preference fields, *Econometrica*, **21**: 63–80.

Groen, JJJ (2000). The monetary exchange rate model as a long-run phenomenon, *Journal of International Economics*, **52**: 299–319.

Groves, GW and EJ Hannan (1968). Time series regression of sea level on weather, *Reviews of Geophysics*, **6**: 129–174.

Hansen, LP and K Singleton (1982). Generalized instrumental variable estimation of nonlinear rational expectations models, *Econometrica*, **50**.

Harrison, PJ and CF Stevens (1976). Bayesian forecasting, *Journal of the Royal Statistical Society Series B*, **38**: 205–247.

Haywood, E (1973). The deviation cycle: a new index of the australian business cycle, 1950–1973, *Australian Economic Review*, 4th Quarter, pp. 31–39.

Hicks, JR (1946). *Value and Capital*, Clarendon Press, Oxford.

Hinich, MJ (1982). Testing for Gaussianity and linearity of a stationary time series, *Journal of Time Series Analysis*, **3**: 169–176.

Hinich, MJ and GR Messer (1995). On the principle domain of the discrete bispectrum of a stationary signal, *IEEE Transactions on Signal Processing*, **43**: 2130–2134.

Hinich, MJ and D Patterson (1985). Identification of the coefficients in a non-linear time series of the quadratic type, *Journal of Econometrics*, **30**: 269–288.

Hinich, MJ and D Patterson (1989). Evidence of non-linearity in the trade by trade stock market return generating process, in W Barnett, J Geweke, and K Shell (eds.), *Economic Complexity: Chaos, Sunspots, Bubbles and Non-linearity, Proc. 4th Int. Symp. on Economic Theory and Econometrics*, Cambridge University Press, Cambridge.

Hoa, TV (1985). A Divisia system approach to modelling monetary aggregates, *Economics Letters*, **17**: 365–368.

Hong, Y (1996). Consistent testing for serial correlation of unknown form, *Econometrica*, **64**: 837–864.

Hooper, P and J Morton (1982). Fluctuations in the dollar: a model of nominal and real exchange rate determination, *Journal of International Money and Finance*, **1**: 39–56.

Hoover, KD and SJ Perez (1994). Post hoc ergo propter once more: an evaluation of "does monetary policy matter? in the spirit of James Tobin, *Journal of Monetary Economics*, **34**: 89–99.

Ishida, K (1984). Divisia monetary aggregates andthe demand for money: a japanese case, *Bank of Japan Monetary and Economic Studies*, **2**: 49–80.

Jones, B, D Dutkowsky and T Elger (2005). Sweep programs and optimal monetary aggregation, *Journal of Banking and Finance*, **29**: 483–508.

Keating, JW (1993). Asymmetric vector autoregressions, *Proceedings of the Business and Economic Statistics Section of the American Statistical Association*, **88**: 68–73.

Keating, JW (2000). Macroeconomic modeling with asymmetric vector autoregressions, *Journal of Macroeconomics*, **22**: 1–28.

Kilian, L (1999). Exchange rate and monetary fundamentals: what do we learn from long-horizon regression? *Journal of Econometrics*, **14**: 491–510.

Kim, CJ and C Nelson (1998). *State-Space Models with Regime-Switching: Classical and Gibbs-Sampling Approaches with Applications*, The MIT Press.

Kocherlakota, N (1996). The equity premium: It's still a puzzle, *Journal of Economic Literature*, **34**: 43–71.

Lamont, O (2000). Economic tracking portfolio, *Journal of Econometrics*, **105**: 161–184.

Lettau, M and S Ludvigson (2001). Resurrecting the (C)CAPM: a cross-sectional test when risk premia are time-varying, *Journal of Political Economy*, **109**: 1238–1287.

Lintner, J (1965). The valuation of risky assets and the selection of risky investments in stock portfolios and capital budgets, *Review of Economics and Statistics*, **47**: 13–37.

Litterman, RB (1986). Forecasting with Bayesian vector autoregression — five years of experience, *Journal of Business and Economic Statistics*, **4**: 25–38.

Lucas, RE (1999). An interview with Robert E. Lucas, Jr., Interviewed by Bennett T McCallum, *Macroeconomic Dynamics*, **3**: pp. 278–291. Reprinted in PA Samuelson and WA Barnett (eds.), (2006). *Inside the Economist's Mind*, Blackwell, Malden, MA.

Lucas, RE (2000). Inflation and welfare, *Econometrica*, **68**(62): 247–274.

MacDonald, R and MP Taylor (1994). The monetary model of the exchange rate: long-run relationships, short-run dynamics, and how to beat a random walk, *Journal of International Money and Finance*, **13**: 276–290.

Mark, NC (1995). Exchange rate and fundamentals: evidence on long-horizon predictability, *American Economic Review*, **8**: 201–218.

Mark, NC and D Sul (2001). Nominal exchange rates and monetary fundamentals: evidence from a small post-bretton woods panel, *Journal of International Economics*, **53**: 29–52.

Marshall, D (1997). Comments on CAPM risk adjustment for exact aggregation over financial assets, *Macroeconomic Dynamics*, **1**: 513–523.

Meese, RA and K Rogoff (1983). Empirical exchange rate models of the seventies: do they fit out of sample? *Journal of International Economics*, **14**: 3–24.

Phlips, L and F Spinnewyn (1982). Rationality versus myopia in dynamic demand systems, in RL Basmann and GF Rhodes (eds.), *Advances in Econometrics*, CT: JAI Press, Greenwich, 3–33.

Poterba, JM and JJ Rotemberg (1987). Money in the utility function: an empirical implementation, in WA Barnett and KJ Singleton (eds.), *New Approaches to Monetary Economics*, Cambridge University Press, Cambridge, 219–240.

Reimers, HE (2002). Analysing Divisia aggregates for the euro area, Discussion paper 13/02, Economic Research Centre of the Deutsche Bundesbank, Frankfurt, May.

Rotemberg, JJ (1991). Commentary: monetary aggregates and their uses, in MT Belongia (ed.), Monetary policy on the 75th Anniversary of the Federal Reserve System, Kluwer Academic: Boston, pp. 232–244.

Rotemberg, JJ, JC Driscoll, and JM Poterba (1995). Money, output and prices: evidence from a new monetary aggregate, *Journal of Business and Economic Statistics*, **13**: 67–83.

Schunk, D (2001). The relative forecasting performance of the Divisia and simple sum monetary aggregates, *Journal of Money, Credit and Banking*, **33**(2): 272–283.

Serletis, A (ed.) (2006). *Money and the Economy*, World Scientific Publishing Co.

Sharpe, WF (1964). Capital asset prices: a theory of market equilibrium under conditions of risk, *The Journal of Finance*, **19**: 425–442.

Sims, CA (1980). Macroeconomics and reality, *Econometrica*, **48**: 1–48.

Spencer, P (1997). Monetary integration and currency substitution in the EMS: the case of a European monetary aggregate, *European Economic Review*, **41**: 1403–1419.

Stokes, H (1991). *Specifying and Diagnostically Testing Econometric Models*, Quorum Books, London.

Stracca, L (2001). Does liquidity matter: properties of a synthetic Divisia monetary aggregate in the auro area, European Central Bank Working Paper no. 79, Frankfurt, October.

Swamy, PAVB and P Tinsley (1980). Linear prediction and estimation methods for regression models with stationary stochastic coefficients, *Journal of Econometrics*, **12**: 103–142.

Swofford, JL (2000). Microeconomic foundations of an optimal currency area, *Review of Financial Economics*, **9**: 121–128.

Swofford, JL and GA Whitney (1987). Nonparametric test of utility maximization and weak separability for consumption, leisure, and money. *Review of Economics and Statistics*, **69**: 458–464.

Taylor, MP and DA Peel (2000). Nonlinear adjustment, long-run equilibrium and exchange rate fundamentals, *Journal of International Money and Finance*, **19**: 33–53.

Theil, H (1967). Economics and information theory, Elsevier, Amsterdam.

Theil, H (1971). Principles of econometrics, John Wiley, New York.

Thornton, D and P Yue (1992). An extended series of Divisia monetary aggregates, *Federal Reserve Bank of St. Louis Review*, **74**: 35–52.

Welch, PD (1967). The use of fast fourier transform for the estimation of power spectra: a method based on time averaging over short modified periodograms, *IEEE Transactions on Audio and Electroacoustics*, **AU-15**: 70–73.

Wesche, K (1997). The demand for Divisia money in a core monetary union, *Federal Reserve Bank of St. Louis Review*, **79**(5): 51–60.

Wolff, CCP (1987). Time-varying parameters and the out-of-sample forecasting performance of structural exchange rate models, *Journal of Business and Economic Statistics*, **5**: 87–97.

Yue, P and R Fluri (1991). Divisia monetary services indexes for Switzerland: are they useful for monetary targeting? *Federal Reserve Bank of St. Louis Review*, **73**: 19–33.

Author Index

Agung, J., 170
Anderson, R.G., 159, 173, 225
Arrow, K.J., 58, 215
Ashley, R., 77, 80

Barnett, W.A., 1, 2, 4–11, 13, 14, 16, 18, 19, 23, 29, 31–34, 36, 39, 40, 44, 51, 53–56, 62, 66, 68–71, 74, 76, 85–88, 90, 91, 95–97, 99, 103–105, 107–109, 111–116, 122, 129, 147–149, 151, 153, 155–157, 166–173, 175, 176, 179, 184, 185, 187, 190, 203–205, 207, 209, 210, 213–216, 218, 219, 225, 246
Batchelor, R., 2
Belongia, M.T., 2, 5, 14, 55, 69, 70, 207, 210, 219, 237
Berkowitz, J., 152
Beyer, A., 168
Bilson, J.F.O., 159
Binner, J., 55, 105, 153, 155
Blanchard, O.J., 115
Boschan, C., 228, 229
Breeden, D., 104
Brock, W.A., 227
Bry, G., 228, 229

Campbell, J.Y., 86, 97, 104
Chae, U., 34, 36, 107, 129
Chalfant, J., 55, 69, 70
Chauvet, M., 1, 6–8, 14, 44, 207, 212, 246
Chen, N.F., 98
Cheung, Y.W., 161
Chinn, M.D., 152, 161
Chrystal, A., 2, 9, 55, 153, 170, 214
Cochrane, J.H., 86, 97, 98
Cockerline, J., 2

de Peretti, P., 11, 216
Dechert, W.D., 227
Diebold, F.X., 151, 161–165
Diewert, W.E., 9, 13, 18, 113, 157, 196, 214, 218
Divisia, F., 2, 4–9, 12, 13, 18, 21, 23, 24, 27, 28, 30, 31, 33, 39–42, 44, 46, 47, 53–55, 66–68, 74–76, 85, 86, 91–93, 97, 103–105, 107–109, 112–117, 147, 151, 153, 157–160, 163, 165–168, 174, 175, 178, 193, 195, 196, 202–205, 207, 209, 210, 212–214, 217, 218, 220, 225, 226, 232, 236, 237, 241, 245–249
Doan, T., 124
Doornik, J.A., 168
Dornbusch, R., 154
Drake, L., 2, 170
Dutkowsky, D., 14, 219

Elger, T., 14, 219
Engel, C., 152

Fama, E.F., 98
Fase, M.M.G., 2, 168
Fayyad, S.K., 69, 72, 73

Feenstra, R.C., 58, 215
Fischer, S., 115, 215
Fisher, D., 2, 5, 9, 12, 17, 55, 70, 100, 113, 153, 157, 182, 210, 214, 217
Fisher, I., 16
Fisher, P., 159
Fluri, R., 2
French, K., 98
Frenkel, J.A., 159
Friedman, M., 18, 29, 30, 50, 245, 246

Gallant, A.R., 76
Geweke, J., 71
Gibbons, M., 104
Goldfeld, S.M., 22
Gorman, W.M., 186
Groves, G.W., 78

Hahm, J.H., 39
Hahn, F., 58, 215
Hannan, E.J., 78
Hansen, L.P., 73
Harrison, P.J., 224
Haywood, E., 228
Hendry, D.F., 168
Hicks, J.R., 3, 208
Hinich, M.J., 41, 53–56, 69, 70, 74, 76, 85
Hoa, T.V., 2
Hong, Y., 80
Hooper, P., 151, 158, 162–165
Hoover, K.D., 126
Hudson, S., 159

Ireland, P., 5, 14, 210, 219
Ishida, K., 2

Jensen, M.J., 13, 31, 32, 53, 54, 62, 68, 76, 85–88, 90, 91, 95, 97, 99, 103, 104, 218
Jones, B.E., 14, 159, 173, 219, 225
Jungeilges, J.A., 76

Kaplan, D.T., 76, 80, 81
Keating, J.W., 34, 36, 107, 124, 129
Kilian, L., 152
Kim, C.J., 7
Kirova, M., 56
Kocherlakota, N., 97
Kwag, C.H., 151

Lamont, O., 98
LeBaron, B., 227
Lettau, M., 103
Lintner, J., 88, 98
Litterman, R.B., 124, 129
Litzenberger, R., 104
Liu, Y., 13, 31, 32, 53, 54, 62, 68, 76, 85–88, 90, 91, 95, 97, 99, 103, 104, 218
Lucas, R.E., 18, 55, 249
Ludvigson, S., 103

MacDonald, R., 9, 55, 153, 161, 170, 214
Mariano, R.S., 151, 161–165
Mark, N.C., 152, 161
Marshall, D., 94
Meese, R.A., 151, 152, 158, 161
Messer, G.R., 78
Morton, J., 151, 158, 162–165
Mullineux, A., 170
Murray, J., 2

Nelson, C., 7
Nesmith, T.D., 159, 173, 225

Offenbacher, E.K., 5, 19, 23, 210

Pascual, A.G., 161
Pasupathy, M., 56
Patterson, D., 77, 80
Peel, D.A., 152
Perez, S.J., 126
Phlips, L., 58, 215
Poterba, J.M., 54, 62, 68, 71, 215
Pradhan, M., 159

Reimers, H.E., 168
Rogoff, K., 151, 158
Roll, R., 98

Ross, S., 98
Rotemberg, J.J., 54, 62, 68, 71, 109, 116, 126, 136, 215

Scheinkman, J.A., 227
Schunk, D., 5, 109, 210
Schwartz, A., 18, 246
Serletis, A., 5, 55, 86, 153, 168, 171, 173, 175, 187, 204, 210, 225
Sharpe, W.F., 88, 98
Sims, C.A., 123, 127
Singleton, K.J., 73
Spencer, P., 168
Spindt, P.A., 5, 19, 23, 210
Spinnewyn, F., 58, 215
Stevens, C.F., 224
Stokes, H, 78, 79
Stracca, L., 168
Sul, D., 152
Swamy, P.A.V.B., 22, 23
Swofford, J.L., 69, 170

Taylor, M.P., 47, 119, 152, 161
Theil, H., 128–133, 135, 175, 196
Tierney, H.L.R., 6–8, 14, 44, 207
Tinsley, P., 22

Weber, W.E., 41
Welch, P.D., 78
Wesche, K., 168
Whitney, G.A., 69
Winder, C.C.A., 168
Wolfe, M., 71
Wolff, C.C.P., 152
Wu, S., 2, 13, 32, 44, 85, 115, 149, 157, 169, 218

Xu, H., 32

Yue, P., 2, 53, 55, 56, 69–71, 74, 85

Zhou, G., 34, 36, 39, 56